Culpeper County, Virginia

Deed Book Abstracts

1781–1783

Ruth and Sam Sparacio

HERITAGE BOOKS
2022

HERITAGE BOOKS
AN IMPRINT OF HERITAGE BOOKS, INC.

Books, CDs, and more—Worldwide

For our listing of thousands of titles see our website
at
www.HeritageBooks.com

Published 2022 by
HERITAGE BOOKS, INC.
Publishing Division
5810 Ruatan Street
Berwyn Heights, Md. 20740

International Standard Book Number
Paperbound: 978-1-68034-504-9

CULPEPER COUNTY, VIRGINIA
DEED BOOK L
(1781-1783)

pp.
1-
3

(On margin: Yowel & Ux. to Champe D. D. to Colo. Champe Jany 23d 1784)

THIS INDENTURE made the Sixteenth day of October in year of our Lord One thousand seven hundred and Eighty one Between JAMES YOWELL, Son to DAVID and MARY his Wife, of County of Culpeper of one part & COLO. WILLIAM CHAMPE of aforesaid County of other part Witnesseth that in consideration of the sum of Two thousand pounds current money of Virginia to them in hand paid by these presents have bargained and sold unto said WILLIAM CHAMPE his heirs & assigns for ever a Certain Tract of land containing One hundred and Eighty nine acres more or less in the foresaid County on the waters of the ROBINSON RIVER and bounded Beg. at two black Jacks Corner to JAMES YOWELL (Son to CHRISR.), thence with his line South eighty degrees West fourteen poles to a red Oak, thence North Eighty degrees West forty four poles to two red Oaks, thence South seventy five degrees West thirty eight poles, thence South fifty five degrees West twenty poles Corn. to red Oak and small Hickory on the ROAD, corner to said YOWELL, thence keepng the said Road North twenty four poles North ten degrees West thirty eight poles corner in said Road in JOHN YOWELLs line, thence with his line North thirty degrees East sixty four poles, Corner in JAMES YOWELLs Plantation in his line, thence South eighty five degrees West twenty two poles to a Dead Poplar on a Branch by said Road, thence North eighty two poles to a white and Spanish Oaks, Corner to said JOHN YOWELL and ROBERT (?)name through a stain) SHOTWELL, thence North ten degrees West sixty six poles to a Chesnut on said Mountain, Corner to said SHOTWELL, thence with a line of PAUL LEATHERER JUNR. South sixty five degrees East One hundred & Sixty six poles, corner to said JAMES YOWELL's (Son to DAVID) Plantation, thence North East seventy poles, Corner to said LEATHERERs Plantation, thence South seventy degrees East fifty one poles to two chesnut Oaks on side of a Mountain by DAVID YOWELL's PATH, thence thirteen degrees West Two hundred & ten poles to the begining togather with all fences houses orchards & all other appurtenances belonging To have and to hold all the aforesaid land and every part from all Incumbrances As Witness our hands and Seals the day & year above written
in presence of

JAMES YOWELL
MARY her mark M YOWELL

Received full satisfaction for the within written Indenture Witness our hands this 16th day of October 1781   JAMES YOWELL

At a Court held for Culpeper County the 15th day of October 1781
This Indenture was acknowledged by the parties and ordered to be recorded the said MARY being privily Examined as the Law directs
Teste   JOHN JAMESON Cl Cur

pp.
3-
5

THIS INDENTURE made this 15th day of October in year of our Lord God One thousand seven hundred and Eighty one Between HENRY BENSON of Parish of (blank) and County of FAUQUIRE of one part and LAZARUS MADDUX of the Parish of Brumswick and County of STAFFORD, both of State of Virginia, of other part Witnesseth that HENRY BENSON in consideration of the just sum of Eight thousand pounds weight of good and merchantable Tobacco to him in hand paid by these presents doth bargain & sell unto LAZARUS MADDUX a certain tract of land lying in the Parish of St. Marks and County of Culpeper in the Great Fork of RAPPAHANNOCK RIVER and bounded begining at two white Oaks on South side of a Branch of FRESHMANS RUN and runeth

thence North ten degrees West Three hundred and twenty poles to three Pines, thence North Eighty degrees East Two hundred poles to two Pines, thence South ten degrees East Three hundred and twenty poles to two white Oaks and a Pine, thence South Eighty degrees West Two hundred poles to the Begining containing (not mentioned) Togather with all woods swamps marshes low grounds meadows mine quarries and all other profits whatsoever to the same belonging To have and to hold said Tract and all it appurtenances unto LAZARUS MADDUX and to his heirs & assigns for Ever and HENRY BENSON doth covenant at all time to warrent and defend the said LAZARUS MADDUX his heirs in the peaceable enjoyment of said land In Witness the said HENRY BENSON hath hereunto affix'd his hand and Seal the day month and year first above written
Sign'd seal'd & acknowledged before   HENRY BENSON
    WM. BRADLEY, HARRY TOLIAFERRO,
    JACOB COMFORT

At a Court held for Culpeper County the 15 day of October 1781
This Indenture was acknowledged by the within HENRY and ordered to be recorded

pp. (On margin: Morriss & Ux. to Morriss D D James 1818)
5- THIS INDENTURE made this 15th day of October One thousand seven hundred and
7 Eighty one Between WILLIAM MORRISS & AMY his Wife of County of Culpeper of one part and THOMAS MORRISS of said County of other part Witnesseth that WILLIAM MORRISS and AMY his Wife for and in consideration of the sum of Two thousand pounds current money of Virginia to them in hand paid by these presents do bargain and sell unto THOMAS MORRISS one tract of land lying in County of Culpeper containing by Estimation One hundred acres more or less bounded begining at a white Oak & Gum near HUNGRY RUN BRIDGE, Corner to DICKIE LATHAM, thence up the RUN with another line of said LATHAMs South twenty three degrees West thirteen poles to five white Oaks (one dead) a Reputed Corner to JOHN SPOTSWOOD Esqr. Deced on the North side of said RUN, thence with SPOTSWOODs line South sixty six degrees West three hun-and seventeen poles (Vizt) thirty four poles to HUNGRY RUN crossing the same three times One hundred & forty eight poles farther to the RUN again, thence up the RUN to the mouth of QUARY BRANCH, thence with FLOYDS PATH to FOX MOUNTAIN ROAD, thence down the ROAD to the begining Togather with all houses Orchards profits whatsoever to the same belonging To have and to hold the said tract of land with the appurtenances unto THOMAS MORRISS his heirs & assigns for ever and WILLIAM MORRISS and AMY his Wife their heirs and assigns will warrent and forever defend these presents against them the said WILLIAM MORRIS and AMEY his Wife and every other persons whatsoever. In Witness whereof WILLIAM MORRISS and AMY his Wife have hereunto set their hands and Seals the day & year above written
At a Court held for Culpeper County the 15th day of October 1781
This Indenture was acknowledged by the parties and ordered to be recorded the within named AMY being privily examined as the Law directs

pp. (On margin: Nooe to Burrage D D TO Thos. Nooe April 84)
7- THIS INDENTURE made the first day of May in year of our Lord One thousand
9 seven hundred and Eighty one Between THOMAS NOE & MARY his Wife of County of Culpeper of one part and EDWARD BURRAGE of said County of other part Witnesseth that for and in consideration of sum of Eight hundred pounds current money of Virginia to him said THOMAS NOOE well & truly in hand paid by these presents have bargained and sold unto EDWARD BURBAGE his heirs and assigns forever one Certain tract of lland containing by Estimation One hundred and fifteen acres be the same more or less lying in County of Culpeper & bounded Begining at two red Oaks thence North

eighty six and half degrees East One hundred and four pole to a white Oak, corner of
JOHN BUTLER & JOHN STRODE near said BUTLER Fence, thence North fifty three half
degrees West Two hundred & sixty poles to red & white Oak on a Hill side, thence South
forty one & half West One hundred & six pole to a red Oak & black Gum, thence South
sixty six degrees East One hundred & ninety pole to the begining Togather with all
houses fences orchards and all other appurtenances belonging To have & to hold the
aforesaid land with every thereof from all Incumbrance of Mortgage, Dowers, Reversion & Reversions by or from us or from any other persons whatsoever & be only to the
use of EDWARD BURRAGE his heirs or assigns forever As Witness our hand & Seal the
day & year above written

in the presence of JOSEPH ROBERTS,   THOMAS NOOE
          JAMES LEACH
   At a Court held for Culpeper County the 15th day of October 1781
This Indenture was acknowledged by the within named THOMAS NOOE & ordered to be
recorded

pp.   THIS INDENTURE made the 15th day of October in year of our Lord One thousand
9-   seven hundred and Eighty one Between JOHN ROUTT and MARY his Wife of Coun-
11   ty of Culpeper of one part and THOMAS LANDRUM of County aforesaid of other
         part Witnesseth that JOHN ROUTT and MARY his Wife for and in consideration of
the sum of Sixty pounds current money of Virginia to him in hand paid by these presents do bargain and sell unto THOMAS LANDRUM one certain tract of land lying in
County of Culpeper and bounded Begining at a white Oak, Corner to THOMAS GINN,
thence North East One hundred & fifteen pole to a red Oak in ROUT's old line, thence
North Twenty two degrees West One hundred and sixty five pole to a Pine, white Oak &
red Oak, thence South forty nine degrees West two hundred & four pole to a Spanish
Oak, red Oak & Hickory, thence South Twenty five degrees East to THOMAS GINNs line,
thence with GINNs line to the beginning containing Two hundred acres be the same
more or less Togather with all ways waters profits and appurtenances whatsoever to the
same belonging To have and to hold the said Tract of land with the appurtenances unto
THOMAS LANDRUM his heirs and assigns and JOHN ROUTT and MARY his wife their
heirs and assigns will warrent and for ever Defend by these presents In Witness
whereof JOHN ROUT and MARY his Wife have hereunto set their hands and Seals the day
and year above written

in presence of   JOHN ROUTT
   At a Court held for Culpeper County the 15th day of October 1781
This Indenture was acknowledged by the said JOHN ROUTT and ordered to be recorded

pp.   (On margin: Brooks & Ux. to Green DD 95)
11-   THIS INDENTURE made the Twentyeth day of October in year of our Lord One
13   thousand seven hundred and Eighty one Between WILLIAM BROOKS and SUSAN-
         NAH his Wife of County of Culpeper of one part and WILLIAM GREEN otherwise
called WILLIAM FOSTER of the County aforesaid of other part Witnesseth that WILLIAM
BROOKS and SUSANNAH his Wife for and in consideration of the sum of Forty five
pounds current money of Virginia to them in hand paid by these presents do bargain
and sell unto WILLIAM GREEN one certain tract of land lying in County of Culpeper and
bounded begining at three red Oaks in JAMES TUTTs line, thence North twenty nine degrees West One hundred & fifty eight pole to a white Oak, thence South sixty one degrees West One hundred and fifty four pole to a red Oak a white Oak and Gum in WIL-
LIAM BROOKS's line, thence South twenty nine degrees East One hundred and fifty eight
pole to two Hickorys in JAMES TUTTs line, thence with that line North sixty one degrees

East One hundred and fifty four poles to the begining containing One hundred and fifty acres be the same more or less Togather with all ways waters profits and appurtenances whatsoever to the same belonging To have and to hold said tract of land with the appurtenances unto WILLIAM GREEN his heirs and assigns and WILLIAM BROOKS & SUSANNAH his Wife shall warrent and forever defend against the claim of any person whatsoever In Witness whereof WILLIAM BROOKS & SUSANNAH his Wife have hereunto set their hands & Seals the day and year above written

in presence of RICHD. YANCEY,
          LEWIS TUTT, JOHN ROUTT,   WILLIAM BROOKS
          P. PENDLETON   SUSANNA BROOKS

   At a Court held for Culpeper County the 19th day of Novr. 1781
This Indenture was acknowledged by the parties & ordered to be recorded, the within named SUSANNAH being privily examined as the Law directs

pp.   (On margin: Spotswood to Roussaw DD to Mr. Cornelius 85)
13-   THIS INDENTURE made the Thirteenth day of March in year of our Lord One
16   thousand seven hundred and Seventy Seven Between JOHN SPOTSWOOD Esqr. on
        one part & JAMES RUSSAW on the other part Witnesseth that JOHN SPOTSWOOD
for and in consideration of the Rents and Covenants herein after mentioned on part of
JAMES RUSSAW & his assigns to be paid and perform'd by these presents doth grant and
to farm let unto JAMES RUSSAW Two hundred and Eighty nine acres of land with the
appurtenances (except all mines minerals and Quarries whatsoever) lying in Parish of
Saint Marks in County of Culpeper and described by a Plot and Survey thereof Indorsed
on the back of this Indenture To have and to hold the Land (except before excepted) to
JAMES RUSSAW and his assigns during the natural lives of JAMES RUSSAW, LUCY(this
name is obscured by a stain) RUSSAW & DAVID RUSSAW and for and during the natural life
of the longest liver of them paying therefore yearly One thousand three hundred and
Eighty pounds of Tobacco with Cask on the twenty fifth day of December One thousand
seven hundred & seventy seven appointed for the payment thereof and the same being
lawfully demanded at the messuage of said JAMES RUSSAW or his assigns upon the said
premises and JAMES RUSSAW or his assigns shall within four years plant upon the
demised premises Three hundred good fruit trees whereof One Third at least to be good
Apple trees and the same will Inclose with a good sufficient and lawfull fence and JOHN
SPOTSWOOD his heirs and assigns shall warrent and defend and keep harmless with
their appurtenances for the yearly rent aforesaid In Witness whereof JOHN SPOTSWOOD
and the said JAMES RUSSAW have hereunto Interchangably set their Hands & Seals the
day and year first above written

in presence of JNO. LONG,   JOHN SPOTSWOOD
     DAVID HENING, HUMPHREY ARNOLD

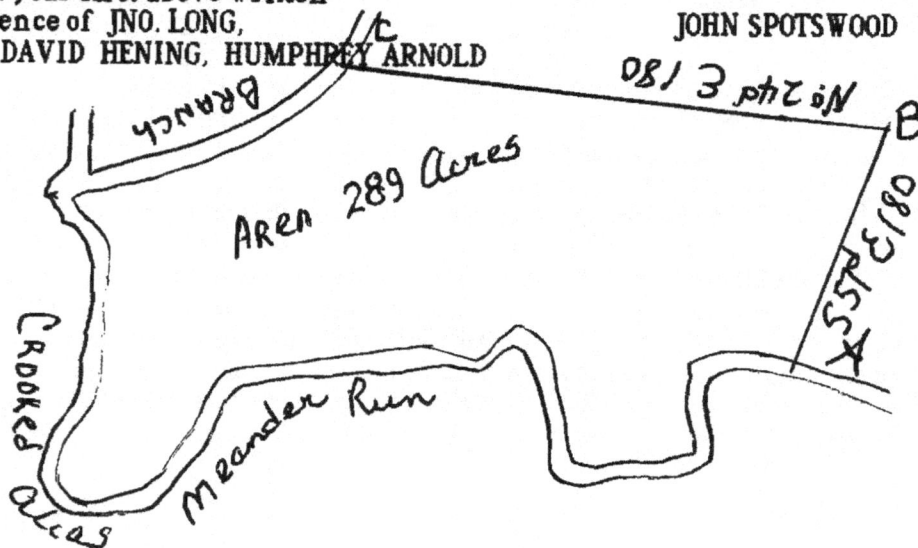

(To go with drawing on previous page) Surveyed by order of Capt. JOHN SPOTSWOOD a Lott of land for JAMES RUSSAW containing Two hundred & eighty nine acres and bounded as follows (Vizt) begining at A two white Oaks on CROOKED RUN thence So. 57 E. 184 pole to B two white and two red Oak saplins th. North 24 East 180 poles to C two white Oaks on the South side of a Branch thence down the Branch to CROOKED alias MEANDER RUN, thence down the sd Run to Beginning

1777   p SAML. CLAYTON JR. C.C.S.

I do assign this Lease over to Mr. ABSOLOM CORNELIUS having received Satisfaction for the same. Witness my hand this 18th of August 1777

Teste WM. ALLEN   JAMES ROUSSAW

At a Court held for Culpeper County Monday the 20th day of October 1777
This Indenture was proved by the Oaths of two of the witnesses thereto; And at a Court held for the said County the 19th day of Novr. 1781, was fully proved and ordered to be recorded

pp. THIS INDENTURE made this Tenth day of September in year of our Lord One thou-
16- sand seven hundred & Eighty one by and Between ROBERT SAUNDERS of Cul-
18   peper County of one part and WILLIAM STEWARD of the County aforesaid of
     other part Witnesseth that for and in consideration of the sum of One hundred
and fifty pounds Specie to him in hand paid by these presents do bargain and sell unto
WILLIAM STEWARD his heirs and assigns all that tract of land lying in County aforesaid
on (name under a stain (?) CEDAR) RUN containing by Estimation One hundred and fifty
acres being one moiety of a Tract of land Willed by the late HUGH SAUNDERS to his Son,
ROBERT & CHARLES SAUNDERS, and bounded as followeth (no description) And all houses
buildings ways and appurtenances whatsoever thereof belonging To have and to hold
said Tract of land and every of the appurtenances unto WILLIAM STEWARD his heirs
and assigns and ROBERT SAUNDERS his heirs will warrent and forever defend by these
presents In Witness whereof ROBERT SAUNDERS hath hereunto sett his hand and Seal
the day and year above written

in presence of SAMUEL CLAYTON,   ROBERT SANDERS
     PETER GATEWOOD, WM. ROBERTSON JUNR.,
     WM. DAVIS

At a Court held for Culpeper County the 19th day of Novr. 1781
This Indenture was proved by the Oaths of SAMUEL CLAYTON, PETER GATEWOOD and
WILLIAM DAVIS witness thereto and ordered to be recorded

pp. THIS INDENTURE made this Nineteenth day of November in year of our Lord One
18- thousand seven hundred & Eighty one Between RICHARD FLYNT JUNR. of County
21   of Culpeper of one part and WILLIAM ROBERTS of other part Witnesseth that for
     and in consideration of Fifty five pounds to him in hand paid by these presents
RICHARD FLYNT and DORATHA his Wife doth bargain and sell unto WILLIAM ROBERTS
his heirs and assigns forever a certain tract of land containing One hundred acres
more or less lying in County of Culpeper in the ROBINSON FORK and is bounded Begining at three small Pines in a Branch corner to MUMFORD STEVENS, runing thence
with one of his lines South Eight degrees East fifty one pole to three small red Oaks in
JOHN FLYNTs Line, thence with his line South sixty nine degrees East One hundred &
sixty pole to a Pine, Corner to AMBROSE JONES, thence North forty five degrees East
Ninety two pole to a white Oak near a Branch in BENJAMIN HAINES line, thence North
forty one degrees West Two hundred and twenty one pole to two Pines, corner to MUM-
FORD STEVENS line, thence South thirty three degrees West One hundred & fifty poles to
the Beginning Togather with all woods ways & appurtenances whatsoever to the said

parcel of land belonging To have and to hold said Parcel of land with their & every of
their appurtenances whatsoever unto WILLIAM ROBERTS his heirs and assigns In Witness whereof we have hereunto set our hands & seals the day and year above written
in presence of   RICHARD FLYNT
                                     DORATHA her mark X FLYNT
   Received full satisfaction for the within mentioned land & premises. Witness my hand
this Nineteenth day of November 1781
Test JOHN PINOR,   RICHARD FLYNT
      GIDEON BROWN
   At a Court held for Culpeper County the 19th Novr. 1781
This Indenture was acknowledged by the parties & ordered to be recorded, the within
mentioned DORATHA being privily examined as the Law directs

pp.   (On margin: Porter to Major DD 1789)
21-   KNOW ALL MEN by these presents that I THOMAS PORTER of Culpeper County for
22   and in consideration of the love good will and natural which I bear to my Son in
         Law, FRANCIS MAJOR & my Daughter, PEGGEY MAJOR his Wife, and for Divers
other good causes and considerations I THOMAS PORTER by these presents do give grant
and confirm unto FRANCIS MAJOR and his heirs & assigns one certain tract of land
lying in County of Culpeper and containing by Estimation Four hundred and twenty
acres be the same more or less lying in the Fork of the ROBINSON RIVER and is bounded
Beginning at some Blazed Pines in FENNEYs SPRING BRANCH, Corner to JOHN MAJOR,
thence West One hundred and Eighty poles to two red Oaks on a Rock near a Branch,
Corner to LAYMAN, thence South fifteen degrees West One hundred & eighteen poles to
a Hickory at the head of a Branch, Corner to ELIOTT BOHANNAN, thence West One
hundred and twenty four poles to a Oak, Corner to the said BOHANNAN, thence North
seventy five degrees West ninety four poles to a black Oak and Hickory, Corner to said
BOHANNON, thence North fifty degrees East Two hundred poles to a white Oak on a
Ridge, Corner to JOHN WAYLAND, thence North fifteen degrees West eighty poles to four
Sycamores on WHITE OAK RUN, thence North forty five degrees West crossing the said
RUN One hundred and six poles to three red Oak Saplins, Corner to NICHOLAS BROYLE,
thence with his line North eighty degrees East eighty eight poles to another Corner of
said BROYLES, thence North five degrees East to a white & red Oak in said BROYLES line
& Corner to JOHN MAJOR, thence with said MAJORs line North eighty five degrees East to
a Sycamore on WHITE OAK RUN, thence down said RUN to said JOHN MAJORs line, thence
with his line South thirty six degrees East poles three Pines Corner to said MAJOR,
thence with his line South forty seven degrees West Fourteen poles to the begining
which said land Togather with the appurtenances belonging I do absolutely give to
FRANCIS MAJOR his heirs & assigns To have and to hold the said land without any
condition whatsoever In Witness whereof I have set my hand and affixed my Seal this
Twenty fourth day of July in year of our Lord One thousand seven hundred and Eighty
one
in presence of SAMUEL MAJOR SENR.,   THOS. PORTER
      SAMUEL DELPH, JOHN MAJOR
   At a Court held for Culpeper County the 20th day of August 1781
This Indenture was aproved by the Oaths of SAMUEL MAJOR SENR., & JOHN MAJOR, two
of the witnesses thereto and ordered to be Certified, And at a Court held for the aforesaid
County the 19th day of November 1781, was fully proved by the Oath of SAML. DELPH &
ordered to be recorded

pp.   THIS INDENTURE made the 15th day of December in year of our Lord One thou-
23-   sand seven hundred & Eighty one Between WILLIAM ROBERTS and JEAN his Wife
28   of County of Culpeper & Colony of Virginia of one part and AZARIAH WATSON of
the same County and Colony of other part Witnesseth that for and in consideration of the sum of Twenty thousand pounds of Crop Tobacco to WILLIAM ROBERTS &
JEAN his Wife in hand paid by these presents do bargain and sell unto AZARIAH WAT-
SON and his heirs a Tract of land containing One hundred and seventy acres of land
being part of a Tract of land purchased of EDMOND BROWNING by WILLIAM ROBERTS
and bounded Begining at a Gum white Oak and a red Oak on the South side of HEDGMAN
RIVER at the mouth of a small Branch, then up the RIVER the several Courses to a white
Oak and red Oak and Hickory saplins on the RIVER just above the Cleared ground where
JOHN NORMAN lived, thence South thirty degrees West to a white Oak red Oak and
Hickory in Mr. ROGER DIXONs back line, then with that line to the begining, And all
houses orchards and appurtenances whatsoever to said premises belonging To have and
to hold the land hereby conveyed with the appurtenances unto AZARIAH WATSON and
of his heirs and assigns forever free of all Incumbrances whatsoever In Witness
whereof the said WILLIAM WATSON & JEAN his Wife have hereunto set their hands and
Seals the day and year first above written

Test JNO. C. COCKE,   WM. ROBERTS
     GEORGE JOHNSTON,   JEAN ROBERTS
     THOMAS McCLANAHAN, ROBERT JOHNSTON

The Commonwealth of Virginia to JOHN SLAUGHTER & JOHN C. COCKE Gentlemen
Greeting (Commission for the private Examinaton of JEAN, Wife of WILLIAM ROBERTS,
dated at the Courthouse the Seventeenth day of December 1781) (Return of Examination dated the 20th day of December 1781 and signed by JOHN SLAUGHTER and JOHN C.
COCKE)

  At a Court held for Culpeper County the 17th day of December 1781
This Indenture was acknowledged by the said WILLIAM ROBERTS and ordered to be recorded, And on the motion of the said AZARIAH WATSON, Its ordered that a Dedimus issue
for the Private examination of the said JEAN ROBERTS which when returned with the
Certificate thereon is also ordered to be recorded

pp.   (On margin: Thomas to Sarah Thomas DD to Jas. Thomas 1787)
28-   TO ALL TO WHOM these presents shall come I RICHARD THOMAS of County of Cul-
29   peper as well for and in consideration of the Natural love & affection which I
have and do bear unto my Daughter, SARAH THOMAS, of said County as well as in
consideration of Five Shillings to me in hand paid by these presents do give grant &
confirm unto my said Daughter, SARAH THOMAS, her heirs & assigns the following
Slaves (to be given up to said SARAH THOMAS her heirs and assigns on the last day of
this present year) to wit, Sucky, Amy, Winney, Colby & Judy, with their future Increase
to hold to my said Daughter, SARAH THOMAS, her heirs & assigns forever. In Witness
whereof I have hereunto set my hand & Seal the 28th day of February 1781
in presence of W. PENDLETON   RICHD. THOMAS
     JAMES BROADUS, JAMES THOMAS

  At a Court held for Culpeper County the 21st day of Jany. 1782
This Indenture of Gift was proved by the Oaths of WILLIAM PENDLETON, JAMES
BROADUS & JAMES THOMAS, witnesses thereto, & ordered to be recorded

p.   (On margin: Thomas to George Thomas D. D. to Geo. Thomas 1787)
29   TO ALL TO WHOM these presents shall come I RICHARD THOMAS of County of
     Culpeper & State of Virginia as well for and in consideration of the Natural love

& affection which I have and do bear unto my Son, GEORGE THOMAS, of County and State
aforesaid as for the consideration of Five shillings to me in hand paid by these presents
hath given & confirmed unto GEORGE THOMAS his heirs and assigns the followng Negro
slaves to wit (to be given up to said GEORGE THOMAS his heirs and assigns on the last day
of this present year) Jack, Claris, Ben & James to hold to him said GEORGE THOMAS his
heirs and assigns forever. In Testimony whereof I have hereunto set my hand and Seal
this 28th day of February 1781
in presence of W. PENDLETON,   RICHD. THOMAS
          JAMES BROADUS, JAMES THOMAS
   At a Court held for Culpeper County the 21st day of Jany. 1782
This Indenture of Gift was proved by the Oaths of WILLIAM PENDLETON, JAMES
BROADUS & JAMES THOMAS, witnesses thereto, and ordered to be recorded

p.   (On margin: Thomas to Richard Thomas DD to Jas. Thomas 1787)
30   TO ALL TO WHOM these presents shall come I RICHARD THOMAS of Culpeper
        County and State of Virginia as well for and in consideration of the Natural love
and affection which I have and do bear to my Son, RICHARD THOMAS, of County and
State aforesaid, as for the consideration of Five Shillings to me in hand paid by these
presents hath given granted and confirm'd unto RICHARD THOMAS his heirs and
assigns the following Slaves to wit: Bob, Abner, Cealia, Moses & Gabriel; To have and to
hold unto him the said RICHARD THOMAS his heirs & assigns forever In Testimony
whereof I have hereunto sett my hand & affix my Seal this Twenty eighth day of February Anno Domini One thousand seven hundred & eighty one
N.B. the said Slaves is to be delivered upon the first day of January next esnuing except
Bob whom he now hath
in presence of W. PENDLETON,   RICHD. THOMAS
          JAMES BROADUS, GEORGE THOMAS
Culpeper County 27th June 1781. I do certify that I have this day exchanged the within
named Gabriel (with my Brother, JAMES THOMAS) for his Negro girl Hannah. Witness
my hand
Teste GEORGE THOMAS   R. THOMAS
   At a Court held for Culpeper County the 21st day of Jany. 1782
This Indenture was proved by the Oaths of WM. PENDLETON, JAMES BROADUS & GEORGE
THOMAS, witnesses thereto, & ordered to be recorded

p.   (On margin: Thomas to Jas. Thomas D D to James Thomas 1787)
31   TO ALL TO WHOM these presents shall come I RICHARD THOMAS of County of Cul-
        peper as well for and in consideration of the Natural love and affection which I
have and do bear unto my Son, JAS. THOMAS, of County aforesaid, as for the consideration of Five Shillings to me in hand paid by these presents hath given granted & confirmed unto JAS. THOMAS his heirs and assigns the following Negro Slave, to wit,
Hannah, To hold to him said JAMES THOMAS his heirs & assigns forever. In Witness
whereof I have hereunto set my hand & Seal this 28th day of February 1781
in presence of W. PENDLETON,   RICHD. THOMAS
          JAMES BROADUS, GEORGE THOMAS
 Culpeper June 27th 1781 I do certify that I have this day swap'd or exchanged the
within mentioned Negro Hannah with my Brother, RICHARD THOMAS, for his Negro boy
Gabriel to have & to hold forever (note there is Memo. made on the said RICHARD THO-
MAS's Deed of said Bargain
Teste GEORGE THOMAS   JAMES THOMAS

At a Court held for Culpeper County the 21st day of Jany 1782
This Indenture was proved by the Oath of WM. PENDLETON, JAMES BROADUS & GEORGE
THOMAS, witnesses thereto, & ordered to be recorded

pp.   (On margin: Crimm to Button D.D. to Self 1785)
32-   THIS INDENTURE made this 9th day of September in year of our Lord One thou-
34   sand seven hundred & Eighty one Between JACOB CRIM and MARY his Wife of
        County of FAUQUIER of one part and WILLIAM BUTTON of County of Culpeper of
other part Witnesseth tht JACOB CRIM and MARY his Wife for and in consideration of
the sum of Twenty eight pounds Current money of Virginia to them in hand paid by
these presents do bargain and sell unto WILLIAM BUTTON one certain tract of land
lying in County of Culpeper and containing by Estimation ninety four acres be the
same more or less being part of a tract granted to WILLIAM HARRISS the 30th day of
May 1749 for Two hundred acres as by the patent from the Proprietors Office may
appear and Beginning at a Pine in a line of JOHN KOONEs land and runing East One
hundred and thirty eight poles to a Pine white Oak & Hickory, thence South thirty four
poles to a white Oak & Hickory, thence South twenty eight degrees West eighty poles to a
Spanish Oak and Hickory, thence South fifty seven degrees Fifty poles to a red Oak near
a Branch, thence North sixty three degrees West eight six poles to a Pine and Spanish
Oak, thence North forty seven East sixty seven poles to three Pines, Corner of JOHN
COONES's land, thence with his line North twenty four poles to the begining, Togather
with all the Houses water courses profits and appurtenances whatsoever to the same
belonging To have and to hold the land and premises herein before mentioned and sold
with apurtenances unto WILLIAM BUTTON his heirs and assigns and JACOB CRIM &
MARY his Wife will warrent and forever defend the said Land before granted against
the claims of all manner of persons In Witness whereof JACOB CRIMM & MARY his Wife
have hereunto set their hands & Seals the day and year first above written
in the presence of us JACOB COONES,   JACOB his mark ⅄ CRIMM
        HARMON his mark ⅄ BUTTON,
        JACOB his mark ✗ HANBACK, HENRY his mark ✗ COONES
     At a Court held for Culpeper County the 21st day of January 1782
This Indenture was proved by the Oaths of JACOB COONES, JACOB HANBACK & HENRY
KOONES witnesses thereto & ordered to be recorded

pp.   THIS INDENTURE made this Twenty sixth day of November in year of our Lord
35-   one thousand seven hundred and Eighty one Between ABRAHAM COOPER and
38   ELIZABETH his Wife of County of Culpeper and State of Virginia of one part and
        WILLIAM ROBERTS Gent. of County and State aforesaid of other part Witnesseth
that ABRAHAM COOPER and ELIZABETH his Wife in consideration of sum of Twenty
pounds current money to them in hand paid by these presents doth bargain and sell
unto WILLIAM ROBERTS his heirs and assigns forever all that tract of land lying in
County and State aforesaid and bounded Begining near the top of the Ridge of the
GIANTS CASTLE at a Corner of CHARLES DUNCAN and a tract of RICHD. NALLE formly now
JOHN KENDALL, thence with a line of the latter to JAMES MURPHEYs Corner, thence
with MURPHEYs line to the land of ISAAC WALL with his line to a Corner of said WALLs
land & in CHARLES DUNCAN's line & with the same up the Ridge of said GIANTS CASTLE
to the begining containing by Estimation Eighty six acres be the same more or less and
to include the whole of a Tract of land taken up by ELIZABETH WATERs Except Two hundred acres the property of ISAAC WALL and JAMES MURPHEY recourse to their Deeds
being had will plainly appear togather with all houses orchards and appurtenances
whatsoever to the same belonging To have and to hold the said tract of land with the

appurtenances unto WILLIAM ROBERTS his heirs and assigns forever and ABRAHAM
COOPER & ELIZABETH his Wife and their heirs the said Tract of land with the appurtenances unto WILLIAM ROBERTS his heirs & assigns wil warrent and forever defend by
these presents against every person whatsoever In Witness whereof the above mentioned ABRAHAM COOPER & ELIZABETH his Wife have herein set their hands & seals the
day & year first above written
in the presence of us EDWARD NEWBY,   ABRAHAM COOPER
        JOHN ROBERTS, WILLIAM BROWNING   ELIZABETH her mark X COOPER
   At a Court held for Culpeper County the 21st day of January 1782
This Indenture was proved by the Oaths of EDWARD NEWBY, JOHN ROBERTS and WIL-
LIAM BROWNING witnesses thereto and ordered to be recorded

pp.   (On margin: Thomas to Thomas D D to JNO. PIPER 1787)
38-   TO ALL TO WHOM these presents shall come I RICHARD THOMAS of County of Cul-
39   peper as well for and in consideration of the natural love & affection which I
        have and do bear unto my Daughter, MILLEY THOMAS, of sd County as well as for
the consideration of Five Shillings to me in hand paid by these presents do give grant &
confirm unto my said Daughter, MILLEY THOMAS, her heirs & assigns the following
slaves (to be given up to said MILLEY THOMAS her heirs & assigns on the last day of this
present year) to wit Jeanny, Nelley, George & Milly with their future increase to hold
to my said Daughter, MILLEY THOMAS, her heirs and assigns forever. In Witness
whereof I have hereunder set my hand & Seal this 28th day of February 1781
in presence of W. PENDLETON,   RICHARD THOMAS
        JAMES BROADUS, JAMES THOMAS
   At a Court held for Culpeper County the 18th day February 1782
This Indenture was proved by the Oaths of WILLIAM PENDLETON, JAMES BROADUS &
JAMES THOMAS witnesses thereto and ordered to be recorded

pp.   (On margin: Lowen to Lowen D. D. to Self 1785)
39-   TO ALL PEOPLE to whom these presents shall come I MARGARETT LOWEN of Cul-
40   peper County Virginia for and in consideration of the love good will & affection
        I have and do bear toward my loving Son, BENJAMIN LOWEN, of said County by
these presents do freely give and grant unto said BENJAMIN LOWEN his heirs & assigns
all my Right of three Negroes known by the name of Austin, Peg & Little Scip, Togather
with their Increases which said Negroes I have delivered unto BENJAMIN LOWEN before
the signing of these presents, To have and to hold the said Negroes and their increase
forever to him BENJAMIN LOWEN and his heirs from henceforth as his proper Negroes
absolutely without any manner of condition In Witness whereof I have hereunto set
my hand & Seal this Seventh day of February One thousand seven hundred & Eighty two
in the presence of JOHN GORE,   MARGARETT her mark Y LOWEN
        ELIJAH THRELKELD, TARPLY SISSON
   At a Court held for Culpeper County 18th day of February 1782
This Deed of Gift was proved by the Oaths of JOHN GORE, ELIJAH THRELKELD and TAR-
PLEY SISSON witnesses thereto and ordered to be recorded

pp.   (On margin: Clyne & Ux. to Leitch D. D. to Leitch the 12th day June 1784)
40-   THIS INDENTURE made the fifteen day of February in year of our Lord One thou-
43   sand seven hundred and Eighty two Between FREDERICK CLYNE and MARY his
        Wife of County of Culpeper in the Colony of Virginia of one part and BENJAMIN
LEITCH of said County and Colony of other part Witnesseth that FREDERICK CLYNE and
MARY his Wife for & in consideration of the Just and full sum of Ninety pounds current

money of Virginia to them in hand paid by these presents doth bargain & sell unto
BENJAMIN LEITCH his heirs and assigns one certain parcel of land containing One hundred & Sixty seven acres lying in Culpeper County and Bromfield Parish in the Great
Fork of RAPPAHANOCK RIVER on the Branches of BUTLERS SWAMP, the same being part
of Three hundred & thirty five acres of land granted to JOHN WYNAL SAUNDERS by the
Right Honourable THOMAS LORD FAIRFAX Proprietor of the Northern Neck of Virginia
by Deed from the Proprietors Office bearing date the Eleventh day of Deember One
thousand seven hundred and forty nine and by JOHN WYNAL SAUNDERS was sold and
convey'd unto EVAN THOMAS and by said EVAN THOMAS & ELINOR his Wife was sold and
convey'd unto NATHANIEL PENDLETON and the said Tract of One hundred and sixty
seven acres of land is bounded begining at a Pine a white Oak and red Oak, a Corner to a
Tract of land granted to WILLIAM TUTT and runs thence with that line South Twenty
three degrees East Two hundred and sixty poles to three pines in the said Line, thence
North forty nine Degrees East One hundred & seventy nine pole to four Pines on a small
branch, a corner to ROBERT COLEMAN, thence with his line North seventy one degrees
West one hundred and eighty five pole to three Pines corner to said COLEMAN, thence
with another of his line North Nineteen degrees East One hundred and ninety pole to
three Pines in said Line thence South forty five degrees West One hundred & seventy
five poles to the begining place with all the houses closures fences meadows to the
same belonging To have and to hold the tract of One hundred and sixty seven acres of
land with the appurtenances thereunto belonging unto BENJAMIN LEITCH his heirs and
assigns and FREDERICK CLYNE & MARY his Wife & their heirs will warrent and forever
defend by these presents against all or any person whatsoever In Witness whereof the
parties to these presents have Interchangeably hereto set their hands & fixt their Seals
the day & year first above written
                                        FREDERICK CLYNE
                                        MARIA CLYNE
    At a Court held for Culpeper County the 18th day of Feby. 1782
This Indenture was acknowledged by the parties and ordered to be recorded the said
MARY being first privily examined as the Law directs

pp.   THIS INDENTURE made this Seventeenth day of October in year of our Lord One
44-   thousand seven hundred and Eighty one Between JONATHAN PRATT of County of
46   MONTGOMARY of the one part and THOMAS PRATT of County of Culpeper of other
           part Witnesseth that JONATHAN PRATT for and in consideration of the sum of
One hundred & fifty pounds Specie in hand paid by these presents doth bargain and sell
unto THOMAS PRATT his heirs and assigns all that tract of land containing One hundred
and fifty acres be the same more or less being a part of a Patent granted to JOHN and
MARTIN DUETT the fifth day of June 1736 for Four hundred acres which said One hun-
dred & fifty acres was by MARTIN DUETT and MARY sold & conveyed to JONATHAN PRATT
the Oldr. and by him giving by a Deed to the said JONATHAN PRATT the Younger and
bounded Begining at the GERMON ROAD where the line of the Late WILLIAM BEVERLEY
Esqr. deced crosses at runing thence with the said BEVERLEYs line North five degrees
East One hundred and Eighty pole to a red Oak corner near a Rock of Stone, thence
South Eighty three degrees East One hundred & fourteen poles to three Pines, thence
South two degrees West Two hundred and Eleven poles to two white Oak standing One on
each side of the said ROAD in MOSES Line, thence up the several turnings of the said
ROAD to the begining with all houses waters profits whatsoever to the same belonging
To have and to hold the One hundred & fifty acres of land more or less with the appur-
tenances thereunto belonging unto THOMAS PRATT his heirs and assigns for ever and
said land shall remain to THOMAS PRATT his heirs and assigns freed and discharged of

and from all Incumbrances whatsoever. In Witness whereof I have hereunto set my
hand & seal the day and date before mentioned
Teste   THOMAS GRAVES JUNR.,   JONATHAN PRATT
        JAMES PRATT, HENRY GAINES
   At a Court held for Culpeper County the 18th day of February 1782
This Indenture was proved by the Oaths of THOMAS GRAVES JUNR., JAMES PRATT &
HENRY GAINES witnesses thereto and ordered to be recorded

pp.   (On margin: Coleman to Pattie D.D. to BENJA. LUCK the 26th day of Augt. 1784)
46-   THIS INDENTURE made the 20th day of January in year of our Lord One thousand
49   seven hundred and Eighty two Between ROBERT COLEMAN of County of Culpeper
         of one part and JAMES PATTIE of same County of other part Witnesseth that
ROBERT COLEMAN for and in consideration of sum of Eighty pounds current money of
Virginia to him in hand paid by these presents do bargain and sell unto JAMES PATTIE
one certain tract of land granted by the Proprietor of the Northern Neck of Virginia to
ROBERT COLEMAN by Patent bearing date the 29th day of June 1748 lying and being in
County aforesaid and bounded Begining at two red Oaks a Chesnut Oak and Hickory on
South side of South Fork of GOURD VINE RIVER, Corner to RICHARD THOMAS, thence
South Forty one degrees West ninety five poles to a large Pine, thence Twenty four de-
grees West fifty nine poles to a white Oak on East side of a Glade, thence North forty
four degrees West eighty eight poles to two Pines & a Hickory, corner to the said THO-
MAS, thence leaving said THOMAS's line South nineteen degrees West Three hundred
poles to a black Stump two chains from two small Pines on the side of a small branch
and one small Pine one chain Westward from said Corner, thence South seventy one
Degrees East One hundred & eighty five poles to four small Pines on East side of a small
Branch, thence North nineteen degrees East Four hundred and thirty five poles to a
Spruce Pine and two red Oak saplins near a Rock of Stone on the River bank, thence up
the said River South sixty six degrees West forty five poles North fifty nine degrees
West thirty two poles to the begining containing Four hundred acres Togather with all
ways profits and appurtenances whatsoever to the same belonging To have and to hold
said land with the appurtenances unto JAMES PATTIE his heirs and assigns And said
ROBERT his heirs and assigns (the above grnted lands & premises with the appurtenances unto JAMES PATTIE his heirs and assigns) will warrent and forever defend In
Witness whereof ROBERT COLEMAN hath hereunto set his hand & Seal the day and year
above written
in presence of CATHARINE PENDLETON,   ROBT. COLEMAN
        HENRY PENDLETON, JAMES PENDLETON
   At a Court held for Culpeper County the 18th day of February 1782
This Indenture was acknowledged by the within ROBERT COLEMAN and ordered to be
recorded

pp.   THIS INDENTURE made this 12th day of May One thousand seven hundred and
49-   Eighty one Between THOMAS MORRISS & MOLLEY his Wife of Culpeper County of
51   one part and JOHN POINDEXTER JUNR. of LOUISA COUNTY of other part Witnesseth
         that THOMAS MORRIS and MOLLEY his Wife for and in consideration of sum of
One thousand five hundred pounds current money of Virginia the receipt whereof
they do hereby acknowledge by these presents do bargain and sell unto JOHN POIN-
DEXTER JUNR. one certain tract of land lying on both sides of HUNGARY RUN adjoining
the Tract of land I now live on containing by Estimation Two hundred acres be the same
more or less and bounded by the lands of JOHN SPOTSWOOD, DAVID HENINGS, THOS.
LATHAM, DICKIE LATHAM & WILLIAM MORRIS, forty three acres of the above land

taken by me which I am to produce a Deed from the Proprietors Office for To have and to hold the said Two hundred acres of land free & clear from all Incumbrances whatsoever and THOMAS MORRIS & MOLLEY his Wife do hereby covenant that they will warrent the fee simple of the said land free and clear of all claims of them the said THOMAS MORRIS and his Wife or from the claim of any person In Witness whereof they the said THOMAS MORRIS and his Wife have hereunto set their hands & Seals the day & year above written

in presence of THOMAS CAMP,   THOS. MORRIS
         JOHN CAMP, HENRY CAMP   MOLLEY X MORRIS

At a Court held for Culpeper County the 18th day of February 1782
This Indenture was proved by the Oaths of THOMAS CAMP, JOHN CAMP & HENRY CAMP witnesses thereto and ordered to be recorded

pp.   (On margin: Dempsey & Ux. to Stevens D. D. to SPICER WILSON June 178(erased)
51-   THIS INDENTURE made the 8th day of September in year of our Lord One thou-
53   sand seven hundred & Eighty one Between WILLIAM DEMPSEY and MILLEY his
           Wife of one part and MUMFORD STEVENS of County of Culpeper Witness that
WILLIAM DEMPSEY and MILLEY his Wife for and in consideration of the sum of Eighty Two pounds hard money of Virginia to them in hand paid have bargained and sold unto MUMFORD STEVENS and to his heirs and assigns forever all that Tract of land that I bought of Capt. AMBROSE POWELL lying on the BEAVER DAM RUN with the SAW MILL & CORN MILL containing Fifty acres in the County of Culpeper & in the Fork of the ROBIN-SON & RAPPADAN joining to Mr. HENRY FREY & AMBROSE POWELL and WILSON and all houses orchards and appurtenances whatsoever to the same belonging To have and to hold said Fifty acres of land with their appurtenances unto MUMFORD STEVENS his heirs ans assigns for ever and WILLIAM DEMPSEY for himself his heirs the said premises with appurtenances unto MUMFORD STEVENS his heirs and assigns against them the said WILLIAM DEMPSEY and MILLEY his Wife their heirs & assigns against all other persons whatsoever & will forever warrent and defend by these presents In Witness whereof the said WILLIAM DEMPSEY and MILLEY his Wife have hereunto set their hands and Seals the 8th day of September of our Lord One thousand seven hundred and Eighty one

in presence of BENJAMIN PETTEY,   WILLIAM DEMCY
         SAMUEL his mark X CERSEY,   MILLEY DEMCY
         ELIZABETH BLEDSOE

At a Court held for Culpeper County the 18th day of February 1782
This Indenture was proved by the Oaths of BENJAMIN PETTEY and SAMUEL CERSEY witnesses thereto who also swore they saw ELIZABETH BLEDSOE subscribe her name as witness thereto and ordered to be recorded

p.   TO ALL PEOPLE to whom these presents shall come I RICHARD QUINN send
54   Greeting. Know ye that I the said RICHARD QUINN of Parish of Brumfield and
           County of Culpeper, Planter, for & in consideration of the love good will and af-
fection which I have and do bear to my two Grand Children (Vizt.) FRANCIS & JOHN QUINN, Children of the deceased THOMAS QUINN of the Parish and County aforesaid by these presents do give grant & confirm unto my two Grand Children One young Negro wench named Rachael and all her future Increase that shall forever hereafter survive from said Negro Rachael to be equily devided as long as one such Negro or Negroes can be found between my two above mentioned Grand Children & their heirs for ever In Witness whereof I have set my hand & Seal this 18th day of February 1782
                                                             RICHARD QUINN

At a Court held for Culpeper County the 18th day of February 1782
This Deed of Gift was acknowledged by the within named RICHARD QUINN and ordered to
be recorded

pp.   THIS INDENTURE made this 18th day of March in year of our Lord Christ One
55-   thousand seven hundred and Eighty two Between LEONARD HART and CATHA-
57   RINE his Wife of Parish of Brumfield and County of Culpeper and Colony of Virginia of one part and PETER WEAVER of the Parish County & Colony aforesaid of
other part Witnesseth that LEONARD HART & CATHARINE his Wife in consideration of
the sum of Thirty Eight pounds current money of Virginia to him in hand paid by these
presents doth bargain and sell unto PETER WEAVER his heirs & assigns for ever a Parcel
of land lying in the Parish & County aforesaid and containing by estimation One hundred acres be the same more or less and bounded Begining at three red Oaks, Corner to
MATTHIAS WEAVER, and runs thence South thirty degrees West One hundred and Eighty
eight poles to three Pines, Corner to said WEAVER, thence South twenty five degrees
East sixty three poles to a white Oak and Pine corner to HENRY CRISTLER, thence North
twenty eight degrees East forty eight poles to three Pines, Corner to said CRISTLER,
thence North a strait line to three red Oaks corner to ADAM BUMBARDNER, thence
North sixty five degrees West to the begining with all appurtenances thereunto belonging To have and to hold the premises aforesaid with the appurtenances unto PETER
WEAVER his heirs and assigns forever and freely discharged of all Incumbrances
whatsoever and LEONARD HART & CATHARINE his Wife and their heirs the premises
aforesaid with the appurtenances to said PETER WEAVER his heirs and assigns against
all persons whatsoever shall warrent and by these presents forever defend In Witness
whereof the parties to these presents have Interchangably set their hands & Seals the
day and year first above written

in the presence of us   LEONARD his mark ✕ HART
                                       KATHARINE her mark ✕ HART

At a Court held for Culpeper County the 18th day of March 1782
This Indenture was acknowledged by the parties and ordered to be recorded, the said
KATHARINE being privily examined as the Law directs

pp.   (On margin: Gaines to Stigler D D 1789)
57-   THIS INDENTURE made this Eighteenth day of March in year of our Lord One
59   thousand seven hundred & Eighty two Between RICHARD GAINES and ELIZABETH
his Wife of one part and JAMES STIGLER of other part Witnesseth that RICHARD
GAINES & ELIZABETH his Wife for and in consideration of sum of Nineteen thousand
pounds of Crop Tobacco to him in hand paid by these presents doth bargain and sell
unto JAMES STIGLER his heirs & assigns for ever a certain Tract of land by estimation
containing One hundred and fifty three acres be the same more or less lying in County
of Culpeper and bounded Begining at a white Oak, Corner to THOMAS GARNETT, thence
North seventy five degrees East Two hundred & twenty six poles to three Pines in a
Bottom, thence South thirty six degrees East fifty six poles to two Pines, thence South
twenty three degrees West One hundred & twenty poles to two Pines and a box Oak,
thence South sixty nine degrees West forty one & half poles to one Pine near the top of
a Hill, thence No. fifty six degrees West Two hundred & eight poles to the Begining Togather with all houses orchards trees watercourses and all other appurtenances thereunto belonging To have and to hold the said Land & Premises with the appurtenances
unto JAMES STIGLER In Witness whereof RICHARD GAINES & ELIZABETH his Wife have
hereunto set their hands & Seals the day & year first above written

RICHARD GAINES
ELIZABETH GAINES

At a Court held for Culpeper County the 18th day of March 1782
This Indenture was acknoweldged by the within RICHARD GAINES and ordered to be recorded

pp.   (On margin: Haywood to Richards D D 1791)
59-   THIS INDENTURE made the Fourteenth day of March in year of our Lord One
62   thousand seven hundred and Eighty two Between GEORGE HAYWOOD of County of
        Culpeper of one part and WILLIAM RICHARDS of said County of other part
Whereas ROBERT SLAUGHTER by his Deed of Bargain & Sale bearing date the fourteenth
day of May in year One thousand seven hundred and Eighty conveyed unto GEORGE
HAYWOOD the fee Simple Estate of Six hundred and Twenty eight acres of land more or
less lying in the Parish of St. Marks and County aforesaid bounded according to the
courses mentioned in said Deed Except the Exceptions & Reservations therein made
respecting the moiety of a GRIST MILL with the appurtenances and priviledges thereto
belonging NOW THIS INDENTURE WITNESSETH that GEORGE HAYWOOD for and in consideration of the sum of One thousand pounds Sterling money of Great Britain or One
hundred and Thirty three thousand three hundred and thirty three pounds of Crop
Tobacco & one third of a Pound to be paid by WILLIAM RICHARDS his heirs by these
presents doth bargain and sell unto WILLIAM RICHARDS his heirs and assigns all his
the said GEORGE HAYWOODs right & Title of and in the aforesaid Tract of land & Premises
Togather with all houses orchards ways Mills Profits and appurtenances to the same
belonging Except the exceptions & Reservations made by said ROBERT SLAUGHTER in his
Deed to GEORGE HAYWOOD as aforesaid To have and to hold the Tract of land & Premises
with the appurtenances unto WILLIAM RICHARDS his heirs and assigns (for ever
crossed out) and GEORGE HAYWOOD & his heirs the above mentioned & sold tract of land
unto WILLIAM RICHARDS his heirs and assigns will warrent and forever defend by
these presents except as before excepted. In Witness whereof GEORGE HAYWOOD hath
hereunto set his hand & Seal the day & year first above written
in presence of EDWARD STEVENS,   GEORGE HAYWOOD
        WILLIAM WALKER, G. BANKS
At a Court held for Culpeper County the 18th day of March 1782
This Indenture was acknowledged by the within GEORGE HAYWOOD and ordered to be
recorded

pp.   THIS INDENTURE made the fifteenth day of March in year of our Lord One thou-
63-   sand seven hundred & Eighty two Between WILLIAM RICHARDS of County of
65   Culpeper of one part and GEORGE HAYWOOD of same County of other part Where-
        as GEORGE HAYWOOD by his Deed dated the Fourteenth Instant did sell and con-
vey to WILLIAM RICHARDS in Fee Simple a certain tract of land lying in parish of St.
Marks and County aforesaid containing Six hundred and twenty eight acres being the
Plantation now in the possession of WILLIAM RICHARDS whereon SIMON MILLER now
lives for the consideration of One thousand pounds Sterling or One hundred & thirty
three thousand three hundred and thirty three pounds of Crop Tobacco & one third as
by said Deed may appear And Whereas WILLIAM RICHARDS hath agreed to Mortgage the
said Tract of land to GEORGE HAYWOOD as Security for the payment of the said Consideration money or Tobacco, NOW THIS INDENTURE WITNESSETH that WILLIAM
RICHARDS for and in consideration of the premises by these presents bargain and sell
unto GEORGE HAYWOOD his heirs and assigns the above mentioned tract of land as
described in the aforesaid Deed is set forth except as to the exceptions & reservations

referred to in said Deed Togather with all houses waters mills profits to the same belonging To have and to hold the said Tract of land with the appurtenances unto GEORGE
HAYWOOD his heirs & assigns PROVIDED Nevertheless that if WILLIAM RICHARDS his
heirs shall well & truly pay GEORGE HAYWOOD his heirs the aforesaid Tobacco or
Sterling money of Great Britain Gold or Silver at the rate of Fifteen shillings Sterling
for every hundred pound weight of said Tobacco and comply with and perform the
condition of a bond dated the same day with these presents executed by WILLIAM
RICHARDS to the said GEORGE HAYWOOD according to the time & in the manner specified
and set forth in the said condition then this Indenture shall become void and of no
effect anything herein contained to the contrary or seeming to the contrary thereof
notwithstanding In Witness whereof the parties have hereunto set their hands & Seals
the day month & year above written
in presence of EDWARD STEVENS,   WILLIAM RICHARDS
         WILLIAM WALKER, G. BANKS   GEORGE HAYWOOD
    At a Court held for Culpeper County the 18th day of March 1782
This Indenture was acknowledged by the parties and ordered to be recorded

pp.   KNOW ALL MEN by these presents that I WILLIAM RICHARDS of County of Cul-
66-   peper am held & firmly bound unto GEORGE HAYWOOD of said County in sum of
68   Two hundred & sixty six thousand six hundred and sixty six pounds of Crop To-
         bacco & two thirds of a pound to which payment well & truly to be made I do
bind myself my heir firmly by these presents In Witness whereof I have hereunto set
my hand and affixed my Seal the Fifteenth day of March One thousand seven hundred &
Eighty two
    The Condition of the above obligation is such that Whereas GEORGE HAYWOOD hath by
Deed of Bargain & Sale dated the Fourteenth day of this Instance sold & conveyed unto
WILLIAM RICHARDS in fee simple a certain tract of land lying in County of Culpeper
for the consideration of One hundred & thirty three thousand three hundred & thirty
three pounds of Crop Tobacco & one third of a pound, If therefore WILLIAM RICHARDS
his heirs do well and truly pay GEORGE HAYWOOD his heirs the said One hundred &
thirty three thousand three hundred & thirty three pounds of Crop Tobacco & one third
of a pound on any Inspection at FALMOUTH or FREDERICKSBURG at the time & manner
following that is to say the same to become due immediately after Peace may be con-
cluded between Great Britain and United States of America or Trade opened between
Britain and Virginia Now if WILLIAM RICHARDS do pay the said Tobacco and provided
said Tobacco is not paid with three months after the time herein limitted for payment
therof the same is to bear and carry Legal Interest from the first day of May One thousand seven hundred and Eighty one untill paid and keep GEORGE HAYWOOD harmless
against the claim of ROBERT SLAUGHTER on account of the aforesaid agreements and
covenants then the above obligation to be void else to remain in force
in presence of EDWARD STEVENS,   WILLIAM RICHARDS
         WILLIAM WALKER, G. BANKS
 At a Court held for Culpeper County the 18th of March 1782
This Bond was acknowledged by the within named WILLIAM RICHARDS and ordered to
be recorded

pp.   (On margin: Slaughter to Slaughter D D to Francis Slaughter 7th April 1784)
68-   TO ALL PEOPLE to whom this present writing shall come, I JOHN SLAUGHTER of
69   Culpeper in Bromfield Parish in the Colony of Virginia send Greeting. Know ye
         that for divers good causes and more especially in consideration of the love good
will and affection which I have and do bear unto my Son, CADWALLADER SLAUGHTER,

for his further and better support and maintainance hereafter in this world, I have given and confirmed unto CADWALLADER SLAUGHTER his heirs & assigns a Tract of land by estimation containing Sixty acres lying in Culpeper County and Brumfield Parish in the GOURD VINE FORK of RAPPAHANOCK RIVER on BLACK WATER RUN in addition to a tract of land I formly gave my Son, CADWALLADER SLAUGHTER, joining BENJAMIN GAINES and ROBERT SLAUGHTER, my Son, and is Bounded begining at two red Oaks and a white Oak on the Road in BEN: GAINES's line and runeth thence South Nineteen degrees West thirty eight poles to two Spanish Oaks, Corner to BEN: GAINES & ROBERT SLAUGHTER, thence South eighty seven degrees East One hundred and forty seven poles to a Hickory, Corner to ROBERT SLAUGHTER, thence South fifty degrees East One hundred pole to two Chesnut Oaks Corner to ROBERT SLAUGHTER, thence North Nineteen degrees East forty six pole to two white Oaks near a large Branch, thence North fifty degrees West sixty pole to a Spanish Oak and HIckory in a Rich Bottom, thence North eighty four degrees West One hundred and sixty pole to the begining, Togather with all houses and improvements arising therefrom to said CADWALLADER SLAUGHTER his heirs or assigns forever without hindrance molestation of denial of any person whatsoever In Witness I have set my hand and Seal this 18th day of March 1782 in the presence of   JOHN SLAUGHTER

At a Court held for Culpeper County the 18th day of March 1782
This Deed of Gift was acknowledged by JOHN SLAUGHTER and ordered to be recorded

pp.   (On margin: Terrell to Medley Dd. Mr. Medley)
70-   THIS INDENTURE made this first day of May in year of our Lord One thousand
72   seven hundred & Eighty one Between JONATHAN TERRELL of County of PRINCE
        EDWARD of one part and AMBROSE MEDLEY of County of Culpeper of other part
Witnesseth that for and in consideration of the sum of Two thousand pounds current money of Virginia to him well and truly in hand paid hath bargained and sold unto AMBROSE MEDLEY his heirs and assigns for ever a certain piece or parcel of land containing by estimation One hundred acres more or less lying in the Fork of the ROBERTSON on the waters of GRIMES's RUN in County of Culpeper and bounded beginning at a Hickory white Oak & black Jack Corner to SOUTHARD, thence North thirty degrees East Four hundred & twenty three poles to three white Oaks in TERRELLs line, thence with his line South eighty five degrees East twenty two poles, Corner to two Pines & red Oak TERRELLs Corner, thence South fifteen degrees West two hundred and sixty poles to two Pines a red & white Oak JACOB MEDLEYs Corner, thence with his line North seventy five degrees West to the Begining togather with all woods ways waters and all other appurtenances belonging To have and to hold the aforesaid land togather with all the Estate right and Title of him the said JONATHAN TERRELL his heirs and assigns In Witness whereof I have hereunto set my hand and Seal the day & year above written
in presence of JNO. HUME,   JONATHAN TERRELL
        LYDDA her mark ─┼─ KLUGG,
        MATTHEW his mark ─┼─┤ HORSLEY
At a Court held for Culpeper County the 21st day of May 1781
This Indenture was proved by the Oaths of LYDDA KLUGG & MATTHEW HORSELEY witnesses thereto and ordered to be Certified; And at a Court held for said County the 18th day of March 1782 was fully proved by Oath of JOHN HUME another witness thereto and ordered to be recorded

pp.   (On margin: Deel to Harris D.D. 5th Sept. 1784)
73-   THIS INDENTURE made the Twentieth day of February in year of our Lord One
76   thousand seven hundred and Seventy Nine Between PETER DEEL of County of

Culpeper in Colony of Virginia of one part and NATHANIEL HARRIS of County and
Colony aforesaid of other part Witnesseth that PETER DEEL for and in consideration of
the full and just sum of Four hundred pounds current money of Virginia to him in hand
paid by the said NATHANAIEL HARRIS by these presents doth bargain and sell unto
NATHANIEL HARRIS his heirs and assigns one certain parcel of land containing Fifty
four acres be the same more or less lying in Culpeper County and Brumfield Parish in
the Great Fork of RAPPAHANOCK RIVER on BLACKWATER RUN being part of Four Hundd.
and ninety nine acres of land granted to PETER DEEL by the Right Honourable THOMAS
LORD FAIRFAX Proprietor of the Northern Neck of Virginia by Deed from the Proprietors Office bearing date the tenth day of May One thousand seven hundred and seventy
seven as by said Deed will more fully appear and said Fifty four acres of land is bounded
begining at a white Oak and red Oak on a Stoney Point on the West side of BLACK WATER
RUN Corner to COLEMAN and CAMPBELL, and run thence with CAMPBELLs line South
East seventy six pole to two white Oaks on BLACK WATER RUN on the South side thereof
near to a Corner of the said HARRISSes, thence with his line North fifteen degrees East
One hundred and forty two pole to two Pines & a Chesnut on a Stoney Point, thence
North sixty five degrees West sixty pole to COLEMAN's line, thence with COLEMAN's line
to the Begining place with all houses orchards improvements profits to the same belonging To have and to hold the aforesaid tract of fifty four acres of land with the appurtenances thereunto belonging unto NATHANIEL HARRIS his heirs and assigns and
PETER DEEL his heirs and assigns the aforesaid tract of land unto NATHANIEL HARRIS
his heirs and assigns shall warrent and forever defend by these presents against any
person whatsoever In Witness whereof the said PETER DEEL hath hereto set his hand &
Seal the day and year first above written
in presence of us JOHN SLAUGHTER   PETER DEAL
         BEN GAINES, BRYAN MAGRATH,
         JOHN McKENNY
    At a Court held for Culpeper County the 18th day of March 1782
This Indenture was proved by the Oaths of JOHN SLAUGHTER, BENJAMIN GAINES &
BRYANT MAGRATH, witnesses thereto, and ordered to be recorded

pp.   THIS INDENTURE made the Twenty third day of March in year of our Lord One
77-   thousand seven hundred and Eighty Two Between GERARD BANKS of County of
78   STAFFORD of one part and GENERAL ALEXANDER SPOTSWOOD of County of SPOT-
       SYLVANIA of other part Witnesseth that GERARD BANKS for and in considera-
tion of seventy thousand pounds of Crop Tobacco to be paid him by ALEXANDER SPOTS-
WOOD by these presents doth bargain and sell unto ALEXANDER SPOTSWOOD his heirs and
assigns forever all that tract of land called FOX NECK lying in Culpeper County containing Three hundred and forty nine acres more or less being the land purchased by
GERARD BANKS of FRANCIS THORNTON relation being had to the Deed will more fully
appear Togather with all houses orchards and appurtenances whatsoever to the same
belonging To have & to hold the tract of land to ALEXANDER SPOTSWOOD his heirs for
ever & GERARD BANKS shall warrent & forever defend by these presents In Witness
whereof the said GERARD BANKS hath hereunto set his hand & Seal the day month and
year above written
in presence of B. BALL,   GER. BANKS
         JAMES TOBIN
    At a Court held for Culpeper County the 15th day of April 1782
This Indenture was acknowledged by the said GERARD BANKS and ordered to be recorded

pp.   (On margin: Maddox & Ux. to Newell D D to Adam Newell 14th June 1784)
78-   THIS INDENTURE made the Twelfth day of March in year of our Lord One thou-
82   sand seven hundred & Eighty two Between LAZARUS MADDOX of County of Cul-
         peper and FRANCES his Wife of one part and ADAM NEWELL of County of Cul-
peper of other part Witnesseth that LAZARUS MADDOX and FRANCES his Wife for and in
consideration of the sum of One hundred pounds current money of Virginia to said
LAZARUS MADDOX in hand paid do by these presents bargain and sell unto ADAM
NEWELL his heirs and assigns for ever a Certain Parcel of land situate in Parish of St.
Mark in County of Culpeper containing by Estimation four hundred acres and is
bounded begining at two white Oaks on South side of a Branch of FLESHMANS RUN and
Runeth thence North ten degrees West Three hundred & twenty poles to two Pines,
thence South ten degrees East three hundred & ten poles to white Oaks and a Pine,
thence South eighty degrees West Two hundred poles to the begining (which said tract
of land was granted to ALEXANDER HOWARD by Patent bearing date from the Proprietors Office the Twenty six day of June in year of our Lord One thousand seven hundred
& thirty One, Togather with all gardens orchards water courses & appurtenances to the
same belonging To have and to hold the Tract of land with the appurtenances unto
ADAM NEWELL his heirs & assigns and LAZARUS MADDOX doth hereby convey the same
freed & discharged of and from all Incumbrances whatsoever (the Quitrents due after
this date only except) In Witness whereof LAZARUS MADDOX and FRANCES his Wife have
hereunto set their hands & affixed their Seals the day and year first above written
in the presence of   LAZARUS MADDUX
                                                FRANCES MADDUX

   MEMORANDUM that on the day and date within mentioned peaceable possession of the
land and premises within mentioned was had & taken by the within LAZARUS MADDOX
and by him delivered to ADAM NEWELL In Witness whereof the said LAZARUS MADDOX
has hereunto set his hand and Seal the day and year within written
Witness   LAZARUS MADDOX
   At a Court held for Culpeper County the 15th day of April 1782
This Indenture was acknowledged by the parties and ordered to be recorded with the
Memorandum endorsed the said FRANCES MADDOX being privily examined as the Law
directs

pp.   (On margin: Slaughter to Slaughter D D to Self 1787)
83-   TO ALL PEOPLE to whom this present writing shall come, I JOHN SLAUGHTER of
84   Culpeper County and Brumfield Parish in Colony of Virginia sends Greeting.
         Know ye that for divers good causes & considerations to me moving but more
especially for and in consideration of the love good will and Effection I have and bear
unto my Son, ROBERT SLAUGHTER, for his better and further support and maintainance
hereafter in this World, I have given and confirmed to my Son, ROBERT SLAUGHTER, his
heirs and assigns that Tract of land by estimation Three hundred and thirty three acres
more or less lying in Culpeper County in Brumfield Parish in the GOURDVINE FORK of
RAPPAHANOCK RIVER joining the lands of JOHN BUTLER, AMON BOHANAN RICE and
CAD. SLAUGHTER and bounded Begining at two Spanish Oaks on the CHURCH ROAD Corner to BEN GAINES and CDW. SLAUGHTER, thence South nineteen degrees West One hundred & fifty four poles to a white Oak and red Oak, thence South forty nine degrees East
Two hundred & fifty poles to a red oak marked C, thence North Nineteen degrees East
Two hundred and fifty two poles to two Chesnut Oaks, Corner to CADW. SLAUGHTER,
thence North fifty degrees West One hundred poles to a Hickory another Corner of
CADW. SLAUGHTER's, thence North Eighty seven degrees West One hundred and forty
seven poles to the begining I do give the aforesaid to my Son, ROBERT SLAUGHTER, his

heirs and assigns the whole of the said land and premises with all houses, fences, water courses profits to the same belonging and ROBERT SLAUGHTER his heirs and assigns shall forever peaceably and quietly enjoy the land without the least suit or molestation In Witness I have hereunto set my hand and Seal this fifteenth day of April One thousand seven hundred & eighty two

in presence of us   JOHN SLAUGHTER
At a Court held for Culpeper County the 15th day of April 1782
This Deed of Gift was acknowledged and ordered to be recorded

pp.   THIS INDENTURE made this 15th day of April in year of our Lord One thousand
84-   seven hundred and Eighty one Between MASON COLVIN of the one part & HENRY
86   SMITH of the other part Witnesseth that said MASON COLVIN for & in considera-
         tion of the sum of Nineteen pounds twelve shillings to him in hand paid by
these presents do bargain & sell unto HENRY SMITH his heirs & assigns forever one
Tract of land containing Fifty six acres lying in County Culpeper & Lower end of STONE
HOUSE MOUNTAIN bounded (no description of land given) together with all houses ways
watercourses profits and commodites to the same belonging To have and to hold the
bargained lands and premises with the appurtenances unto HENRY SMITH his heirs &
assigns for ever and MASON COLVIN his heirs &c. against the claim of any other person
whatsoever will warrent and forever defend by these presents In Witness whereof the
said MASON COLVIN hath hereunto set his hand & Seal the day & year above written
in presence of   MASON COLVIN
At a Court held for Culpeper County the 15th day of April 1782
This Indenture was acknowledged by the within mentioned MASON COLVIN and ordered
to be recorded

pp.   THIS INDENTURE made the 17th day of May in year of our Lord One thousand
86-   seven hundred & Eighty two Between JACOB HANBACK and SARAH his Wife of
89   County of Culpeper of one part and ROBERT McMEKEN of the aforesaid County of
         other part Witnesseth that JACOB HANBACK & SARAH his Wife for and in con-
sideration of the sum of Twenty five pounds current money of Virginia to them in hand
paid by these presents do bargain and sell unto ROBERT McMEKEN one certain Tract of
land lying in County of Culpeper containing by Estimation One hundred and ten acres
be the same more or less being part of a Patent granted to JOHN BUTTON Deced the 7th
day of September 1753 for Four hundred and seventy two acres as by the Patent from
the Proprietors Office may appear and Begining at a Chesnut and white Oak in a line of
said Tract and runing with said line West Twenty five poles to two Pines, thence South
One hundred & thirty six poles to two Pines and a red Oak, thence West forty nine Poles
to two Pines and a red Oak Corner to SAMUEL SCOTT and COLO. FAIRFAX, thence North
five degrees East One hundred and Twenty nine poles to a Pine marked F X in GREEN's
line, thence with his line North fifteen degrees East thirty two poles to a white Oak on a
Branch, thence South sixty five degrees East One hundred and Eighty five poles
between a white Oak & Spanish Oak th. South sixty four poles to the begining. Togather
with all houses buildings water courses profits and appurtenances whatsoever to the
same belonging To hold the said land herein before mentioned and sold with their and
every of their rights members & appurtenances unto ROBERT McMEKEN his heirs and
assigns forever and said JACOB HANBACK and SARAH his Wife will warrant and forever
defend the said land before granted against the claim of all manner of persons In Witness whereof JACOB HANBACK & SARAH his Wife have Interchangeably set their hands
and Seals the day and year first above written

acknowledged before us JACOB COONES,   JACOB his mark X HANBACK
   HENRY his mark Y COONES
  At a Court held for Culpeper County the 20th day of May 1782
This Indenture was acknowledged and ordered to be recorded

pp.   (On margin: Slaughter &c. to Slaughter &c. DD to John Slaughter April 1784)
89-   TO ALL PEOPLE to whom this present writing shall come Wee WILLIAM BROWN
91   & JOHN SLAUGHTER of Culpeper County and Brumfield Parish & Colony of Vir-
      ginia sends greeting. Know ye that for divers good causes and considerations us
thereunto moving but more especially for and in consideration of the good will and affection which we have and bear unto our Son & Daughter, JOHN SUGGETT SLAUGHTER
and SUSANAH his Wife, and for their better & further support and maintenance hereafter in this World, we have given granted and Confirm'd and by these presents do
freely & absolutely give and confirm unto JOHN SUGGETT SLAUGHTER and SUSANNAH
his Wife the following Slaves and land distinguishing the Gifts by said BROWN & said
SLAUGHTER. I WILLIAM BROWN do freely and absolutely give unto my Son in Law, JOHN
SUGGETT SLAUGHTER, and SUSANAH his Wife the following Slaves Vizt. Sam, Fanney and
Pegg and will forever maintain a good right or title of the aforesaid Slaves to JOHN
SUGGETT SLAUGHTER and SUSANNAH his Wife their heirs and assigns. I JOHN SLAUGH-
TER do freely and absolutely give unto my Son, JOHN SUGGETT SLAUGHTER & SUSANNAH
his Wife the following Slaves and Land Vizt. Charles and Rachael and Two hundred
acres of land more or less lying in Culpeper County and Brumfield Parish and GOARD-
VINE FORK of RAPPAHANNOCK RIVER and bounded Beginning at three red Oaks and a
Gum at the foot of DAVICES MOUNTAIN, thence South thirty East Two hundred pole to a
red Oak & two Hickories near a Branch, thence North thirty East fifty two poles to two
Gum and a Hickory on the ROAD thence up the ROAD North eleven West forty eight pole
to a Spanish Oak on the Road Side, thence North thirty East sixty pole to three Locases in
an old Field thence North forty eight East ninety two poles to two Maples in a Branch in
the back, thence with said Back line to the begining containing by Estimation Two
hundred acres and will forever maintain good Right or Title of the Land & Slaves to my
Son, JOHN SUGGETT SLAUGHTER and SUSANNAH his Wife, their heirs or assigns. We the
said WILLIAM BROWN & JOHN SLAUGHTER for ourselves our heirs &c. doth grant that
the land & slaves with their Increase shall be to the only use of JOHN SUGGETT SLAUGH-
TER and SUSANNAH his Wife their heirs and assigns. We shall and will warrent & forever defend good right or title of the Slaves and their Increase as also the abovementioned lands shall be peaceably and Quietly held by JOHN SUGGETT SLAUGHTER and
SUSANNAH his Wife their heirs and assigns without the least suit or molestation forever
In Witness we have hereunto set our hands & Seals this Twentieth day of May One
thousand seven hundred and Eighty two
in the presence of us   W. BROWN
                                JOHN SLAUGHTER
  At a Court held for Culpeper County the 20th day of May 1782
This Indenture was acknowledged by the within mentioned WILLIAM BROWN & JOHN
SLAUGHTER and ordered to be recorded

pp.   (On margin: Christopher &c. Bond to Chelfe Dd your order May 1810)
92-   KNOW ALL MEN by these presents that we MORTON CHRISTOPHER, JOHN CLORE
93   JUNR. and MICHAEL WILHOITE of County of Culpeper are held & firmly bound to
      PHILIP CHELFE of aforesaid County in the full and just sum of Three thousand
pounds in Gold or Silver to which payment well and truly to be made we bind ourselves
our heirs and assigns in the Penal sum of Six thousand pounds of the before mentioned

money

The Condition of the above Obligation is this that the said PHILIP CHELFE some years
ago purchased a tract of land of Mr. JAMES BELFORD containing Five hundred forty
eight acres lying on the foot of the DOUBLE TOP MOUNTAIN on the Waters of the ROBIN-
SON RIVER in said County which said Tract of land the said CHELFE never obtained any
right of the said BELFORD than the purchase now part of the said Tract of land the said
CHELFE conveyed to the said CLORE, but with no other right than that which the said
CHELFE obtained of the said BELFORD, the other part of said Tract is at this time in possession of the said CHRISTOPHER but he the said CHRISTOPHER hold the said land by no
other right than that before mentioned. Now the said CLORE and CHRISTOPHER do by
these presents agree to and with PHILIP CHELFE to acquit him the said CHELFE and his
heirs and assigns from makeing any other Right to them the said CLORE and CHRISTO-
PHER or their heirs or assigns than the above mentioned and that if any dispute or disturbance shall hereafter arise concerning the above mentioned land, they the said
CLORE and CHRISTOPHER do by these presents oblige themselves to Defend the said
CHELFE and his heirs from any damage that may come against the said CHELFE or his
heirs concerning the said land. Now if the said CHRISTOPHER and CLORE shall well and
truly comply with this agreement according to the tenor of the above Bond that then
this obligation shall be void and of no Effect otherwise to remain in full force power
and virtue as Witness our hands and Seals the (blank) day of (blank) 1782.
in presence of JOHN SAMPSON,   JOHN CLORE JUNR.
         JOHN HANESEFER   MORTON his mark 𝑚 CHRISTOPHER
                                        MICHAEL WILHOITE

At a Court held for Culpeper County the 20th day of May 1782
This Bond was proved by the Oaths of JOHN SAMPSON & JOHN HANESEFER Witnesses
thereto & ordered to be recorded

pp.   (On margin: Wright & Ux. Deed to TOLIAFERRO D D to Self 1787)
94-   THIS INDENTURE made the 20th of May One thousand seven hundred and Eighty
95   Two Between THOMAS WRIGHT & ANN his Wife of Culpeper County of one part &
       HARRY TALIAFERRO of the said County of other part Witnesseth that for and in
consideration of the sum of Twenty two pounds Ten shillings to THOMAS WRIGHT in
hand paid by these presents doth bargain and sell unto HARRY TALIAFERRO his heirs
and assigns one certain tract of land lying in Culpeper begining at two water Oaks in a
Glade, Corner to his Father in a line of a Patent granted to JOHN FINLESON thence with
that line South seventy seven degrees East eighty four poles to a Box Oak in the said
line Corner to HENRY FIELDS, thence with his line North Ten degrees East One hundred
& thirty two poles to a water Oak & white Oak in said line, Corner to JOHN JOHNSON, then
with JOHNSONs line North seventy seven degrees West sixty six poles to two white Oaks &
a Hickory, corner to RICHARD WRIGHT in the said line, then with his line South twenty
one degrees West One hundred & thirty poles to the begining containing Sixty acres
more or less together with all rights members & appurtenances thereunto belonging To
have and to hold the said land with the appurtenances unto HARRY TOLIAFERRO his
heirs & assigns forever and THOMAS WRIGHT & ANN his Wife & their heirs will warrent
and forever defend by these presents In Witness whereof the said THOMAS WRIGHT &
ANN his Wife has hereunto set their hands and Seals the day and year before mentioned
                                        THOMAS WRIGHT
                                        AN WRIGHT

At a Court held for Culpeper County the 20th day of May 1782
This Indenture was acknowledged by the parties & ordered to be recorded, the said ANN
being privately examined as the Law directs

pp.   (On margin: Rootes to Berry DD JOEL YOWELL Feby 1796)
96-   THIS INDENTURE made the 28th day of March in year of our Lord One thousand
99   seven hundred & Eighty two Between GEORGE ROOTS of County of FREDERICK &
      ELIZA. his Wife of one part and ACREY BERRY of County of Culpeper of other
part Witnesseth that GEORGE ROOTS & ELIZA. his Wife for and in consideration of the
sum of Twenty pounds good & lawfull money of Virginia to them in hand paid by these
presents do bargain and sell unto ACREY BERREY and to his heirs and assigns forever
all that Tract of land containing Three hundred and three acres be the same more or
less lying in Culpeper County on the Branches of the ROBINSON RIVER and is bounded
Begining at the Lower end of WILLIAM GRAYSONs Plantation at a Dogwood & Hickory
cut down, thence with his line North twenty six degrees West One hundred and two pole
to two Chesnuts and Chesnut Oak corner to GRAYSON on the Top of the MILL RIDGE,
thence down the several courses of MILL RIDGE to three Spanish Oaks, thence along the
said RIDGE to a Poplar and red Oak, Corner to JASPER STARR, thence with the said
STARRs line South four degrees East One hundred & seventy pole to a white Oak by a
Branch thence South thirty one degrees West forty six pole to two red Oaks by the Old
Road, Corner to MARK FINKS, thence with FINKS line South nineteen degrees West One
hundred & forty five pole to a dead red Oak in FINKS line being a Corner of a tract surveyed for WILLIAM CHAPMAN, thence with said CHAPMANs line North fifty seven degrees West One hundred & sixty two pole to two Chesnut Oaks, thence North eighty five
degrees West Eight eight poles to the beginning and all and singular the houses buildings orchards gardens meadows pastures and appurtenances whatsoever to the same
belonging To have and to hold the said Three hundred and three acres of land more or
less unto ACREY BERREY his heirs and assigns for ever and GEORGE ROOTS shall forever
warrent & defend by these presents In Witness whereof the said GEORGE ROOTS have
hereunto set his hand & Seal this 28th day of March in the year of our Lord One thousand seven hundred & eighty two
in presence of JOHN COLLINS,   GEO. ROOTES
        JOHN his mark X TAYLOR, WILLIAM CHAPMAN
   Received of the within named ACREY BERREY the sum of Seventy pounds lawfull
money being the consideration within mentioned as Witness my hand this 20th day of
March 1782
Test JOHN COLLINS   GEO. ROOTS
        WILLIAM CHAPMAN
   If my Wife ever claims Dower in the within lands I bind myself my heirs to pay Mr.
BERREY one full third part of the value I reced for it
Test JOHN COLLINS   GEO. ROOTES
        WILLIAM CHAPMAN
   At a Court held for Culpeper County the 20th May 1782
This Indenture was proved by the Oaths of the Witnesses thereto & ordered to be
recorded

pp.   (On margin: Rotts &c. to Hume DD JOEL YOWELL Feby 1796)
99-   THIS INDENTURE made the 28th day of March in year of our Lord One thousand
102   seven hundred & Eighty two Between GEORGE ROOTS of County of FREDERICK &
      WILLIAM CHAPMAN of County of Culpeper of one part and GEORGE HUME of
County of Culpeper of other part Witnesseth that GEORGE ROOTS & WILLIAM CHAPMAN
for and in consideration of the sum of Fifty pounds good & lawfull money of Virginia to
them in hand paid by these presents do fully clearly & absolutely bargain and sell unto
GEORGE HUME and to his heirs and assigns for ever all that Tract of land containing One
hundred & Thirty seven acres be the same more or less lying and being in Culpeper on

the Branches of the ROBINSON RIVER and is bounded beginning at a Chesnut & Hickory Corner to said HUME North twenty nine pole to a Gum on a Branch corner to WILLIAM GRAYSON, thence with his line North twenty four degrees East sixty eight pole to a Dogwood & Hickory cut down, thence South eighty five degrees East eighty four pole to two Chesnut Oaks, thence South fifty seven degrees East One hundred and fifty four pole to a red Oak dead standing in MARK FINKS line, thence with his line South thirty degrees West One hundred & five poles to a Gum & Chesnut Oak by a large Rock, thence South seventy degrees West sixty four pole to a Chesnut & Dogwood Corner to said GEORGE HUME, thence with the lines of that tract, thence North One hundred & fourteen pole to two red Oaks and a Spanish Oak by a small Branch, thence West One hundred and twenty seven pole to the Begining and all houses orchards gardens & appurtenances whatsoever to the same belonging To have and to hold the said One hundred & thirty seven acres of land more or less and GEORGE ROOTS & WILLIAM CHAPMAN their heirs & assigns against all other persons whatsoever shall for ever defend by these presents In Witness whereof the said GEORGE ROOTS & WILLIAM CHAPMAN have hereunto set their hands and Seals this 28th day of March in the year of our Lord One thousand seven hundred & Eighty two

in presence of ACREY BERRY,   GEO: ROOTES
        JOHN COLLINS,   WILLIAM CHAPMAN
        JOHN his mark B TAYLOR
Reced of the within named GEORGE HUME the sum of Fifty pounds lawfull money being the consideration within mentioned as Witness my hand this 28th day of March 1782
        JOHN COLLINS   GEO: ROOTS
At a Court held for Culpeper County the 20th day of May 1782
This Indenture was proved by the Oaths of ACREY BERRY, JOHN COLLINS & JOHN TAYLOR Witnesses thereto and ordered to be recorded

pp. (On margin: Haynie & Ux. to Camps DD 1792)
102- ARTICLES of AGREEMENT entered into this 15th day of February in year of our
105 Lord Christ One thousand seven hundred and Eighty two Between RICHARD HAYNIE and ANN his Wife (formly ANN CAMP, Widow & Relick of AMBROSE CAMP deceased) of County of Culpeper and State of Virginia of one part & THOMAS CAMP WILLIAM CAMP, JOHN CAMP & HENRY CAMP, Surviving Children of the deceased of other part. Whereas AMBROSE CAMP by his last Will & Testament date the (blank) day of (blank) 17( ) and duly recorded in the County Court of Culpeper reference being thereunto had will more fully appear did after devising to his Son, THOMAS CAMP, One hundred acres of land and two Negroes named Phill & Sall, and directed a certain tract of his land containing Two hundred acres be sold for purpose therein mentioned Bequeath the residue of his land & slaves to his Wife, ANN CAMP, during her natural life and at the Decease directed the residuary land to be sold and the money arising therefrom together with all the Slaves to be equally divided between her Six youngest children, to wit WILLIAM CAMP, JOHN CAMP, HENRY CAMP, JAMES CAMP, MARSHELL CAMP & BETSEY CAMP, the three youngest of which Children being now dead before any division made whereby the Reversion of the said Estate is vested in THOMAS CAMP, WILLIAM CAMP, JOHN CAMP & WILLIAM CAMP, Surviving Children of the said AMBROSE CAMP deceased. And Whereas the said ANN CAMP is since intermarried with RICHARD HAYNIE, a party hereto, NOW THESE ARTICLES OF AGREEMENT Witnesseth that RICHARD HAYNIE and ANN his Wife for and in consideration of the Benefit of having three Negroes to wit Old Robin, Lett & Frank, Son of Bett, that is to say, Robin & Lett during the natural life of said ANN HAYNIE and the said Frank during the natural life of said RICHARD HAYNIE and ANN his Wife or the life of the longest liver of them and

for the further consideration of THOMAS CAMP, WILLIAM CAMP, JOHN CAMP & HENRY
CAMP agreeing to clear the said RICHARD HAYNIE & ANN his Wife from the payment of
any Debt or Debts due from the Estate of AMBROSE CAMP deceased to any person whatever do hereby give up to be divided all the other Estate of the said deceased between
THOMAS CAMP, WILLIAM CAMP, JOHN CAMP & HENRY CAMP according to an Agreement between the said parties and RICHARD HAYNIE and ANN his Wife do hereby oblige
themselves to give up all the said Estate (except as before excepted) unto the said Surviving Children free and clear from the Claim of them the said RICHARD HAYNIE & ANN
his Wife for the full performance of these Articles the parties to these presents have
hereunto set their hands & Seals the day month & year first above written

in the presence of D. JAMESON JUNR.,   RICHD. HAYNIE
    RICHARD GAINES,   ANN her mark X HAYNIE
    EDWARD WATKINS,   THOS. CAMP
    JAMES NASH   WM. CAMP
                                 JOHN CAMP
                                 HENRY CAMP

  At a Court held for Culpeper County the 20th day of May 1782
These Artices of Agreement was proved by the Oath of DAVID JAMESON JUNR., EDWARD
WATKINS & JAMES NASH, witnesses thereto, And ordered to be recorded

pp.   (On margin: Camp Bond to Camp &c. DD to Self)
105-   KNOW ALL MEN by these presents that I THOMAS CAMP of Culpeper County am
107   held and firmly bound unto WILLIAM CAMP, JOHN CAMP & HENRY CAMP of said
       County in the full & Just sum of Two thousand pounds current money of Vir-
ginia to which payment well & truly to be made to said WILLIAM CAMP, JOHN CAMP &
HENRY CAMP their heirs I bind myself my heirs firmly by these presents Witness my
hand & Seal this 15th day of February 1782
  The Condition of the above Obligation is such Whereas the above bound THOMAS CAMP
Son and Heir at Law of AMBROSE CAMP deceased and Heir at Law of JAMES CAMP, MAR-
SHELL CAMP & BETSEY CAMP deceased, Children of said AMBROSE CAMP deceased, hath
agreed to take an equal part or one forth part of said AMBROSE CAMP deceased according to a Division this day made. Now if THOMAS CAMP and his heirs do well & truly
abide by the said Division and do not molest the others in their part, then this obligation to be void, Else to remain in full force Power & Virtue

in presence of D. JAMESON JUNR.,   THOS. CAMP
    RICHARD GAINES, JAMES NASH

  At a Court held for Culpeper County the 20th day of May 1782
This Bond was proved by the Oaths of D. JAMESON JUNR. and JAMES NASH Witnesses
thereto and ordered to be recorded
  The Division of the Slaves belonging to the Estate of AMBROSE CAMP deced as agreed
between the parties the 15th day of February 1782
  To THOMAS CAMP his part: Lure, Jim & Little Dick
  To WILLIAM CAMP his part, Joe, Frank & Jinney
  To JOHN CAMP his part Old Dick, Agg, Kike & Mingo
  To HENRY CAMP his part Winn, Bob & John
  This Division was made and agreed to between the parties and also that the money
arising from the sale of the lands of the said Estate is to be equally divided between the
aforesaid THOMAS CAMP, WILLIAM CAMP, JOHN CAMP & HENRY CAMP
Test D. JAMESON JUNR.

At a Court held for Culpeper County the 20th of May 1782
This Division of the Estate of AMBROSE CAMP Deced was returned and ordered to be
recorded

pp.   (On margin: Johnston to Wood Junr., D. D. 1788)
107-   THIS INDENTURE made this 17th day of June in year of our Lord One thousand
110   seven hundred and Eighty two Between ANDREW JOHNSTON of County of Culpe-
        per of one part and JOSEPH WOOD JUNR. of aforesaid County of other part Wit-
nesseth that for and in consideration of the sum of Four hundred pounds current
money of the Commonwealth of Virginia well and truly in hand paid to said ANDREW
JOHNSTON he hath bargained and sold unto JOSEPH WOOD JUNR. his heirs & assigns for
ever a certain Tract of land containing by Estimation Three hundred and twenty acres
lying in the said County and on COMICAL RUN, a Branch of DEEP RUN, and bounded
Begining at three Pines standing near the WIDOW STANSIFER's House, thence South
Twenty eight degrees East Two hundred & thirty poles, Corner to two pines, thence No.
Eighty two degrees West thirty poles to three Pines on a Ridge, thence South fifteen
degrees West seventy four poles, Corner to two red Oaks, a Corner of ROBERT FLOYD in a
line of the Old Tract, thence with his line South eighty nine degrees West One hundred
& three poles to one white Oak & Hickory, thence South thirty six degrees West Sixteen
poles to three white Oaks, thence South Seventeen degrees West seventy two poles to a
red & white Oak, thence South twenty degrees East sixty five poles to one Pine & red Oak
in MICHAEL HUFMANs line, thence with his line North eighty three degrees West One
hundred & sixty four poles to two white Oaks & Pine, Corner to the WIDOW HUFMAN,
thence with her line of the Begining, Togather with all woods waters orchards and all
other appurtenances belonging To have & to hold all the aforesaid Land with every
part thereof from all Incumbrances of Mortgages, Dowers, Reversions by or from us or
from any other persons whatsoever In Witness whereof I have hereunto set my hand &
Seal the day & year above written
in presence of GOODRICH LIGHTFOOT,   ANDR. JOHNSTON
        THOS. C. FLETCHER, JOHN STEVENS,
        D. JAMESON JUNR.
    At a Court held for Culpeper County the 17th day of June 1782
This Indenture was acknowledged by the within ANDREW JOHNSTON and ordered to be
recorded

pp.   (On margin: Lightfoot & Ux. to Strode D. D. CHS. CARTER 1818)
110-   THIS INDENTURE made the Eighth day of March in year of our Lord One thou-
113   sand seven hundred & Eighty two Between WILLIAM LIGHTFOOT of One part &
        JOHN STRODE of other part Witnesseth that WILLIAM LIGHTFOOT for and in con-
sideration of the sum of Six hundred pounds Specie to him in hand paid by JOHN STRODE
by these presents doth bargain and sell unto JOHN STRODE his heirs and assigns for
ever all that Tract of land containing by Estimation Three hundred be the same more or
less purchased by WILLIAM LIGHTFOOT as followeth: One hundred acres of JOHN READ,
one other hundred acres of JOHN RYAN, and the other hundred acres of JAMES TUR-
NER as by TURNER's Deed recorded in the General Court and READs & RYANs Deeds recorded in Culpeper Court relation being thereunto had will more fully appear, Together with all buildings orchards gardens meadows and appurtenances whatsoever to
the same belonging To have and to hold the said Tract or parcell of land with the appurtenances unto JOHN STRODE his heirs & assigns forever and WILLIAM LIGHTFOOT &
his heirs the aforesaid bargained and sold premises with the appurtenances unto JOHN
STRODE his heirs and assigns from the claim and demand of him the said WILLIAM

LIGHTFOOT his heirs & from the claim of every other person shall warrent & for ever
defend In Witness whereof the said WILLIAM LIGHTFOOT hath hereunto set his hand
and Seal the day month & year first above written
in presence of PETER ABELL,   WM.LIGHTFOOT
        ROBERT COLEMAN JUR.   ELIZABETH LIGHTFOOT
        GOODRICH LIGHTFOOT,
        ANTHONY FOSTER, G. BANKS
  MEMORANDUM that on the 8th day of March One thousand seven hundred and Eighty
two peaceable and quiet possession of the within mentioned lands & premises was delivered by the within named WILLIAM LIGHTFOOT to the within named JOHN STRODE by
the Delivery of Turf and Twigg
in presence of us (same witnesses)   WM.LIGHTFOOT
  At a Court held for Culpeper County the 17th day of June 1783
This Indenture was acknowledged by the within parties and ordered to be recorded, the
said ELIZABETH LIGHTFOOT being privily examined as the Law directs

pp.   (On margin: Clayton &c. to Camp D D to Self 1787)
114-   THIS INDENTURE made the 17th day of June in year of our Lord One thousand
117   seven hundred and Eighty two Between SAMUEL CLAYTON, Surviving Executor
      of AMBROSE CAMP deced, WILLIAM CAMP and FRANCES his Wife, JOHN CAMP and
SARAH his Wife, HENRY CAMP & ELIZABETH his Wife of County of Culpeper of one part
and THOMAS CAMP of County aforesaid of other part Whereas AMBROSE CAMP by his
last Will and Testament bearing date the (blank) day of March 1769 did devise to his Son,
THOMAS CAMP, one hundred acres of land to be laid off at the upper end of the Tract
whereon he then lived and by said Will directed Two hundred acres of land at the Lower
end be sold and the money ariseing therefrom to be applied to the payment of his Debts
the Ballance of said Tract containing One hundred and fifteen acres he let to his Wife
ANN CAMP during her natural life and after her decease the said land to be sold & the
money ariseing from such sale to be equally divided between his six youngest Children,
(to wit) WILLIAM CAMP, JOHN CAMP, HENRY CAMP, JAMES CAMP, MARSHELL CAMP &
BETSEY CAMP & their heirs, three youngest of which is since dead and the said ANN
CAMP having Intermarried with RICHARD HAYNIE in Consequence of which marriage
the said RICHARD HAYNIE came into possession of the said Land and the said RICHARD
HAYNIE and ANN his Wife by their Articles of Agreement bearing date (blank) for the
consideration therein expressed have given up their right to the said land which by
the Will of said AMBROSE CAMP deced and by Agreement of said THOMAS CAMP, WIL-
LIAM CAMP, JOHN CAMP & HENRY CAMP, the Surviving Children of said AMBROSE CAMP,
& the Consent of the said Exrs. the land was to be sold and the money divided equally
between them in pursuance of which agreement the said land was set up to the highest
bidder & the said THOMAS CAMP became the Purchaser for the sum of Six hundred
pounds One hundred and Fifty pounds of which purchase being one fourth or his equal
part. THIS INDENTURE THEREFORE WITNESSETH that SAMUEL CLAYTON, Exr. &c., WIL-
LIAM CAMP & FRANCES his Wife, JOHN CAMP & SARAH his Wife, HENRY CAMP & ELIZA-
BETH his Wife for and in consideration of the sum of Four hundred and fifty pounds
Current money to said WILLIAM CAMP, JOHN CAMP & HENRY CAMP in hand paid by
these presents do bargain and sell unto THOMAS CAMP his heirs and assigns forever
One tract or parcell of land containing One hundred and fifteen acres of land be the
same more or less being the residue of the tract of land whereon the said AMBROSE
CAMP formerly lives in Culpeper County and bounded begining at a Pine Corner to sd
THOMAS CAMP, thence South thirty five degrees East ninety four pole, thence South
seventy five degrees East thirty eight pole to a small box Oak Corner to DICKIE LATHAM

thence with line (blank) thence North fifty six degrees West One hundred & eighty pole to some Bushes near a Pine, thence North fifty degrees East One hundred & fifty four poles to the begining being the land which was lent to ANN CAMP by the Will of AMBROSE CAMP deced, the Ballce. of the Tract whereon she lived at the time of her marriage, together with all houses profits and commodities to the same belonging To have and to hold the said Tract of land with the appurtenances unto THOMAS CAMP his heirs and asssigns forever and SAMUEL CLAYTON Exr. &c. WILLIAM CAMP and FRANCES his Wife, JOHN CAMP & SARAH his Wife, HENRY CAMP & ELIZABETH his Wife for themselves and their heirs the said land with the appurtenances unto THOMAS CAMP his heirs & assigns shall warrent and for ever defend by these presents In Witness wherefof the said SAMUEL CLAYTON Exr. &c., WILLIAM CAMP & FRANCES his Wife, JOHN CAMP and SARAH his Wife, HENRY CAMP and ELIZABETH his Wife have hereunto set their hands & Seals the day and year first within written
in presence of

      SAML. CLAYTON WM. CAMP, JOHN CAMP, SARAH CAMP, HENRY CAMP (no signature for FRANCES and ELIZABETH CAMP).

     At a Court held for Culpeper County the 17th day of June 1782
This Indenture was acknowledged by the parties thereto and ordered to be recorded

pp.   THIS INDENTURE made the Seventeenth day of November in year of our Lord One
117-   thousand seven hundred & Eighty One Between SAMUEL LEATHERER of County of
122   Culpeper and MARY his Wife of the one part and WILL. JINKINS of the foresaid
           County of other part Witnesseth that for and in consideration of the sum of Two hundred pounds current money of Virginia to them in hand paid have bargained and sold unto WILL JINKINS his heirs and assigns for ever a certain tract of land containing Three hundred twenty five acres more or less lying on the Waters of POPHAMS RUN in said County and bounded begining at a hickory in a line of a Tract granted to ROBERT KING thence with his line South fifty six poles to a forked Chesnut and red Oak saplin thence East One hundred pole to a Chesnut Locust and Chesnut Oak near the top of the LONG MOUNTAIN thence North twenty six degrees East One hundred and eighty two poles to a Chesnut and Poplar thence North thirty degrees West Forty seven poles to a Poplar and red Oak, Corner to the DUTCH QUARTER LAND, thence with the said DUTCH QUARTER LAND South thirty five degrees West thirty eight poles to a red Oak and hicory Corner of said DUTCH LAND, thence with another line of the said LAND South sixty five degrees West One hundred and fifty two poles to a Chesnut, another Corner to the said LAND, thence with another line of said QUARTER LAND North thirty one degrees West One hundred and eighty six poles to a red Oak, Corner to the said LAND, thence South eighty seven degrees West sixty four poles to a Chesnut and red Oak on the Top of a Mountain, Corner to JOHN THOMAS and SEAL, thence with a line of said SEALs South thirty eight degrees West seventy poles to a red Oak in JOHN SAMPSONs deced line thence with the said line South forty degrees East Twenty poles to a white Oak corner to said SAMPSON, thence South seventy degrees East sixty four poles to a Chesnut Oak and two red Oaks near a parcel of Rocks, thence South sixty poles to a gum by LEWIS RENDERs Fence, thence with RENDERs line South forty two degrees East thirty six poles to a red Oak and Gum, Corner to said RENDER, thence South Forty degrees West eighteen poles to a Chesnut, Corner to said RENDERs, thence South fifty six degrees East sixty four poles, Corner to a white Bush on the Road, thence North fifteen degrees West two poles to a Dogwood white Oak and Hicory, Corner to PAUL LEATHERER, thence with PAUL LEATHERERs line East to a chesnut Oak and Sassifrass, thence to the begining together with all houses fences orchards and all other appurtenances belonging To have and to hold the aforesaid land with every part thereof from all Incumbrances unto WILLIAM

JINKINS his heirs and assigns forever Witness our hands and Seals the day and year above written

in presence of   JOHN EDWARDS,   SAMUEL LEATHERER
                 GEORGE CRUMP, WM. HUGHES,   MARY her mark X LEATHERER
                 JOHN SLAUGHTER

Recd full satisfaction for this within written Indenture Witness my hand this 17th day of November 1781
                 JOHN SLAUGHTER,   SAML. LEATHERER
                 HENRY HILL

MEMORANDUM that on the same day of the date of the within written Indenture Quiet and peacible posseession was made and given by the said SAMUEL LEATHER and Wife to the said WILLIAM JINKINS in presence of us whose names are under written
        JOHN SLAUGHTER, JOHN EDWARDS,   SAMUEL LEATHER
        GEORGE CRUMP, WILLIAM HUGHS   MARY her mark + LEATHER

The Commonwealth of Virginia to JOHN SLAUGHTER and HENRY HILL Gentlemen Greeting (Commission for the private examination of MARY, the Wife of SAMUEL LEATHER dated the 16th day of November 1781 in the Sixth year of the Commonwealth) Return of the private examination dated the 17th day of Novr. 1781 and signed by JOHN SLAUGHTER and HENRY HILL)

At a Court held for Culpeper County the 17th day of June 1782

This Indenture proved by the Oaths of JOHN EDWARDS, GEORGE CRUMP & JOHN SLAUGHTER witness thereto and ordered to be recorded with the Commission thereto annexed and the Certificate thereon

pp.   (On margin: Abell to Lightfoot D D 1787)
122-   THIS INDENTURE made the 17th day of June in year of our Lord One thousand
124   seven hundred and Eighty two Between PETER ABEL and LUCEY his Wife of the
       County of Culpeper of one part and WILLIAM LIGHTFOOT of the aforesaid County of other part Witnesseth that PETER ABEL and LUCEY his Wife for and in consideration of the sum of Four hundred and twenty two pounds current money of Virginia to them in hand paid by these presents doth bargain and sell unto WILLIAM LIGHTFOOT a certain tract of land lying in said County; it being the Tract whereon the said ABEL now lives and containing by Estimation Two hundred and nineteen acres be the same more or less and bounded Begining at a dead red Oak in BUCKNERs line, thence North seventy degrees East one hundred and eighty one poles to a hicory, thence South twelve degrees East One hundred and ninety eight poles to three white Oaks, thence South seventy five degrees Fifteen minutes West One hundred and thirty eight poles to a white Oak and Ash near the Run, thence up the meanders of the Run Twenty eight poles, thirty two poles, twenty six poles and thirty poles to a Stake near the Run on the South side, a Corner to LAURENCE CATTLETTs, thence Eighty six poles to the Begining Together with all houses fences and advantages whatsoever belonging To have and to hold the said Tract of land with all appurtenances unto WILLIAM LIGHTFOOT his heirs and assigns and PETER ABEL and LUCEY his Wife doth hereby warrant and will forever defend the said tract of land and premises with all the appurtenances before mentioned unto WILLIAM LIGHTFOOT his heirs or assigns free from all incumbrances In Witness whereof the said PETER ABEL and LUCY his Wife have hereunto set their hands and Seals the day and year above written

in the presence of   PETER ABELL
                                                  LUCY ABELL

At a Court held for Culpeper County the 17th day of June 1782
This Indenture was acknowledged by the within PETER ABELL and ordered to be
recorded
At a Court held for Culpeper County the 15th day of July 1783
LUCEY ABELL, Wife of PETER ABELL, came into Court and acknowledged a Deed of Bargain and Sale from her said Husband to WILLIAM LIGHTFOOT being first privily Examined as the Law directs

pp.   (On margin: Green to Green D D JAS. WILLIAMS 1789)
124-   THIS INDENTURE made this 15th day of July in year of our Lord One thousand
126   seven hundred and Eighty two Between JOHN GREEN of County of Culpeper and
             State of Virginia of one part and WILLIAM GREEN, Son of the said JOHN, of the
County and State aforesaid of other part Witnesseth that JOHN GREEN for and in consideration of the natural love good will and affection which he hath for his said Son,
WILLIAM GREEN, and for the farther consideration of the sum of Five shillings current
money of Virginia to him in hand paid by these presents doth give bargain and sell
unto WILLIAM GREEN his heirs and assigns two tracts of land lying in County of Culpeper, One tract containing by Estimation Seventy acres bounded Beginning at three
white Oaks on the North side of the North Fork of the GOARD VINE RIVER, thence North
fifty five degrees West eighty four poles to a white Oak in a branch, thence South fifty
degrees West One hundred and four poles to a Pine, thence South forty degrees East
eight four poles to a white Oak on the said RIVER, thence down the RIVER the several
Courses to the begining; Also one other tract of land containing by estimation Four
hundred and seventy eight acres bounded begining at a Pine, Corner to Green between
three blazed Pines near the top of a Ridge, thence North sixty degrees West two hundred and thirty eight poles to two white Oaks and a Chesnut on a Hill side near a branch
of CROOKED RUN, thence North seventy four degrees East three hundred and twenty
poles to two white Oak saplins in a Value between two Blazed Pines, thence South sixteen degrees East two hundred and fifteen poles between a Pine and Spanish Oak near a
Blazed white Oak saplin, thence South seventy four degrees West One hundred and
seventy three poles to a white Oak on the side of the North Fork of the GOARD VINE
RIVER, Corner to ROBERT GREEN, thence with his line North fifty seven degrees West
Eighty six poles to a Oak on a branch side, thence South forty three degrees thirty
minutes West One hundred and six poles to the beginning Together with all houses
fences orchards or improvements whatsoever to the same belonging To have and to
hold the said Tract of land with all appurtenances thereunto belonging unto WILLIAM
GREEN and JOHN GREEN doth hereby warrent and will forever defend the said land with
appurtenances unto WILLIAM GREEN his heirs and assigns free from the claim of any
person whatever In Witness whereof the said JOHN GREEN hath hereunto set his hand
and Seal the day and year first above written
in the presence of   JOHN GREEN
At a Court held for Culpeper County the 15th day of July 1782
This Deed of Gift was acknowledged by the within mentioned JOHN GREEN and ordered to
be recorded

pp.   (On margin: Foster & Ux. to Stevens D. D. to Genl. Stevens 1785)
126-   THIS INDENTURE made the Fifteenth day of August in year of our Lord One thou-
128   sand seven hundred and Eighty two Between ANTHONY FOSTER and ROSEY his
             Wife of County of Culpeper of one part and EDWARD STEVENS of the same County
of other part Witnesseth that said ANTHONY FOSTER and ROSEY his Wife for an in consideration of the sum of Four hundred and forty eight pounds to them in hand paid by

the said EDWARD STEVENS the receipt whereof the said ANTHONY FOSTER and ROSEY his Wife doth hereby acknowledge have granted bargained and sold by these presents doth grant bargain sell and confirm unto EDWARD STEVENS his heirs and assigns forever a certain tract of land containing Two hundred and twenty four acres being the land whereon I now live and bounded begining at or between five white Oaks, Corner to HUNTER, thence South seventy seven degrees East One hundred and seventy six poles to a white Oak and red Oak saplin, thence South forty six degrees East eighty poles to two Box Oaks and red Oak saplin in COLEMANs line, thence with that line South forty three & half degrees West One hundred and ninety poles to a Hicory and Dogwood on MOUN-TAIN RUN, thence up the RUN the several courses to a small white Oak and persimmon on the said RUN, corner to EDWARD STEVENS, thence with the said STEVENS up PAYTONs SPRING BRANCH to HUNTERs line near a small Ash, thence with HUNTERs line North twenty degrees East One hundred and thirty five poles to the beginning, Together with all houses buildings Orchards gardens and appurtenances whatsover to the same be-longing To have and to hold the said Tract of land with the appurtenances unto said EDWARD STEVENS his heirs and assigns forever and ANTHONY FOSTER and ROSEY his Wife for themselves their heirs the said land and premises with the appurtenances unto the said EDWARD STEVENS his heirs and assigns shall warrant and forever defend by these presents against any person whatsoever and that the lands and premises shall forever remain unto EDWARD STEVENS his heirs and assigns forever freely and clearly discharged of all other bargains, sales, Debts, Judgments, Dower and title of Dower and all other right and Estates In Witness whereof the said parties have hereunto set their hands and Seals the day and year first above written

ANTHONY FOSTER
ROSEY FOSTER

At a Court held for Culpeper County the 15th day of July 1782
This Indenture was acknowledged by the within ANTHONY FOSTER and ordered to be recorded, the said ROSEY being privily examined as the Law directs

pp.
128-
132

(On margin: Medley & ux. to A. Medley Dd. Mr. Medley)
THIS INDENTURE made this fifteenth day of April in year of our Lord One thou-sand seven hundred and Eighty two Between JACOB MEDLEY and SUSANNAH his Wife of one part and AMBROSE MEDLEY of other part Witnesseth that JACOB MEDLEY and SUSANNAH his Wife in consideration of the sum of Five hundred pounds Specie to them in hand paid by AMBROSE MEDLEY by these presents doth bargain and sell unto AMBROSE MEDLEY his heirs and assigns forever one Certain Tract of Land in Culpeper County and on which JACOB MEDLEY now lives containing by Estimation Seven hundred and one acres be the same more or less and was purchased by JACOB MEDLEY of the following persons: One hundred and fifty acres of WILLIAM BARTON and WILLIAM WHITEMAN, Two hundred acres of MAY BURTON and Three hundred and fifty one acres of CHARLES and BENJAMIN GRIMES, with all and singular the appurtenances belonging and all the Estate Right title and demand of them the said JACOB MEDLEY and SUSANNAH his Wife To have and to hold the aforesaid lands with their appurtenances unto AMBROSE MEDLEY his heirs and assigns forever and JACOB MEDLEY and SUSAN-NAH his Wife the aforesaid lands and premises with appurtenances will for ever war-rant and defend against the claim of any person In Witness whereof the said JACOB MEDLEY and SUSANNAH his Wife have hereunto set their hands and affixed their Seals the day and year above written
in presence of JAMES BARBOUR,   JACOB MEDLEY
        ZACHARIAS GIBBS, ROBT. ALCOCK   SUSANNAH MEDLEY

The Commonwealth of Virginia to JAMES BARBOUR and ROBERT ALCOCK Gentleman Greeting (for the private examination of SUSANNAH, the Wife of JACOB MEDLEY, dated at the Courthouse the 16th day of April 1782 and in the Sixth year of the Commonwealth) (The return of the private examination dated the 18th day of April 1782 and signed by JAMES BARBOUR and ROBERT ALCOCK)

At a Court held for Culpeper County the 20th day of May 1782
This Indenture was partly proved by the Oaths of JAMES BARBOUR and ZACHARIAS GIBBS witnesses thereto which is to be Certified; And at a Court held for the aforesaid County the 15th day of July 1782 was fully proved by the Oaths of ROBERT ALCOCK, a witness thereto, and ordered to be recorded with Commission thereto annexed and Certificate thereon

pp. (On margin: Medley & Ux. to R. Medley D D. GEORGE CHRISTLER Sept. 1785)
132- THIS INDENTURE made this fifteenth day of April One thousand seven hundred
136 and Eighty two Between JACOB MEDLEY and SUSANNAH his Wife of the one part & REUBEN MEDLEY of the other part Witnesseth that JACOB MEDLEY and SUSANNAH his Wife in consideration of the sum of Five hundred pounds Specie to them in hand paid by these presents doth bargain and sell unto REUBEN MEDLEY his heirs and assigns forever one Certain Tract of land on the ROBINSON RIVER in Culpeper County on which lands the said REUBEN MEDLEY now lives containing by Estimation Two hundred and thirty four acres be the same more or less One hundred & fifty acres of which was purchased by JACOB MEDLEY of JACOB BLANKENBECKER and the other Seventy eight acres was purchased by JACOB MEDLEY of GEORGE HOTT with all the appurtenances thereunto belonging To have and to hold the above said lands with their appurtenances unto REUBEN MEDLEY his heirs and assigns forever and JACOB MEDLEY and SUSANNAH his Wife the aforesaid land will forever warrent and defend against the claim of any persons In Witness whereof the said JACOB MEDLEY and SUSANNAH his Wife have hereunto set their hands and affixed their Seals the day and year above written
in presence of JAS. BARBOUR, JACOB MEDLEY
ROBT. ALCOCK, ZACH. GIBBS SUSANA ✗ MEDLEY

The Commonwealth of Virginia to JAMES BARBOUR & ROBERT ALCOCK Gentlemen Greeting (Commission for the private examination of SUSANNAH, Wife of JACOB MEDLEY dated at the Courthouse the 15th day of April 1782 & sixth year of the Commonwealth) (Return of the private Examination dated 18th day of April 1782 and signed by JAMES BARBOUR and ROBERT ALCOCK)

At a Court held for Culpeper County the 20th day of May 1782
This Indenture was partly proved by the oaths of JAMES BARBOUR and ZACHARIAS GIBBS witnesses thereto which is to be Certified; And at a Court held for Culpeper County the 15th day of July 1782 was fully proved by the Oath of ROBERT ALCOCK, a witness thereto, and ordered to be recorded with Commission thereto annexed and Certificate thereon

pp. (On margin: Threlkeld to Jameson D.D. 1788)
137- THIS INDENTURE made this 15th day of August One thousand seven hundred and
138 eighty two Between THOMAS THRELKELD and ELEANOR his Wife of County of Culpeper of one part and DAVID JAMESON of said County of other part Witnesseth that THOMAS THRELKELD and ELEANOR his Wife for and in consideration of the sum of Forty Shillings current money to them in hand paid by these presents do bargain and sell unto DAVID JAMESON one half acre Lot of land in TOWN of FAIRFAX in the said County called and known in the plan of the said TOWN by the number Twenty which said half acre Lot was purchased by THOMAS THRELKELD of NATHANIEL PENDLETON

Gent. and conveyed by a Deed of Bargain and Sale from NATHANIEL PENDLETON and
BETTY his Wife bearing date the 15th day of June 1778 and recorded in County Court of
Culpeper Referrence being had thereto will more fully appear, To have and to hold the
said Lot of land and all the appurtenances thereunto belonging to DAVID JAMESON In
Witness whereof the said THRELKELD and Wife have hereunto set their hands and Seals
the day and month above written

in presence of BIRKETT DAVENPORT,   THOS. THRELKELD
          RICHD. YANCEY, ROBT. COLEMAN JR.

At a Court held for Culpeper County the 19th of August 1782
This Indenture was acknoweldged by the within THOMAS THRELKELD and ordered to be
recorded

pp.   (On margin: Marsh & Ux. to Barnes D D H. BARNES 1794)
138-   THIS INDENTURE made the 20th day of August One thousand seven hundred and
140   eighty two Between EDWARD MARSH and ELEANOR his Wife of Culpeper County
          of one part and LEONARD BARNES of the said County of other part Witnesseth
that for and in consideration of the sum of Forty pounds by LEONARD BARNES to
EDWARD MARSH in hand paid by these presents doth bargain and sell unto LEONARD
BARNES his heirs and assigns one certain tract of land containing One hundred and
Twenty five acres be the same more or less being the same that was formerly the
property of BENNETT NOOE as his Deed will shew bearing date April 20th 1780, Together
with all houses gardens orchards and advantages whatsoever to the same belonging To
have and to hold the premises hereby bargained and sold unto LEONARD BARNES his
heirs and assigns forever and EDWARD MARSH and ELEANOR his Wife and their heirs
shall warrant and forever defend these presents In Witness whereof the said EDWARD
MARSH and ELEANOR his Wife have hereunto set their hands and Seals the day and year
above mentioned   EDWARD MARSH
                                                     ELEANOR MARSH

At a Court continued and held for Culpeper County the 20th day of August 1782
This Indenture was acknowledged by the parties and ordered to be recorded, the said
ELEANOR being privily examined as the Law directs

pp.   (On margin: Green to Slaughter D D Self Jany 1809)
140-   THIS INDENTURE made this the nineteenth day of June in year of our Lord One
145   thousand seven hundred and Eighty Between JOHN GREEN, Acting Executor of
          the Last Will and Testament of WILLIAM GREEN, Gent. deceased, of County of Cul-
peper and State of Virginia of one part and ROBERT SLAUGHTER JUNIOR of the County
and State aforesaid of other part Witnesseth that Whereas the said WILLIAM GREEN in
his life time in and by his last Will and Testiment duly made and published bearing date
the Twenty fourth day of August One thousand seven hundred and sixty three and recorded in the County Court of Culpeper (Referance being thereunto had will more fully
appear) did among other things Impower & require his Executors therein named (of
whom the said JOHN GREEN is the only Acting Person) to mortgage or sell any of his unintailed lands for the payment of his Just debts and Legacies or to act otherwise as they
should think best for the support of the decedents Wife and Children, And the said
Acting Executor thinking it most Expedient to sell part of the said unintailed land did on
the fifteenth day of November One thousand seven hundred and seventy nine being
Culpeper Court Day expose a parcell thereof for sale being the place whereon the said
Decedent lived of which GEORGE HAYWOOD of the County aforesaid became a purchaser
as the highest bidder for the sum of Seven thousand One hundred pounds current
money of Virginia and has since let the ROBERT SLAUGHTER JUNR. have. Now the said

JOHN GREEN by vertue of the power to him given by the said Will and for the sum of
Seven thousand and One hundred pounds current money of Virginia to him in hand
paid by ROBERT SLAUGHTER JUNR. by these presents doth bargain and sell unto ROBERT
SLAUGHTER JUNR. his heirs and assigns forever one certain tract of land lying on both
sides of MOUNTAIN RUN in County of Culpeper and State of Virginia being the place
whereof the said WILLIAM GREEN deced lived, being in two separate tracts bought by
WILLIAM GREEN deced, the one of Colo. THOMAS SLAUGHTER of County of Culpeper and
the other of JOHN TRIPLETT of same County, the boundaries of which tracts may appear
by refering to the Deeds recorded in the County Court of Culpeper containing by the
said Deeds Three hundred and sixty four acres be the same ore or less and also all trees
woods profits and appurtenances whatsoever to the said land belonging To have and to
hold the said Tract of land containing Three hundred and sixty four acres the same
more or less as aforesaid and all the premises with the appurtenances unto ROBERT
SLAUGHTER JUNIOR his heirs and assigns discharged of all Incumbrances whatsoever
which may be alledged in consequence of any act or acts thing or things committed or
done by the said WILLIAM GREEN in his life time or by his heirs since his Death And
JOHN GREEN by these presents doth warrant and will forever defend the said land and
premises unto ROBERT SLAUGHTER JUNIOR his heirs and assigns forever against the
claim of any person whatsoever In Witness whereof the said JOHN GREEN hath hereunto set his hand and Seal the day and year first within written
in presence of R. SLAUGHTER,   JOHN GREEN
        JAMES GREEN. LAWRENCE SLAUGHTER
    This is to Certify that I do relinquish all my Right and title of Dower to the within
mentioned three hundred and sixty four acres of land to ROBERT SLAUGHTER JUNIOR his
heirs and assigns forever. In Witness whereof I have set my hand and Seal this the
Nineteenth day of June One thousand seven hundred and Eighty
in presence of ROBERT SLAUGHTER,   ANN GREEN
        JAMES GREEN, LAURENCE SLAUGHTER
    Received of ROBERT SLAUGHTER JUNIOR the sum of Seven thousand one hundred
pounds current money of Virginia being the consideration within mentioned as Witness my hand this the Nineteenth day of June One thousand seven hundred and Eighty
Witness ROBERT SLAUGHTER,   JOHN GREEN
        JAMES GREEN, LAURENCE SLAUGHTER
    I do hereby relinquish to ROBERT SLAUGHTER JUNIOR any Right I may have to the
above said Land as the first Purchaser In Witness whereof I have set my hand this
Nineteenth day of June One thousand seven hundred and eighty
Witness ROBERT SLAUGHTER,   GEORGE HAYWOOD
        JAMES GREEN, LAURENCE SLAUGHTER
    I do hereby oblige my self my heirs &c. to allow a Burying Ground sufficient for the
said Decedents Family and witness whereof I have hereunto set my hand and seal this
the Nineteenth day of June Seventeen hundred and eighty
Witness   ROBERT SLAUGHTER JUNR.
    At a Court held for Culpeper County the 17th day of July 1780
This Indenture with the Certificates and Receipt thereon was proved by the Oaths of
JAMES GREEN & LAWRENCE SLAUGHTER as to JOHN GREEN, ANN GREEN & GEORGE HAY-
WOOD and acknowledged as to ROBERT SLAUGHTER JUNR. and ordered to be Certified, And
at a Court held for the said County the 20th day of August 1782 was further proved by
ROBERT SLAUGHTER and ordered to be recorded

pp.   (On margin: Thornton to Cocke D D Jno. C. Cocke Dec 1797)
145-   THIS INDENTURE made the thirteenth day of May in year of our Lord One thou-
149   sand seven hundred and seventy eight and in the Second year of the Common-
        wealth of Virginia Between PETER PRESLY THORNTON of NORTHUMBERLAND
COUNTY Esquire of one part and JOHN CATESBY COCKE Esquire of other part Witnesseth
that PETER PRESLY THORNTON for and in consideration of the sum of Three hundred and
fifty pounds current money to him in hand paid by JOHN CATESBY COCKE by these presents doth bargain and sell JOHN CATESBY COCKE and his heirs all that tract or parcel of
land containing Seven hundred acres, it being part of a Tract lately divided between
the said PETER PRESLY THORNTON and his Brother, PRESLY THORNTON, Situate in
County of Culpeper and on a branch of RAPPAHANOCK called and known by the name of
EASTHAMS RIVER, begining at a Spanish Oak, red Oak and Hickory near a branch and
on CHESTERS GAP ROAD on the North West side thereof, thence down the ROAD according to the several courses thereof to two small red Oak saplings on the North West side
thereof and Corner to Mr. HICKMAN, thence South fifty nine degrees West Two hundred and eight poles to two white Oaks and one red Oak near a Branch, thence North
twenty degrees Forth five minutes West One hundred and twelve poles to a red Oak,
thence North thirty eight degrees West Forty poles to a Maple standing in a branch,
thence North eighty one degrees West thirtyeight poles to a red Oak on the side of a Hill,
thence North seventy four degrees West forty one poles to two Swamp Spanish Oaks,
thence South seventy three degrees West twenty two pole to a Spanish Oak and Hickory,
thence North forty six degrees West thirty pole to two white Oaks on LIZARD BRANCH
side, thence up the meanders thereof according to the several courses to two Spanish
Swamp Oaks standing on said Branch, thence North seventy one degrees West fifty pole
to three Spanish Oaks in a Pond, thence North twenty one degrees West One hundred
and twenty pole to a red Oak on EASTHAMs RIVER aforesaid, thence down the said RIVER
according to the several courses thereof to a white and red Oak Stump standing on said
RIVER bank, Thence leaving the RIVER South twenty degrees East twenty pole to a post,
thence North sixty five degrees East One hundred and four pole to a white Oak, red Oak
and Hickory, thence North Ten degrees East One hundred and sixty eight pole to five
white Oaks standing on a Ridge, thence South eighty four degrees East One hundred
pole to the begining which said Dividend or parcel of land with all houses buildings
yards gardens orchards water courses commodities and appurtenances to the same belonging To have and to hold the said Dividend Tract and parcel of land and premises
with every of their appurtenances unto JOHN CATESBY COCKE his heirs and assigns and
PETER PRESLY THORNTON and his heirs will warrent and forever defend the said Dividend Tract & Parcell of land unto JOHN CATESBY COCKE his heirs and assigns against the
claim of every person whatsoever In Witness whereof the parties to these presents
have hereunto set their hands and Seals the day and year first above written
in presents of JOHN WORMELY,   PETER PRESLY THORNTON
        RO. WORMELY CARTER, ROBT. HAMILTON,
        JOHN TAYLOR HAMILTON, REUBEN BEALE
Reced May 13th 1778 of JOHN CATESBY COCKE the full and just Sum of Three hundred &
fifty pounds, it being the consideration money mentioned within to be by him paid to
Witness JOHN MACKAY,   PETER PRESLY THORNTON
        JNO. THORNTON, JOHN TAYLOR HAMILTON,
        REUBIN BEALE
At a Court held for Culpeper County the 16th day of November 1778
This Indenture was proved by the Oath of REUBIN BEALE a witness thereto and ordered
to be Certified; At a Court held for said County the 17th day of April 1780, was further
proved by the Oath of ROBERT HAMILTON, a witness thereto, which is to be Certified;

And at a Court held for the aforesaid County the 16th day of September 1782 was fully
proved by the Oath of JOHN TAYLOR HAMILTON, another witness thereto, and ordered to
be recorded

pp.   (On margin: Shackleford to Freeman D D Self 1801)
149-   THIS INDENTURE made the 23d day of January One thousand seven hundred and
151   eighty two Between JOHN SHACKLEFORD of County of Culpeper of one part and
         ROBERT FREEMAN (Son of ROBERT) of same County of other part Witnesseth that
JOHN SHACKLEFORD for sum of sixty pounds current money to him in hand paid by
ROBERT FREEMAN by these presents doth bargain and sell unto ROBERT FREEMAN his
heirs and assigns a certain Tract of land situate on the Little Fork and County aforesaid
containing Thirty one acres be the same more or less bounded begining at a Pine on
the West side of a Hill, Corner WILLIS old Survey and runing with his Line South fifty
seven degrees West forty four poles to a Hickory Saplin on the West side a Hill Corner to
WILLIAM BOWMER and FREEMAN, then with FREEMANs line South thirty degrees East
eighty eight poles to two box Oaks on a Hill, Corner to JESSE PARSONS, thence with PAR-
SONs line North forty seven degrees East Eighty two poles to his Corner two red Oak saplins on the East side of a Hill, thence with HANKEN READs line North fifty five degrees
West Eighty one pole to the begining, Together with all houses Orchards and improvements to the same belonging To have and to hold to the said ROBERT FREEMAN his heirs
and assigns forever and JOHN SHACKLEFORD for himself his heirs doth warrant and
defend the said land and premises unto ROBERT FREEMAN his heirs and assigns against
the claim of any person whatever In Witness whereof the said JOHN SHACKLEFORD hath
hereunto set his hand and Seal the day and year first above written
in presence of WILLIAM HAYNIE,   JOHN SHACKLEFORD
         JOHN FREEMAN, CATY her mark X BLACKWELL
    At a Court held for Culpeper County the 16th day of September 1782
This Indenture was proved by the Oaths of WILLIAM HAYNIE, JOHN FREEMAN & CATY
BLACKWELL witnesses thereto and ordered to be recorded

pp.   (On margin: Newman to Henshaw D.D. to Saul (?) Henshaw Sept. 1806)
151-   THIS INDENTURE Witnesseth that I JAMES NEWMAN of ORANGE COUNTY for divers
153   good causes and considerations to me thereunto but more especially for the
         natural love and affection which I have and do bare unto my Son in Law, JOHN
HENSHAW, and my Daughter, PATTY, his Wife of County of Culpeper by these presents
doth give grant and confirm unto JOHN HENSHAW and PATTY his Wife their heirs and
assigns forever One certain tract of land lying and being in Parish of Brumfield in
County of Culpeper, it being all and every part of that tract of land which I purchased
from JOHN BROYLES lying on DEEP RUN and containing by Estimation Four hundred and
sixty two acres be the same or less bounded Begining at a red Oak and Hickory on the
South side of HAY STACK BRANCH by ADKINS's, runing thence North seventy degrees
West Two hundred and twenty eight poles to three Black Oaks Corner to MICHAEL
MANKSPILE, thence with his line North twenty seven degrees East One hundred and
forty four poles to a red and two Box Oaks on a Ridge in MANKSPILEs Old Patent line,
thence North seventy degrees East Two hundred and Sixty pole to three Pines, Corner of
the Old Patent, thence South forty five degrees East One hundred and sixty six pole to
two large Pines Corner to HENRY AYLOR, thence South fifty degrees West three hundred pole along another of the Old Patent lines to the begining, Together with all and
singular the appurtenances thereunto belonging To have and to hold the premises
aforesaid with the appurtenances to said JOHN HENSHAW and PATTY his Wife their heirs
and assigns forever. In Witness whereof I have hereunto set my hand and Seal this

16th day of September One thousand seven hundred and Eighty two
in presence of us   JAMES NEWMAN
  At a Court held for Culpeper County the 16th day of September 1782
This Deed of Gift was acknowledged and ordered to be recorded

pp.   (On margin: Buford to Lewis D. D. to Jno. Lewis 14 Sept 94)
153-   THIS INDENTURE made this twenty sixth day of July in year of our Lord One
155   thousand seven hundred and Eighty two Between JOHN BUFORD of Parish of
         Bromfield in County of Culpeper of one part and JOHN LEWIS of Parish and
County aforesaid of other part Witnesseth that JOHN BUFORD for value received of him
the said JOHN LEWIS by these presents doth bargain and sell to JOHN LEWIS his heirs
and assigns forever one Tract of land lying and being in the Parish and County aforesaid contained by Estimation Three hundred and eighty eight acres be the same more or
less the said parcel of land being a Tract granted to JOHN BUFORD by Patent bearing date
the Ninth day of August One thousand seven hundred and thirty five and bounded Begining at a red Oak two white Oaks and a Pine on BEAUTIFUL RUN and runing thence
South twenty five degrees West ninety six pole to a Beach and a Pine, thence South
seventy five degrees East One hundred and seventy poles to three Pines, thence North
eighteen poles to two pines, thence East One hundred poles to three Pines, thence North
twenty degrees East three hundred poles to a white Oak Pine and a Hickory in GIBBs line
thence with said line South seventy degrees West three hundred and forty pole to a
Pine on BEAUTIFUL RUN, thence down the several Courses of said BEAUTIFUL RUN to the
begining with all the appurtenances thereunto beloning and all Estate right title and
demand whatsoever of him the said JOHN BUFORD to have and to hold the premises with
appurtenances to JOHN LEWIS his heirs and assigns forever In Witness whereof I have
hereunto set my hand and seal the day and year first above written
in presence of us SAMUEL BROOKING,   JOHN BUFORD
         ROBERT BROOKING, SIMEON BUFORD
  At a Court held for Culpeper County the 16th day of Sept. 1782
This Indenture was proved by the Oaths of SAMUEL BROOKING, ROBERT BOOKING and
SIMEON BUFORD witnesses thereto and ordered to be recorded

p.   KNOW ALL MEN by these presents that I WILLIAM CHAMPE of County of Culpeper
156   and Bromfield Parish hath bargained sold and delivered one Negro girl named
         Judah to ELISHA CHEECK of the aforesaid County and Parish and will forever
warrant and defend the right or Title of said Negroe Judah and her Increase unto said
ELISHA CHEECK or his heirs forever, I bind myself my heirs &c. in the full sum of One
thousand pound Specie in support of the above title of said Negroe in Witness I have
unto set my hand and Seal this 22d day of June 1782
Test BEN. GAINES   WILLIAM CHAMPE
         WM. PENDLETON
  At a Court held for Culpeper County the 16th day of Sept. 1782
This Bill of Sale was proved by the Oaths of BENJAMIN GAINES and WILLIAM PENDLETON
witnesses thereto and ordered to be recorded

pp.   THIS INDENTURE made this 16th day of Septr. in year of our Lord One thousand
157-   seven hundred and Eighty two Between CYRUS BROYLE and MARY his Wife of
160   County of Culpeper of one part and WILLIAM HERNDON of aforesaid County of
         other part Witnesseth that for and in consideration of Twenty five pounds cur-
rent money of Virginia to him the said CYRUS BROYLE and MARY his Wife well and
truly in hand paid hath bargained and sold unto WILLIAM HERNDON his heirs and

assigns for ever a certain Tract of land containing by Estimation Two hundred acres be the same more or less situate in County aforesaid and on the Waters of the ROBINSON RIVER and bounded Begining at two red Oaks and Pine, thence North fifteen degrees East One hundred and sixty poles to three Pines, thence North seventy five degrees West Two hundred poles to two white Oaks, Corner to FLESHMAN, thence South fifteen degrees West One hundred and sixty poles to three Pines, thence South seventy five degrees East Two hundred poles to the Begining, Together with all houses water courses Orchards and all other appurtinances belonging or in any wise appertaining To have and to hold the aforesaid land from all Incumbrances whatsoever to WILLIAM HERNDON his heirs and assigns forever In Witness whereof we have hereunto set our hands and seals the day and year above written
in presence of

SYRUS his mark + BROYLE
MARY her mark + BROYLE

Reced full satisfaction for the within written Indenture Witness our hands this 16th day of September 1782

SYRUS his mark + BROYLE

Memorandum that on the same day of the date of the within written Indenture Quiet and peaceble possission of the land and premises within mentioned was made and given by the said CYRUS BROYLE and MARY his Wife to the said WILLIAM HERNDON in presence of us whose names are underwritten

SYRUS his mark + BROYLE

The Commonwealth of Virginia to JAMES BARBOUR and WM. WALKER Gentlemen Greeting (Commission for the private examination of MARY, Wife of CYRUS BROYLE, dated at the Courthouse the 16th day of Septr. 1782) (Return of the private Examination dated the 27th day of Septr. 1782 and signed by JAS. BARBOUR and WILLIAM WALKER)
At a Court held for Culpeper County the 16th day of Septr. 1782
This Indenture was acknowledged by the said BROYLE & ordered to be recorded with Commission thereto annexed and certificate thereon

pp. (On margin: Crigler & Ux. to Sampson D. D. to Self 1786)
161- THIS INDENTURE made the 16th day of Septr. in year of our Lord One thousand
163 seven hundred and Eighty Between CHRISTOPHER CRIGLER and CATHARINE his Wife of County of Culpeper and Colony of Virginia of one part and JOHN SAMPSON of the County and Colony aforesaid of other part Witnesseth that CHRISTOPHER CRIGLER and CATHARINE his Wife for and in consideration of the sum of Eight Hundred pounds current money of Virginia to them in hand paid by these presents doth bargain and sell unto JOHN SAMPSON his heirs and assigns one certain piece or parcel of land lying in the County of (blank) containing by Estimation One hundred and fifty seven acres (more or less) and bounded Begining at a gum two white oaks and one red oak standing on the North side the ROBINSON RIVER runing thence down the several Courses of the said RIVER One hundred and forty eight poles to a Sycamore, Poplar and Maple on the said RIVER bank at the Lower end of an ISLAND, thence crossing a prong of said RIVER North fifteen degrees East eighty four pole crossing also KITTS RUN to two Pines on a Ridge, thence North One and a half degrees West Eighty two poles to two Chesnuts on a Ridge, thence North fifteen degrees East forty poles to a Forked Chesnut and Chesnut Oak on the side of the Ridge, thence North fifteen degrees West forty four poles to a Chesnut Oak and red Oak in the back line of the Pattent, thence with the back line North seventy five degrees West sixty four poles to four red Oaks on the West side of a Branch, Corner to the Pattent, thence with another of the Pattent South fifteen degrees West two hundred pole to the begining Together with all houses fences waters and appurtenances whatsoever belonging To have and to hold the said Land and pre-

mises with the apurtinances unto JOHN SAMPSON his heirs and assigns forever free and
clear of all former Incumbrances whatsoever and CHRISTOPHER CRIGLER and CATHA-
RINE his Wife doth warrnt and forever defend the said land against the claims of any
person In Witness whereof the said CHRISTOPHER CRIGLER and CATHARINE his Wife
have hereunto set their hands and Seals the day and year first above written
in presence of   CHRISTOPHER his mark *K* CRIGLER
                                                  KATHARINE CRIGLER *K*
    At a Court held for Culpeper County the 16th day of September 1782
This Indenture was acknowledged by the parties and ordered to be recorded the said
KATHARINE CRIGLER being privily examined as the Law directs

pp.   THIS INDENTURE made the Eighteenth day of September in year of our Lord One
163-   thousand seven hundred and Eighty two by and Between CHRISTOPHER CRIGLER
16**J**   and CATHARINE his Wife of the County of Culpeper of one part and GEORGE
        WILHOIT of the County aforesaid Witnesseth that CHRISTOPHER CRIGLER and
CATHARINE his Wife for and in consideration of the sum of Fifty pounds current money
of Virginia to him in hand paid by GEORGE WILHOIT by these presents do bargain and
sell unto GEORGE WILHOIT his heirs and assigns forever a certain Devidend Tract or
parcel of land containing One hundred acres being a part of a greater tract Formerly
granted to THOMAS DIMMACK and by him conveyed to PHILIP ROOTS Gent. deceased,
formerly of KING & QUEEN COUNTY and by him in his last Will and Testament in writing
bearing date the (blank) One thousand seven hundred and sixty five among other
things devised the said Tract to his Son, GEORGE ROOTS, party to these presents, as by the
said Will remaining in the Court of KING and QUEEN Recoarse being thereunto had may
more fully appear lying in the Little Fork of RAPPAHANOCK RIVER on the Dreans of
waters of the ROBINSON RIVER in the County aforesaid and is bounded Begining at a
Locust Dogwood and Hickory a Corner to the said DIMMACKs Patent and runing thence
with the Pattent line North One hundred pole to two white Oaks and hickory in said line
near a branch, thence leaving the Pattent line North seventy two degrees East seventy
two pole to a large Chesnut Gum and Locust on the West side of a Branch, thence down
the said Branch South eighty five degrees East seventy pole to a Hickory and three
Chesnuts, thence South to the line of the Patent on a high Spur of the GERMAN RIDGE,
thence with the line of the Patent West to the begining, Together with all the houses
buildings gardens orchards meadows pastures mines minerals Quarries and appurtenances whatsoever to the same belonging To have and to hold the said Land with every
of their appurtenances unto GEORGE WILHOIT his heirs and assigns forever and CHRIS-
TOPHER CRIGLER and CATHARINE his Wife for themselves and their heirs the said premises with the appurtenances to the said GEORGE WILHOIT his heirs and assigns & all
other persons whatsoever shall warrant and forever defend by these that GEORGE WIL-
HOIT his heirs and assigns shall at all times forever hereafter have hold possess and
enjoy the said premises with appurtenances without the disturbance or hindrance of
said CHRISTOPHER CRIGLER and CATHARINE his Wife their heirs or assigns In Witness
whereof CHRISTOPHER CRIGLER and CATHARINE his Wife hath hereunto set their hands
and seals the day and year above written
in presence of   CHRISTOPHER CRIGLER
                                                  CATHARENE CRIGLER
    Received of the within named GEORGE WILHOIT the sum of Fifty pounds current money
of Virginia being the consideration within mentioned to be paid to me as witness my
hand and Seal this   CHRISTOPHER CRIGLER
                                                  CATHARINE CRIGLER

At a Court held for Culpeper County the 16th day of September 1782
This Indenture was acknowledged by the within CHRISTOPHER CRIGLER and ordered to
be recorded, the said CATHARINE being privily Examined as the Law directs

pp.   (On margin: Crigler & Ux. to A. Crigler D D yr Order 96)
167-   THIS INDENTURE made the Eighth day of Sept. in year of our Lord One thousand
169   seven hundred and Eighty two Between CHRISTOPHER CRIGLER and CATHARINE
       his Wife of County of Culpeper of one part and ARON CRIGLER of the aforesaid
County of other part Witnesseth that for and in consideration of the sum of Fifty pounds
current money of Virginia to him the said CHRISTOPHER CRIGLER well and truly in
hand paid have bargained and sold unto ARON CRIGLER his heirs and assigns forever a
certain piece of land containing by Estimation Eighty nine acres lying at the foot of the
GARMAN RIDGE and on the waters of ROBINSON RIVER and in the said County and
bounded Begining at a Locust Stake and in an old Field and in a line of a tract of land
belonging to GEORGE HUME, thence with that line East One hundred pole to a Corner of
DIMMICKs Cut down, then with a line of that Pattent South forty pole to SMITHs line,
thence with his line South fifty five degrees East eighty pole to two Chesnuts in said
line, thence South forty five degrees West sixty pole to a Chesnut and Chesnut Oak,
thence North forty six degrees West thirty seven pole to a large red Oak, thence leaving
the Pattent lines and runing with a line of COLO. JAMES BARBOURs North eighty two degrees West One hundred pole to two Chesnuts and a Dogwood in OUTZs line and by a
Branch, thence North to the begining Together with all houses fences water courses
orchards and all other appurtenances belonging To have and to hold the aforesaid land
from all Incumbrances of mortgages Dowers Reversion by or from us or from any
other person whatsoever and to the only use of him the said AARON CRIGLER his heirs
and assigns As witness our hands and Seals the day and year above written
in presence of   CHRISTOPHER CRIGLER
                                      CATHRINE CRIGLER
At a Court held for Culpeper County the 16th day of Sept. 1782
This Indenture was acknowledged by the within CHRISTOPHER CRIGLER and ordered to
be recorded the said CATHARINE being privily examined as the Law directs

pp.   THIS INDENTURE made the Sixteenth day of Sept. in year of our Lord Christ One
170-   thousand seven hundred and Eighty two Between LEWIS BOOTEN and ELEANOR
172   his Wife of County of Culpeper (grantee not shown here as usual in such Deeds) Wit-
       nesseth that said LEWIS and ELEANOR his Wife for and in consideration of the
sum of Two hundred and seventy pounds good and Lawfull money of the State to them in
hand paid by these presents do bargain and sell unto ARMSTEAD MINOR his heirs and
assigns forever one certain tract of land lying in County and Colony aforesaid and in
the Fork of the RAPID ANN and ROBINSON RIVERs and is bounded Begining at two Poplars on a Branch, Corner to JAMES ARCHER, thence South twenty five degrees West Two
hundred and eighty poles crossing BEAUTIFUL RUN to a Black Oak, Corner to the said
ARCHER, thence South fifty degrees East One hundred and ninety poles to a Corner, the
tree or trees whreof not mentioned in the Plott, thence South twenty five degrees East
One hundred and sixty poles to a Pine and white Oak on a Branch, thence crossing the
Branch South sixty five degrees East twenty poles to a white Oak and black Oak, corner
to AMBROSE BOHANNON, thence North thirty nine degrees West Two hundred and fifty
poles to the first mentioned beginning Together with all the profits commodites and
appurtenances to the said tract of land belonging to have and to hold the aforesaid land
with all its appertinances unto him the said ARMSTEAD MINOR his heirs and assigns
forever and that by Virtue of these presents the said tract of land and premises with all

its appurtinances is become the actual Estate and Inheritance of him the said ARM-
STEAD MINOR his heirs and assigns forever and said LEWIS and ELEANOR his Wife will
forever warrant and defend the said land with all its appurtinances unto ARMSTEAD
MINOR his heirs and assigns and that the same is freely and clearly discharged of and
from all incumbrances whatever In Witness whereof the parties to these presents have
set their hands and Seals the day and date above written

in presence of us RICHARD VAWTER,   LEWIS BOOTEN
       JOHN BOOTEN, TRAVES BOOTEN   ELEANOR BOOTEN

At a Court held for Culpeper County the 16th day of Sept. 1782
This Indenture was acknowledged by the within LEWIS BOOTEN and ordered to be recorded the said ELEANOR being privily examined as the Law directs

pp.   (On margin: Huffman & Ux. to Fray D D John Fray 1798)
172-   THIS INDENTURE made this Nineteenth day of August in year of our Lord One
174   thousand seven hundred and Eighty two Between HENRY HOFFMAN and ELIZA-
       BETH his Wife of County of Culpeper and State of Virginia of one part and JOHN
FRAY of the said County of other part Witnesseth that HENRY HOFFMAN and ELIZABETH
his Wife for and in consideration of the sum of Sixty pounds to them in hand paid by
these presents do bargain and sell unto JOHN FRAY his heirs and assigns forever one
certain tract of land containing Sixty acres lying in County of Culpeper and Bromfield
Parish and is bounded Begining at a Stone in the Old Field being a Corner of said HUFF-
MANs in HENRY BACKs line, thence with his line South Forty nine degrees East Two
hundred and twenty poles to a Corner of VALENTINE HARTs in the said Line, thence
with said HARTs line South seventy nine degrees West fifty three poles to a Poplar on a
Branch, thence down the several Courses of the said Branch to a red and white Oak,
thence leaving the said Branch South fifty five degrees West Twenty poles to two Pines,
thence to the begining. Together with all profits commodites and appurtinances to the
said land belonging To Have and to hold the aforesaid land with every of it appurtinances unto JOHN FRAY his heirs and assigns forever now in possession of him the said
JOHN FRAY and by Virtue of these presents is become the actual Estate and Inheritance
of him the said JOHN FRAY his heirs and assigns forever and that the same is freely and
clearly discharged of all manner of Incumbrances, the Quit rents and taxes hereafter to
become due only excepted. In Witness whereof the parties to these presents have set
their hands and Seals this day and year above written

in presence of us   HENRY HUFMAN
                                ELIZABETH HUFMAN

At a Court held for Culpeper County the 16th day of Sept. 1782
This Indenture was acknowledged by the within HENRY HUFMAN and ELIZABETH his
Wife and ordered to be recorded, the said ELIZABETH being privily examined as the Law
directs

pp.   (On margin: Greenhill to Bourn d d to Mr. WHARTON)
175-   THIS INDENTURE made the nineteenth day of December in year of our Lord One
176   thousand seven hundred & Eighty Between AMBROSE GREENHILL of County of
       ESSEX of one part and ANDREW BOURN JUNR. of County of Culpeper of other part
Witnesseth that AMBROSE GREENHILL for and in consideration of Fifteen hundred &
fifty pounds current money of Virginia to him in hand paid by these presents doth
bargain and sell unto ANDREW BOURN JUNR. his heirs and assigns one certain Parcell
of land lying in County of Culpeper and bounded Beginning at two Hickories and a Box
Oak corner to GREENs by WAGGONER, thence So. thirty eight degrees East, one hundred
and seventy eight poles to a red Oak and Spanish Oak, thence South thirty six degrees

East sixty poles to three white Oaks, thence South fifty three degrees East, thirty eight poles to other three white Oaks, thence North fifty degrees East One hundred & seventy poles to two Pines & a white Oak, Corner to HUGH SAUNDERS, thence North thirty six degrees West Eighty six poles to an Ash and a white Oak saplin, thence South seventy degrees West One hundred and twelve poles to one white Oak, thence North thirty two degrees West forty three poles to CABBIN BRANCH, thence up the Branch to the Begining Togather with all ways water courses commodities and appurtenances whatever to the same belonging To have and to hold the above mentioned tract of land with the appurtinances unto ANDREW BOURN JUNR. his heirs and assigns and AMBROSE GREENHILL for himself his heirs and assigns the above mentioned granted land unto ANDREW BOURN JUNR. his heirs and assigns against the claim of every person whatsoever shall warrant and forever defend. In Witness whereof AMBROSE GREENHILL hath hereunto set his hand and Seal the day and year above written
in presence of JAMES THOMAS   AMBROSE GREENHILL
        JOHN TAYLOR, JOHN McDONALD
   At a Court held for Culpeper County the 20th day of May 1781
This Indenture was proved by the Oath of JAMES THOMAS which is to be Certified; And at a Court held for the said County the 16th day of Sept. 1783 was fully proved by the Oath of JOHN McDONALD who swore he saw JOHN TAYLOR subscribe his name to the within Deed and its ordered to be recorded

pp.   THIS INDENTURE made the 22d day of August in year of our Lord One thousand
176-   seven hundred and Eighty two Between WILLIAM ROBERTSON and ELIZABETH his
178   Wife of County of Culpeper and State of Virginia of one part and JAMES YOWELL
           of the County & State aforesaid of other part Witnesseth that WILLIAM ROBERT-
SON and ELIZABETH his Wife for and in consideration of the sum of One hundred and Eighty two pounds Ten Shillings current money of Virginia to them in hand paid by JAMES YOWELL have bargained and sold unto JAMES YOWELL his heirs and assigns for ever two certain tracts of land in the said ROBERTSONs possession whereon he now lives containing One hundred and Ninety three acres (more or less) situate lying and being in County aforesaid on the South Fork of MOUNTAIN RUN and bounded the first tract of Ninety one acres formly the property of RICHARD SHIP (decd) Begining at a Pine in FIELDs & PARKERs line and runing thence No. twenty seven degrees East One hundred and fourteen poles to two Pines, thence North fifty poles to three Pines, Corner to PAR-KER. thence North seventy five degrees East fifty two poles to two pines in ROWEs line, thence South seven degrees East One hundred & fifty pole to two Pines and a white Oak, Corner to HENNINGER, thence South thirty degrees West seventy eight pole, thence North seventy seven degrees West fourteen poles to a white Oak and red Oak, Corner to HENNINGER, thence North fifty five degrees West eighty two pole to three white Oaks, Corner to FIELDs, thence to the beginning; The other tract of One hundred and two acres which RICHARD STEVENS purchased of BEN ROWE Begs. at a Pine and white Oak sapplins Corner to the other Tract in HENNINGERs line thence North seven degrees One hundred and ninety four pole to a Pine and two white Oak sapplins, thence North seventy degrees East forty eight pole to a Pine, thence South sixty four degrees East sixty six poles to two Pines near the top of a Hill, thence South twenty degrees East sixty four pole to two Pines & a white Oak, thence South sixteen degrees West forty eight pole to three white Oaks, Corner to WRIGHT, thence South seventy degrees West One hundred & six poles to a white Oak and Pine, Corner to HENNINGER, thence South thirty degrees West eight poles to the Beginning with all the Estate right Interest whatsoever belonging and WILLIAM ROBERTSON and ELIZABETH his Wife shall warrent and by these presents defend the said land and premises with the appurtenances thereunto be-

longing unto JAMES YOWELL his heirs and assigns freed and cleared of all Incumbrances whatsoever Quitrents hereafter to become due only excepted. In Witness
whereof the parties to these presents have Interchangeably set their hands and Seals
the day and year within written
in presence of AMBROSE COLEMAN   WM. ROBERTSON
        RICHARD PARKER, JOHN SUTTON
        WILLIAM COX
    Received of JAMES YOWELL the sum of One hundred & Eighty two pounds Ten Shillings
Specie it being in full the consideration money mentioned in the within Deed
(same witnesses)   WM. ROBERTSON
    At a Court held for Culpeper County the 16th day of Septr. 1782
This Indenture was proved by the Oath of AMBROSE COLEMAN, RICHARD PARKER & JOHN
SUTTON, Witnesses thereto, and Ordered to be recorded

pp.   (On margin: Watts to Doggett D D JNO. WOODROW 1791)
179-   THIS INDENTURE made the Twentieth day of July in year of our Lord One thou-
182   sand seven hundred and Eighty two Between PETERS WATTS, an Attorney to
        WILLIAM WATTS of the State of NORTH CAROLINA and County of GUILFORD, of
one part and REUBIN DOGGETT of Culpeper County in Virginia of other part Witnesses
that PETER WATTS, Attorney to WILLIAM WATTS, for and in consideration of the sum of
Fifty pounds current money of Virginia in hand paid by REUBIN DOGGETT by these presents doth bargain and sell unto REUBIN DOGGET his heirs and assigns a Tract of land
with the appurtenances lying in the Parish of St. Marks and County of Culpeper containing One hundred and twenty eight acres be the same more or less bounded Begining at two white Oaks and a Pine running thence North Thirty two degrees West One
hundred and eighteen poles to two white Oaks, thence South 75 degrees W. 76 poles to 3
white Oaks in AMELIA ROAD, thence along the said ROAD to two white oaks, thence
North fifty nine degrees East One hundred and seventy two poles to two Maples and a
Ash on WATTS's BRANCH, thence down the said Branch to the begining Corner to JOHN
MEGANNON Together with all houses yards gardens orchards and appurtenances whatsoever to the land (bounded as above) belonging To have and to hold the said Hundred
and Twenty eight acres of land be the same more or less with the appurtenances hereby bargained and sold or intended to be hereby bargained and sold unto REUBIN DOG-
GET his heirs and assigns & that PETER WATTS an Attorney of WM. WATTS his heirs &c.
will forever warrant and defend the land and appurtenances aforesaid unto REUBIN
DOGGETT his heirs &c. forever In Witness whereof the said PETER WATTS has hereunto
set his hand and Seal this Twentieth day of July 1782
in presents of RICHARD WAUGH,   PETER his mark ┼ WATTS
        ROBERT POLLARD, WM. BRADLEY,
        JNO. WHARTON, JOHN LONG, THOMAS FARISH
    Recd of the within named REUBIN DOGGETT the within mentioned sum Fifty pounds
current money of Virginia being the consideration money mentioned in the within
deed to be paid by him on the perfection thereof Witness my hand this Twentieth day
of July 1782
        (same witnesses)   PETER his mark ┼ WATTS
    At a Court held for Culpeper County the 16th day of September 1783
This Indenture was proved by the Oaths of RICHARD WAUGH, WM. BRADLEY & JOHN
LONG witnesses thereto and ordered to be recorded

pp.   (On margin: Gatewood & Ux. to Taliaferro D. D. to Self Jany 1785)
182-   THIS INDENTURE made the 23d day of August One thousand seven hundred and
186   eighty two Between PETER GATEWOOD and SARAH his Wife of Culpeper County of
         one part and NICHOLAS TALIAFERRO of ORANGE COUNTY of other part WHEREAS
PETER GATEWOOD and Wife doth hereby covenant bargain and sell the above NICHOLAS
TALIAFERRO a certain tract of land situate in Culpeper County containing One hundred
and eighty eight acres Fifty acres run as follows Beginning at three Hickorys Corner to
GRINNAN, thence North thirty seven degrees West sixty two poles to three white Oaks,
thence North East forty six poles to a red Oak in SPOTSWOODs line thence with that line
South seventy four degrees East eighty poles to (blank) thence South seventeen degrees
Ninety poles to (blank) in the said GATEWOODs line, thence with his line North sixty
seven degrees West eighty poles to a forked White Oak & red Oak, thence South eighty
two degrees West Twenty two poles to the begining, the One hundred and thirty eight
acres runs as follows Begining at a white Ask & Hickory on CEDAR RUN, Corner to
FOSHEE, thence with his line North fifty six degrees East One hundred and eighty six
poles to a Box Oak in a Glade another Corner of the said FOSHEE's, thence the same Course
continued thirty eight poles to a Spanish Oak & forked white Oak, thence North sixty
seven degrees West one hundred and forty three pole to a forked white Oak and red Oak,
thence South eighty two degrees West twenty two pole to three Hickorys, Corner to
DANIEL GRINNAN in a glade, thence with his line South thirty six degrees West twenty
eight pole to a Spanish and white Oak, thence South forty seven degrees West One hundred and sixteen pole to two white Oaks in the said Glade, thence South four degrees East
thirty six pole to a Hickory & Elm near CEDAR RUN, thence leaving the said GRINNAN
down the said RUN the several Courses thereof to the Begining NOW THIS INDENTURE
witnesseth that for & in consideration of Four hundred pounds in hand paid by NICHO-
LAS TALIAFERRO said PETER GATEWOOD & SARAH his Wife by these presents do bargain
& sell unto NICHOLAS TALIAFERRO and his heirs the aforesaid One hundred and eighty
acres of land according to the bound aforementioned with all ways waters profits and
advantages to the same belonging To have and to hold the land hereby bargained and
sold with the appurtenances unto NICHOLAS TALIAFERRO his heirs & assigns forever
and PETER GATEWOOD & SARAH his Wife shall and will warrant and forever defend In
Witness whereof the said parties have hereunto set their hands and seals the day & year
first above written
in the presence of GEORGE NEWMAN,   PETER GATEWOOD
         RICHARD WAUGH, JOHN SLEET,   SARAH her mark + GATEWOOD
         ROBT. COLEMAN JR., SAMUEL CLAYTON
   Received on the day of the date of the within Deed of NICHOLAS TALIAFERRO therein
named, the sum of Four hundred pounds it being the consideration within mentioned to
be by him paid to me
Witness SAMUEL CLAYTON, RICHARD WAUGH,   PETER GATEWOOD
         JOHN SLEET, GEORGE NEWMAN
   The Commonwealth of Virginia to SAMUEL CLAYTON, RICHARD WAUGH & JAS. HORD
Gent. Greeting (Commission for the private examination of SARAH, Wife of PETER GATE-
WOOD dated at the Courthouse the 23d day of August 1782 and Seventh year of the Com-
monwealth) (Return of examination dated 23d day of August 1782 and signed by SAM.
CLAYTON and RICHD. WAUGH)
   At a Court held for Culpeper County the 16th day of September 1782
This Indenture was proved by the Oaths of three witnesses thereto and ordered to be
recorded with the Commission thereto annexed and Cirtificate thereon

pp.   WHEREAS by the Last Will and Testament of JOHN CARPENTER dest. bearing the
187-   29th day of June 1782, he lent unto his Wife, ANN BARBARA CARPENTER one
188   third part of his Estate & the Residue of his Estate to be equally divided his four
        Sons, JOHN, ANDREW, WILLIAM & MICHAEL, and after the death of said Widow
then her one third to be divided in the same manner for as much as it was disagreable
to the said Widow that the Estate should be appraised and so large a part would be rather
an incumbrance to her in her old age, the said heirs being all of Lawfull age and
thoroughly persuaded that the said Estate was free and clear from debt, do cordially &
unanimusly together with the consent of the said Widdow without the formality of an
Order of Court to make a division among themselves which they the said Heirs & Widdow
do by these presents agree shall forever stand to them and their heirs forever (Except
the part alloted to the Widow, which after her death to be equally divided among the
said Four Sons) that is to say, to JOHN CARPENTER his heirs &c., Eve, Jack, Jacob &
Franky, To ANDREW CARPENTER his heirs &c. Adam, Elizabeth & Rose; To WILLIAM CAR-
PENTER his heirs &c. Tom, Mary, Lewis & Nanny; To MICHAEL CARPENTER his heirs &c.
Christopher, George, Adam & Eave, to ANN BARBARA CARPENTER (widow) Bet, which
Negros alloted and divided as above mentioned we the said heirs have now in actual
possession who together with the said ANN BARBARA acknowledge ourselves fully
sattisfied & contented, and to the end that the memory of the said Division shall be per-
petuated to prevent any dispute that might in futer arise the same is desired to be recorded In Testimony whereof we the Subscribers do hereunto fix our hands and Seals
the 12th day of October 1782
in presents off GEORGE UTTZ, Younger,   JOHN his mark + CARPENTER
        GEORGE UTTZ, SENR.   ANDREW his mark + CARPENTER
                                              WILLIAM his mark +CARPENTER
                                              MICHAEL his mark + CARPENTER
                                              BARBARA her mark + CARPENTER
    At a Court held for Culpeper County the 21st day of October 1782
These Articles of Agreement was acknowledged by JOHN & ANDREW CARPENTER and
proved as to other by the Oath of the witnesses thereto and ordered to be recorded

pp.   KNOW ALL MEN by these presents that I THOMAS (SLAUGHTER omitted) of County of
188-   Culpeper, Heir at Law of LAWRENCE SLAUGHTER deced, for divers good causes
189   and considerations to me moving have this day and by these presents ordained
        and appointed BENJAMIN ROBERTS of County aforesaid my right and Lawfull
Attorney for me and in my name as well in the said County and in any other County in
this State to act in all manner of suits that shall in my behalf be commenced after the
consealing of these presents and in my name to issue all and all manner of Process for
me and in my name to Execute which shall be as good and authentick for me my heirs to
us as tho I had in person acted the same, and I do by these presents as aforesaid Constitute and appoint said BENJAMIN ROBERTS my lawfull Attorney In Witness whereof I
have hereunto set my hand and seal this Twenty first day of October One thousand
seven hundred and Eighty two
in the presence of   THOMAS SLAUGHTER
    At a Court held for Culpeper County the 21st day of October 1782
This Power of Attorney was acknowledged by the within THOMAS SLAUGHTER and
ordered to be recorded

pp.   (On margin: Triplett & Ux. to Purvis D. D. Triplett 1790)
189-   THIS INDENTURE made the 18th day of October One thousand seven hundred and
192   Eighty two Between JOHN TRIPLETT & ELIZABETH his Wife of County of Culpeper
          of one part and WILLIAM PURVIS JUNR. of County aforesaid of other part Wit-
nesseth that JOHN TRIPLETT & ELIZABETH his Wife for and in consideration of the sum
of Thirty pounds current money to them in hand paid by these presents do bargain and
sell unto WILLIAM PURVIS JUNR. his heirs & assigns forever One tract of land lying in
County of Culpeper containing by Estimation Forty five acres be the same more or less
being part of the tract of land whereon the said TRIPLETT now lives & bounded Begining at a Beech & Dogwood on the South side of BLACKWATER at the Mouth of the
Branch, thence up the said Branch the several courses to a white Oak red Oak & Hickory
on a Stony Point in said TRIPLETTs line, thence North thirty four degrees West seventy
pole to TRIPLETTs Corner on BLACKWATER, thence down the RUN the several courses to
the begining together with all houses outhouses orchards & water courses to the same
belonging To have and to hold the said land and premises with the appurtenances unto
WILLIAM PURVIS JR. his heirs and assigns forever and JOHN TRIPLETT & ELIZABETH his
Wife for themselves and their heirs the said Land with the appurtenances unto WM.
PURVISS JR. his heirs and assigns shall warrent & forever defend by these presents
against the claim of any person In Witness whereof JOHN TRIPLETT & ELIZABETH his
Wife have hereunto set their hands and Seals the day year first above written
in presence of JAMES PENDLETON,   JOHN TRIPLETT
          JOHN SLAUGHTER, RICHARD PARKS   ELIZABETH TRIPLETT
  The Commonwealth of Virginia to JOHN SLAUGHTER, JAMES PENDLETON & JOHN WIG-
GINTON Gentlemen Greeting (Commission for the private examination of ELIZABETH, the
Wife of JOHN TRIPLETT dated at the Court house the 15th day of October 1782 & in the
seventh year of the Commonwealth) (Return of the private examination dated the 18th
day of October 1782 and signed by JOHN SLAUGHTER and JAMES PENDLETON)
  At a Court held for Culpeper County the 21st day of October 1782
This Indenture was acknowledged by the within JOHN TRIPLETT and ordered to be re-
corded with Commission thereto annexed and Certificate thereon endorsed

pp.   (On margin: Landrum to Orr D.D. to Saml. Orr 12th July 84)
192-   THIS INDENTURE made the 21st day of October in year of our Lord One thousand
194   seven hundred and Eighty two Between THOMAS LANDRUM of County of Culpe-
          per of one part and SAMUEL ORR of County aforesaid of other part Witnesseth
that THOMAS LANDRUM for and in consideration of a Negro girl named Esther to him
delivered by SAMUEL ORR, the Receipt whereof I the said THOMAS LANDRUM doth hereby acknowledge, by these presents doth bargain and sell unto SAMUEL ORR his heirs
and assigns forever one certain tract of land containing two hundred acres lying in
County of Culpeper and bounded Begining at a white Oak, Corner to THOMAS GINN,
thence North East One hundred and fifteen pole to a red Oak in ROUTES old Line, thence
North twenty two degrees West one hundred and sixty five pole to a Pine, Oak and red
Oak, thence South forty nine degrees West two hundred and four poles to a Spanish Oak
red Oak and Hickory, thence South twenty five degrees East to THOMAS GINNs line,
thence with the said GINNs line to the begining, together with all houses gardens
orchards fences profits whatsoever to the said land belonging To have and to hold unto
SAMUEL ORR his heirs and assigns and THOMAS LANDRUM do and will warrant and forever defend by these presents against the claim of himself his heirs &c. As Witness
whereof to these presents hath hereunto set my hand and Seal the day and year first
above written
in presence of   THOMAS LANDRUM

At a Court held for Culpeper County the 21st day of Octr. 1782
This Indenture was acknowledged by the within THOMAS LANDRUM and ordered to be recorded

pp.   (On margin: Barbee to Jett D.D. yr Son 1789)
195-   KNOW ALL MEN by these presents that I JOHN BARBEE of County of Culpeper for
196   diverse good causes & considerations me hereunto moved and especially that
        I am about to remove from the said County to the Back Country on the Waters of
OHIO & it being necessary that some few persons should be authorized to manage and
transact my affairs in my absence as well in the disposal of my effects to be left behind
me and collecting of the Debts that may be due to me as to the payment of those that am
owing & particularly a Debt due to GAVIN LAWSON of the same County as by Bond and
settlement therefore of this date I have therefore nominated and appointed as I do by
these presents nominate & appoint JAMES JETT of said County of Culpeper to be true and
lawfull Attorney for me and in my name to ask for sue for levy & receive of all and sun-
dry persons whatsoever all debts and demands due to me or that I have against all and
every person whatsoever and to sell and dispose of all or any of my property and
effects that may be left behind and also to discharge all debts and just demands against
me and in general due everything in the same manner as if I was personally present
hereby ratifying and confirming all and whatever my said Attorney shall do or cause
to be done in the premises In Testimony whereof I have set my hand and Seal this
seventeenth day of August in the year 1782
in presence of GAVIN LAWSON,   JOHN BARBEE
        ROBT. LATHAM
    At a Court held for Culpeper County the 21st day of October 1782
This Power of Attorney was proved by the Oath of ROBERT LATHAM a witness thereto
and ordered to be recorded

pp.   THIS IS TO CERTIFY that I GEORGE LAYMAN of Culpeper County Virginia have
196-   Impowered my Son, MICHAEL LAYMAN, to receive three bonds for Fifty pounds
197   each due me from FREDERICK WINTER, TULPEHOKIN TOWNSHIP, BERKS COUNTY,
        PENSYLVANIA which bonds I lodged in the hands of PETER SPEAKER of the said
County and Township and if PETER SPEAKER has received the money of the money due
on the said bonds, I hereby empower my said Son to receive the said money for my use
and in case the said MICHAEL LAYMAN shall think it necessary to bring any Sute or
Suits for the recovery of the said bonds or for the recovery of the money due thereon, I
the said GEORGE LAYMAN do hereby fully empower and authorize the said MICHAEL
LAYMAN to bring any Suit in my name against any person for the purpose aforesaid
and to prosecute or discontinue any action or actions as MICHAEL LAYMAN shall think
proper and to make any agreement compromises or acquittance respecting the same
ratifying whatever the said MICHAEL LAYMAN shall do in the premises and hereby
confirm this Power of Attorney irrevocable and do revoke all other Powers and War-
rants of Attorney by me hereafter given or executed Witness my hand and Seal this
(blank) day of October 1782
In presence of us FRANCIS MAJOR,   GEORGE LAYMAN
        JOHN DUNCAN, WILLIAM WALKER
    At a Court held for Culpeper County the 21 day of October 1782
This Power of Attorney was proved by the Oaths of FRANCIS MAJOR & JOHN DUNCAN
witnesses thereto & ordered to be recorded

pp.   (On margin: Wright & Ux. to Camp DD 1787)
197-   THIS INDENTURE made this the 15th day of July in the year of our Lord One thou-
199   sand seven hundred and Eighty two Between THOMAS WRIGHT and ANN his Wife
           of County of Culpeper of one part and WILLIAM CAMP of County aforesaid of
other part Witnesseth that THOMAS WRIGHT and ANN his Wife for and in consideration
of the sum of Twenty five pounds current money of Virginia to them in hand paid by
WILLIAM CAMP by these presents doth bargain and sell unto WILLIAM CAMP his heirs
and assigns forever a certain tract or parcel of land containing One hundred acres
lying in the County aforesaid and on the South side of MOUNTAIN RUN and is bounded
Begining at two Pines and a Rock Stone, thence South seven degrees thirty minutes East
One hundred and twenty four poles to a white Oak North seventy two degrees East
twenty two poles to two Pines on a Ridge Corner to EDWARD WATKINS, thence with his
line to a Poplar on the South of the MARSH BRANCH, thence North seventy seven degrees West (blank) pole to a Hickory a red Oak & Pine Saplins in WRIGHTs line, thence
with his line to the Begining together with all houses Orchards gardens water courses
& appurtenances whatsoever to the same belonging To have and to hold the said tract of
land with the appurtenances unto WILLIAM CAMP his heirs and assigns forever the
said THOMAS WRIGHT and ANN his Wife for themselves and their heirs the said lands
and premises with their and every of their appurtenances unto WILLIAM CAMP his
heirs and assigns shall and will warrant and forever defend by these presents against
any person whatsoever In Witness whereof the said parties to these presents have
hereunto set their hands and Seals the day and year first above written
in presence of us WILLIAM ALLAN,   THOMAS WRIGHT
        JOHN NALL, THOS. BROWN   ANN WRIGHT
     Received July 15th 1782 of WILLIAM CAMP the full and just sum of Twenty five pounds
current money of Virginia being the consideration mentioned in the within Deed
                                            Recd p   THOMAS WRIGHT
     At a Court held for Culpeper County the 21st day of October 1782
This Indenture was acknowledged by the within THOMAS WRIGHT & ordered to be recorded, the said ANN being privily Examined as the Law directs

pp.   (On margin: Lillard to Champe 1851 Ocxto 12 die to B. BERRY)
199-   THIS INDENTURE made the Twentieth day of Septr. in year of our Lord One thou-
204   sand seven hundred and Eighty two Between JOHN LILLARD & SUSANNAH his
           Wife of County of Culpeper & State of Virginia of one part and WILLIAM CHAMPE
of County and State aforesaid of other part Witnesseth that for and in consideration of
the sum of One hundred and fifty pounds current money of Virginia to him the said
JOHN LILLARD in hand paid by WILLIAM CHAMPE hath bargained & sold unto WIL-
LIAM CHAMPE his heirs & assigns a certain parcel of land containing One hundred and
fifty acres (more or less) lying in County aforesaid & is part of a greater Tract of land
formerly the Property of MARTIN HARDEN, which said Tract is bounded begining at a
large Hickory and red Oak, Corner in a line of Colo. FRANCIS THORNTON and Runs
thence with the said THORNTONs line South twenty seven degrees West twenty eight
poles to a red Oak and Hickory, thence South fifteen degrees East forty two poles to a
Poplar, thence South forty eight degrees East sixty four poles to a red Oak, thence South
seventy six degrees East forty pole to two Spanish Oaks, thence South thirty two degrees
East fifty poles to a Hickory white Oak and red Oak, corner to said THORNTON, thence
leaving his line South Eighty two degrees East thirty six pole to a Hickory and three
white Oaks in a line of another tract of said THORNTON & WILLIAM GREEN thence with
said GREENs line North seventy degrees West sixty pole to two white Oaks & one red Oak
Corner to the said GREEN & WETHERALL, thence with said WETHERALLs line North forty

degrees West One hundred & ninety four pole to three Hickories in the said WETHER-
ALLs line, thence North One hundred & fifty four poles to three Chesnuts at the head of
a hollow near the top of a Mountain on the North side, thence East to the begining with
all the Estate Right Title &Interest whatsoever thereunto belonging Except two hundred
acres which was taken from the said recited Tract and was conveyed by JOHN LILLARD
& SUSANNAH his Wife to JOHN BRADLEY & THOMAS LILLARD (One hundred acres of
which to each) the residue of said recited Tract being One hundred and fifty acres
whereon said JOHN LILLARD now lives which he had sold and confirmed to the said
WILLIAM CHAMPE and JOHN LILLARD and SUSANNAH his Wife and their heirs will
warrant and by these presents forever defend the said land and premises with appurtenances thereunto belonging unto him the said WILLIAM CHAMPE his heirs and
assigns forever freed and cleared of all Incumbrances whatsoever In Witness whereof
the parties to these presents have hereunto set their hands and seals the day and year
above written

in the presence of JOHN SLAUGHTER,   JOHN LILLARD
            HENRY HILL, BENJAMIN LILLARD,   SUSANNAH LILLARD
            ROBT. SLAUGHTER

    The Commonwealth of Virginia to JOHN SLAUGHTER, HENRY FIELD & HENRY HILL
Gentlemen Greeting (Commission for the private Examination of SUSANNAH, Wife of
JOHN LILLARD, dated at the Courthouse the Twentieth day of September 1782 and in the
Seventh year of the Commonwealth)
    Memorandum That on the Twentieth day of Septr. One thousand seven hundred &
Eighty two peaciable & Quiet possession & Seizen of the within mentioned land & premises was held by the said JOHN LILLARD and SUSANNAH his Wife & was by them de-
livered the said WILLIAM CHAMPE to be held by him his heirs & assigns forever according to the true intent and meaning of the within Deed Witness my hand & Seal the day
and year first above written
Test HENRY HILL, BENJAMIN LILLARD,   JOHN LILLARD
            JOHN SLAUGHTER
    Recd of WILLIAM CHAMPE One hundred & fifty pounds current money of Virginia it
being in full the consideration mentioned in the within Deed
Test HENRY HILL, BENJAMIN LILLARD,   JOHN LILLARD
            JOHN SLAUGHTER
    Culpeper Sct. By Virtue of the within Commission to us the subscribers directed, we did
personally go to the within named SUSANNA and her did Examine & she did acknowledge that she without the persuasion or threats of the said JOHN her Husband did desire
the annexed Deed should be recorded in the County Court of Culpeper Given under our
hands & Seals the 20th day of Septr. 1782   JOHN SLAUGHTER
                                                     HENRY HILL

    At a Court held for Culpeper County the 21st day of Octr. 1782
This Indenture was acknowledged by the within JOHN LILLARD with Commission
thereto annexed & Certificate thereon & ordered to be recorded

pp.   (On margin: Lillard to Gray D D 1790)
204-   THIS INDENTURE made the Twentyeth day of September in year of our Lord One
207   thousand seven hundred and Eighty two Between JOHN LILLARD & SUSANNAH
            his Wife of County of Culpeper of one part and GEORGE GRAY of aforesaid County
of other part Witnesseth that for and in consideration of the sum of Four and Fifty
pounds current money of Virginia to him the said JOHN LILLARD in hand paid have
bargained & sold unto GEORGE GRAY his heirs and assigns a certain Tract of land containing Seven hundred & sixty three acres situate on the HAZEL RIVER in the aforesaid

County and is bounded Begining at two white oaks marked thus ℗ standing on the HAZEL RIVER at the mouth of CABIN BRANCH, being a Corner of Colo. WILLIAM THORNTON, thence with his line up the said Branch North eighty five degrees West fifty seven pole to two Spanish Oaks on the said Branch, thence crossing the same South fifty seven degrees West Eighty five pole to a white Oak on a Hill, thence South eighteen degrees West One hundred and twenty five pole to a Blazed white and red Oak & Hickory, thence South seventy seven degrees West One hundred and eighteen pole to a blazed white Oak by the Road, thence South twenty five degrees East Four hundred and twelve pole to a Poplar and white Oak by the SCOOLHOUSE OLD FIELD thence leaving THORNTONs lines North thirty three degrees East four hundred and fifty five pole to the HAZLE RIVER near a large Rock, thence up the several Courses of the said River to the Beginning, Together with all the Estate right title and Interest whatsoever thereunto belonging and JOHN LILLARD and SUSANNAH his Wife and their heirs will warrant and by these presents forever defend the said land and premises with the appurtenances thereunto belonging unto GEORGE GRAY his heirs & assigns Freed and Cleared of all Incumbrances whatsoever In Witness whereof the parties to these presents have hereunto set their hands and Seals the day and year above written

in the presence of HENRY HILL,   JOHN LILLARD
        BENJAMIN LILLARD, JOHN SLAUGHTER,   SUSANNA LILLARD
        ROBT. SLAUGHTER

Memorandum that on the same of the date of the within written Indenture, Peaceable and quiet possession of the within mentioned land and premises was made and given by the said JOHN LILLARD & SUSANNAH his Wife to the said GEORGE GRAY in the presence of us whose names are under written
Test HENRY HILL,   JOHN LILLARD
        BENJAMIN LILLARD, JOHN SLAUGHTER

Recd of GEORGE GRAY Four hundred & fifty pounds Current money it being in full the consideration money mentioned in the within Deed
Test HENRY HILL,   JOHN LILLARD
        BENJAMIN LILLARD, JOHN SLAUGHTER

The Commonwealth of Virginia to JOHN SLAUGHTER, HENRY FIELD & HENRY HILL Gentlemen Greeting (Commission for the private Examination of SUSANNA, Wife of JOHN LILLARD dated at the Courthouse the 21st day of September 1782 and Seventh year of the Commonwealth)(Return of the Examination dated the 20st day of September 1782 and signed by JOHN SLAUGHTER and HENRY HILL)
At a Court held for Culpeper County the 21st day of Octor. 1782
This Indenture was acknowledged by the within JOHN LILLARD, with a Commission thereto annexed & Certificate thereon endorsed & ordered to be recorded

pp.   (On margin: Whitesides & Ux. to Adams D D 1789)
208-   THIS INDENTURE made this Eighteenth day of November in year of our Lord One
211   thousand seven hundred and Eighty two Between JOHN WHITESIDES and KATHARINE his Wife of County of Culpeper and Colony of Virginia of one part and JOHN ADAMS of County and Colony aforesaid of other part Witnesseth that for and in consideration of Seven hundred pounds of Crop Tobacco in hand paid by JOHN ADAMS by these presents them the said JOHN WHITESIDES and KATHARINE his Wife doth bargain and sell unto JOHN ADAMS his heirs and assigns one certain tract or parcel of land lying in County of Culpeper containing Seventeen acres and binding Beginning at two pines in a small valley and running South ten degrees West forty four pole to three Pines in old line near a Path, thence near and with said Path North sixty four & half degrees East Eleaven poles to two red Oaks, thence North sixty eight degrees East thirty

one poles to two red Oaks and a Hickory, thence North fifty four degrees East fifty two
poles to two red Oaks and a white Oak, thence North seventy two poles and a half degrees East twenty poles to two Pines, thence North fifty six degrees East twenty eight
poles to a Pine and Chesnut on said Path in another old line, thence with said line South
seventy four degrees West one hundred and twenty three poles to the beginning, together with all houses orchards water courses profits and appurtenances whatsoever to
the said premises hereby granted belonging To have and to hold the lands hereby conveyed and every of their appurtenances unto JOHN ADAMS his heirs forever and JOHN
WHITESIDES and KATHARINE his Wife have good power and lawfull authority to grant
and convey the same to JOHN ADAMS and that the premises now are and so hereafter
forever shall remain and be free and clear of & from all Encumbrances whatsoever In
Witness whereof the said JOHN WHITESIDES and KATHARINE his Wife have hereunto set
their hands and Seals the day and year first above written
In presence of   JOHN WHITESIDES
                                                      CATHARINE WHITESIDES
    Received of JOHN ADAMS the full just sum of seven hundred pounds of Crop Tobacco
being in full for the acknowledgment of the within Deed of Indenture as Witness our
hands this 16th day of November 1782
                                                      JOHN WHITESIDES
    At a Court held for Culpeper County the 18th day of November 1782
This Indenture with the Receipt thereon was acknowledged by the within JOHN WHITE-
SIDES and ordered to be recorded the said KATHARINE being first privily Examined as
the Law directs

pp.   THIS INDENTURE made this Eighteenth day of Novr. One thousand seven hun-
211-   dred and Eighty two Between GEORGE FANT and MARY his Wife of STAFFORD
214   COUNTY of one part and ARTHUR MORSON of said County of other part Witnesseth
          that GEORGE FANT and MARY his Wife for and in consideration of the sum of
Ninety two pounds Five shillings and ten pence half penny current money to them in
hand paid by ARTHUR MORSON by these presents do grant sell & confirm unto said
ARTHUR MORSON in his actual possession now being and his heirs forever One tract of
land lying & being in County of Culpeper and bounded Begining at a white Oak saplin
by a path on the North side of ELK RUN, thence South fifteen degrees West eighty two
poles to two white Oak saplins, thence South West One hundred and twenty six poles to
three Chesnuts on a Ridge, thence North Ten degrees West two hundred poles to a white
and red Oak, thence to the begining containing One hundred acres more or less together with all the appurtinances thereunto belonging To have and to hold the said Tract
of land and appurtinances unto ARTHUR MORSON his heirs and assigns forever and
GEORGE FANT and MARY his Wife shall forever warrant and defend by these presents In
Witness whereof the said GEORGE FANT and MARY his Wife have hereunto set their
hands and seals the day and year first above written
in presence of GERARD BANKS,   GEORGE FANT
       HARRIS HOOE, JOSEPH FANT   MARY FANT
    Commonwealth of Virginia to GERARD BANKS, HARRIS HOOE & WILLIAM HEWIT
Gentlemen Justices of STAFFORD COUNTY Greeting (Commission for the private Examination of MARY, the Wife of GEORGE FANT, dated at the Courthouse the 18th day of Novr.
1782 and seventh year of the Commonwealth) (Stafford County Sct: Return of private
examination of MARY FANT dated 5th day of February 1783 and signed by GER. BANKS
and HARRIS HOOE
       (The recording information of this entry does not appear)

pp.   (On margin: Kamper & Ux. to Whitesides D D to Whitesides 1785)
214-   THIS INDENTURE made this 18th day of November and in year of our Lord One
216   thousand seven hundred & Eighty two Between JOHN KAMPER and ANNE his Wife
         of County of FAUQUIRE of one part and JOHN WHITESIDES of County of Culpeper
of other part Witnesseth that JOHN KAMPER and ANNE his wife for and in consideration
of the sum of One hundred and twenty four pounds current money of Virginia to them
in hand paid by the said JOHN WHITESIDES by these presents do bargain and sell unto
JOHN WHITESIDES one certain tract or parcel of land lying in County of Culpeper containing by estimation fifty three acres which said tract is part of a tract descended to
ANNE KEMPER, Wife of said JOHN, by virtue of the Last Will and Testament of TILMAN
WEAVER deced, and bounded Beginning at a red Oak and white Oak sapling and runing
North seventy six degrees West twelve poles across a large branch to three white Oak
saplings, thence North One degrees West forty eight poles to a Pine and two red Oak saplins on the East side of said Branch, thence North twenty seven & half degrees West Two
hundred and five poles to three Pines in the old line near the RIDGE PATH, thence with
said line North Ten degrees East twenty poles to four Chesnuts a red Oak & white Oak,
Corner to said WHITESIDES other tract, thence with a line thereof South twenty degrees
West seventy two poles to the beginning, containing Fifty three acres as above Together with all the houses water courses profits and appurtenances whatsoever to the
same belonging To have and to hold the said land and premises with every appurtenances unto JOHN WHITESIDES his heirs & assigns and JOHN KEMPER and ANNE his Wife
will warrant and forever defend the said land and premises before granted against the
claim of all manner of persons In Witness whereof the said JOHN KEMPER and ANNE his
Wife have interchangeably set their hands & Seals the day and year first above written
                                        JOHN KAMPER
                                        ANN her mark ✗ KAMPER
    June 17th 1782 Then recd of JOHN WHITESIDES the within consideration of One hun-
dred & twenty five pounds Virginia Currency and acknowledged myself to be fully
satisfied   reced p me   JOHN KAMPER
    The Commonwealth of Virginia to JOSEPH BLACKWELL & FRANCIS TRIPLETT Gent.
Greeting (Commission for the private Examination of ANNE, Wife of JOHN KAMPER,
dated at the Courthouse the 18th day of Nov. 1782 and seventh year of the Commonwealth). (Return of private Examination of said ANNE KAMPER dated the 25th day of
November 1782 and signed by JOS. BLACKWELL and FRANCIS TRIPLETT)
    At a Court held for Culpeper County the 18th day of Nov. 1782
This Indenture was acknowledged by the within JOHN KAMPER and ordered to be recorded with Commission returned thereto annexed & Certificate thereon

pp.   (On margin: Delp to Delp D D 1785)
217-   TO ALL PEOPLE to whom these presents shall come I CONROD DELP do send
219   Greeting. Know ye that I the said CONROD DELP together with ANNA MAGDA-
         LINE my Wife of Parish of Brumfield in County of Culpeper for divers good
causes and considerations but more especially for and in consideration of the natural
love good will and affection which we bear toward our Loving Son, HENRY DELP of the
same Parish and County have given and by these presents do freely give and grant
unto HENRY DELP his heirs and assigns for ever a certain piece of land situate in the
foresaid Parish and County and on the Waters of LITTLE DARK RUN being part of the
same Tract whereon I now live, containing by estimation eighty two acres be the same
more or less and bounded Beginning at three red Oaks in SAMUEL DELP's line, thence
South Fifty seven degrees East two hundred and thirty four poles to three red Oak
bushes in the said COONROD DELPs line, thence with his line North forty five degrees

East eighty six poles to a white Oak, thence North thirty five degrees West Eighteen poles to LITTLE DARK RUN, thence up said RUN to the mouth of a Branch on North side of said RUN, thence up the Branch to three Maples in said Branch, Corner to ZACHORY SIMS, thence with said SIMS's line South seventy one degrees West twenty four poles to two red Oaks, thence North seventeen degrees West twenty four poles, North five degrees West forty four poles to two black Oaks, thence North twelve poles to three white Oaks on a Branch, thence North eighty three degrees West ninety six poles to two white and one red Oak in the said SAMUEL DELP's line, thence with his line to the Beginning which said tract of land (before signing of these presents) we have delivered into his actual possession and do and will warrant and forever defend the said land from the Lawfull claim of any person whatsoever To have and to hold the aforesd land and premises to him the said HENRY DELP his heirs or assigns from henceforth as his or their own property absolutely without any manner of condition In Witness whereof we have hereunto set our hands & Seals this (blank) day of (blank) in year of our Lord One thousand seven hundred and eighty two
in presence of
                                           COONROD DELP
                                           ANNA MAGLDALINE

   At a Court held for Culpeper County the 18th day of Novr. 1782
This Indenture was acknowledged by the parties and ordered to be recorded, the said ANNA MAGDALINE being privily examined as Law directs

pp.   (On margin: Watts & Ux. to Wale D D 1790)
219-   THIS INDENTURE made the Eighteenth day of November in year of our Lord One
221   thousand seven hundred and Eighty two Between FREDERICK WATTS and ELIZA-
       BETH his Wife of County of Culpeper of one part and TIMOTHY WALE of the said
County of other part Witnesseth that FREDERICK WATTS and ELIZABETH his Wife for and in consideration of Service Done before the ensealing and delivery of these presents by these presents doth bargain and sell unto the said TIMOTHY WALE a tract or parcell of land lying in County of Culpeper containing Fifty acres and is bounded Begining at a large Pine on South side of the OLD AMELIA ROAD, thence with the said ROAD North twenty one degrees East thirty two poles to a white Oak in RICHARD CHELTONs line, thence with the said Line No. fifty five degrees West fifteen poles to two red Oaks and Poplar, Corner to CHELTON in WILLIAM KABLERs line, thence with said KABLERs line South twenty one degrees West thirty pole to a large white Oak, corner to the said KABLERs, thence with the said Line North seventy five degrees West ninety nine poles to a branch of POTATO RUN, thence up the several courses of said RUN thirty poles to an Oak and Pine on the South side of said RUN, thence South thirty nine degrees East fifty eight poles to three large white Oaks by the side of a Path, thence South twenty two degrees East fifty eight poles to a Pine Dogwood and Oak, thence North forty three degrees East One hundred & two poles to the beginning, And all houses orchards water courses profits commodities and appurtenances whatsoever & also the Estate, Right, Title & Demand whatsoever of said FREDERICK WATTS of and into the said premises and all Deeds Evidences and Writings touching or in any ways concerning the same To have and to hold the tract of land hereby granted & released and every of their appurtenances unto TIMOTHY WALE his heirs and assigns and FREDERICK WATTS and ELIZABETH his Wife his heirs and assigns will warrent and forever defend by these presents In Witness whereof the said FREDERICK WATTS & ELIZABETH his Wife hath hereunto set their hands and Seals the day and year first above written
in presence of SAMUEL REEDS,   FREDERICK WATTS
     JAMES RAWSON, JOHN GORE   ELIZABETH WATTS

MEMORANDUM that full and peaceable possession and Seizen of and in the lands and Tenements within mentioned was taken and delivered by said FREDERICK WATTS to said TIMOTHY WALE this Eighteenth day of November 1782

                                    FREDERICK WATTS

Recd of TIMOTHY WALE full serve as within mentioned by him to me Witness my hand this 18th day of Novr. 1782

                                    FREDERICK WATTS

At a Court held for Culpeper County the 18th day of November 1782
This Indenture was acknowledged by the parties and ordered to be recorded, the said ELIZABETH being first privily examined as the Law directs

pp.   (On margin: Broyle & Ux. to Major D D 1787)
221-   THIS INDENTURE made the Twentieighth day of September in year of our Lord
224   One thousand seven hundred & Eighty two Between NICHOLAS BROYLE & DOLLY
         his Wife of County of Culpeper of one part and FRANCIS MAJOR of the aforesaid
County of other part Witnesseth that for and in consideration of the sum of One hundred and fifty five pounds current money of Virginia to him in hand paid hath bargained and sold unto FRANCIS MAJOR his heirs & assigns forever a certain piece or parcell of land lying in County aforesaid on the Waters of the ROBINSON RIVER and bounded Beginning at a small white and red Oak, Corner to CHRISTOPHER MAJOR and JOHN MAJOR in ADAM YAGERs line, thence with said YAGERs line South sixty five degrees East One hundred & nine poles to two red and one white Oak, thence South seven degrees West Two hundred poles to three red Oak saplins, thence North sixty five degrees West One hundred and nine poles to two red and one Spanish Oak saplins in the said MAJORs line, thence with MAJORs line North seven degrees East to the Beginning, Togather with all woods water courses Orchards and all other appurtenances belong To have and to hold all the aforesaid land with every parcel thereof from all Incumbrances to the only proper use of him the said FRANCIS MAJOR his heirs & assigns forever In Witness whereof we have hereunto set our hands & Seals the day and year above written
in presence of JAMES BARBOUR,   NICHOLAS his mark VB BROYLE
         WILLIAM WALKER, MICHAEL SMITH,   DOLLY her mark X BROYLE
         SAMUEL MAJOR SENR., JOHN DUNCAN
Rec'd full satisfaction for the within written Indenture Witness our hands this 28th day of September 1782
         JAS. BARBOUR,   NICH. his mark VB BROYLE
         WILLIAM WALKER
Memorandum. That on the same day of the date of the within written Indenture Quiet and peaceable possession of the within mentioned land and premises was made and given by said NICHOLAS BROYLE and DOLLY his Wife to the said FRANCIS MAJOR in presence of us whose names are under written
         JAS. BARBOUR   NICH. his mark VB BROYLE
         WILLIAM WALKER
The Commonwealth of Virginia to JAMES BARBOUR & WILLIAM WALKER Gentlemen Greeting (The Commission for the private Examination of DOLLY, the Wife of NICHOLAS BROYLE dated at the Courthouse the 28th day of September 1782 and in the seventh year of the Commonwealth)(The return of the private Examination of DOLLY BROYLE dated the 4th day of October 1782 and signed by JAS. BARBOUR and WILLIAM WALKER)
At a Court held for Culpeper County the 21st day of October 1782
This Indenture was partly proved by the Oaths of MICHAEL SMITH & JOHN DUNCAN two of the witnesses thereto and ordered to be Certified, And at a Court held for the said

County the 18th day of November 1782 was fully proved by JAMES BARBOUR another
Witness thereto and ordered to be recorded with Commission thereto annexed and certificate thereon

pp.   (On margin: Kemper to Kemper D D to MARTIN KEMPER Exr. of Peter Kemper
224-   March 1832)
226   THIS INDENTURE made this 18th day of November in year of our Lord One thousand seven hundred and Eighty two Between JOHN KEMPER and ANNE his Wife of
County of FAUQUIER of the one part and PETER KEMPER of the County of Culpeper of
other part Witnesseth that JOHN KEMPER and ANNE his Wife for and in consideration of
the sum of Two hundred pounds current money of Virginia to them in hand paid by
PETER KEMPER by these presents do bargain & sell unto PETER KEMPER one certain
tract of land lying in County of Culpeper containing by estimation One hundred & fifty
nine acres and bounded Begining at three Pines, Corner to JOHN WHITESIDES and
runing thence South ten degrees West Three hundred and forty seven poles to a Pine
on a Poison Hill, thence North seventy eight degrees East One hundred & fifty six poles
to two box Oaks near a small branch, Corner to JOHN BUTTONs land, thence North thirty
one degrees West thirteen poles to two white Oaks, thence North eighteen degrees East
twenty eight poles to a white Oak & red Oak sapling, Corner to JOHN WHITESIDES, thence
with his line North seventy six degrees West twelve poles across a Branch to three
white Oak saplins, thence North one degree West forty eight poles to a Pine and two red
Oak saplins, thence North twenty seven and half degrees West Two hundred and five
poles to the Begining, Togather with all houses water courses profits commodites and
appurtenances whatsoever to the same belonging To Hold the said land and premises
hereinbefore mentioned and sold with their appurtenances unto PETER KEMPER his
heirs and assigns and JOHN KEMPER and ANNE his Wife will warrent and forever defend the said land & premises before granted against the claim of any manner of person In Witness whereof the said JOHN KEMPER and ANNE his Wife have Interchangably set their hands & seals the day and year first above written
acknowledged before us   JOHN KAMPER
  June 17th 1782 Then received of PETER KEMPER the within consideration of Two hundred pounds Virginia Currency and acknowledge myself to be fully satisfied
                          Rec'd p me   JOHN KAMPER
  At a Court held for Culpeper County the 18th day of November 1782
This Indenture was acknowledged by the within mentioned JOHN KEMPER and ordered
to be recorded

pp.   THIS INDENTURE made this Seventh day of August in year of our Lord One thou-
226-   sand seven hundred & Eighty two Between JOHN MINOR and MARY his Wife of
228   County of Culpeper of one part and WILLIAM DUVALL, Attorney of the County of
        HANOVER, of other part Witnesseth that they the said JOHN MINOR and MARY his
Wife for & in consideration of the sum of Five hundred pounds in Specie to them in
hand paid by these presents do bargain and sell WILLIAM DUVAL his heirs and assigns
a certain tract of land lying in the Parish of Brumfield in County of Culpeper and containing One thousand acres be the same more or less, it being all the land which one
SEBASTIAN HATTLER bought of COMPTON and bounded beginning at three Box Oaks at
JACOBY's corner, thence runing North eighty five degrees East Eleven poles to three
Corner Hickories in COMPTON's line, thence North eighteen degrees East sixty six poles
to three corner white Oaks on the Spur of a Mountain, thence North eighty five degrees
East Three hundred & twenty seven poles to three Corner red Oaks, thence South nineteen degrees East One hundred & forty poles to a Branch in CAPTAIN KENERLIEs line,

thence South One hundred & twenty poles to two white Oaks, Corner to KENERLY & GOUGE's, thence South seven degrees East One hundred and twenty six poles to a Poplar and white Oak in CHAPMANs line, thence South seventy degrees West One hundred and fifty poles to three white Oaks, thence North seventy nine degrees West to DANIEL JACOBY's Corner, thence from the said Corner long JACOBY's line to the first station with all the appurtenances thereto belonging To have and to hold all the said Land with all and every of its appurtenances to him the said WILLIAM DUVALL his heirs & assigns And they the said JOHN MINOR and MARY his Wife the said tract of land with all its appurtenances against themselves & their heirs and against the claim of all persons whatsoever to him the said WILLIAM DUVAL his heirs and assigns do by these presents warrent and forever defend. In Witness whereof they the said JOHN MINOR and MARY his Wife have hereunto set their hands & affix'd their seals the day month and year above written

in presence of us JNO. C. COCKE,   JOHN MINOR
        EZEKIEL NORMAN, GEORGE GREEN   MARY MINOR
    Memorandom This Seventh day of August 1782 Then Livery of Seisen of the within sold land and premises was made by the within mentioned JOHN MINOR and MARY his Wife to the within named WILLIAM DUVALL
Teste JNO. C. COCKE,   JOHN MINOR
        GEORGE GREEN, EZEKIEL NORMAN   MARY MINOR
    Memorandom This Seventh day of August 1782 Then received of the within named WILLIAM DUVAL Five hundred pounds in Specie in full payment of the within sold land & premises
Teste JNO. C. COCKE,   JOHN MINOR
        GEORGE GREEN, EZEKIEL NORMAN   MARY MINOR
    At a Court held for Culpeper County the 18th day of March 1782
This Indenture was partly proved by the Oath of GEORGE GREEN, a witness thereto, which is ordered to be Certified; And at a Court held for the said County the 18th day of November 1782 was acknowledged by the within parties And ordered to be recorded, the said MARY being first privily examined as the Law directs

pp.   TO ALL PEOPLE to whom these presents shall come I DANIEL BRADFORD send
228-   Greeting. Know ye that I DANIEL BRADFORD of the County of FAUQUIER and
230   State of Virginia for and in consideration of the natural love good will and affection which I have and do bear unto my Loving Son, ENOCH BRADFORD of the County of Culpeper and State aforesaid, by these presents do freely clearly and absolutely give grant & confirm unto my said Son, ENOCH BRADFORD, his heirs and assigns forever a certain Dividend or tract of land in the County of Culpeper and on GREAT BATTLE RUNN and bounded Beginning at two Pines and a white Oak, Corner to WILLIAM ROBERTS, thence North twenty two degrees East Two hundred & seven poles to GREAT BATTLE RUNN where the Road crosses the same, thence up the said RUNN according to its meanders on the North side (including all Islands in said RUNN) to a Sycamore, Corner to JOHN BRADFORD near where JOHN ROBERTS formly had a MILL, then leaving the RUNN South West One hundred & thirty two poles to two Spanish Oaks & a white Oak, thence South East One hundred and ninety eight poles to the Begining, containing One hundred and sixty acres be the same more or less, Togather with all houses gardens Orchards meadows pastures profits commodities & appurtenances whatseover to the same belonging To have and to hold the said land with their appurtenances unto ENOCH BRADFORD his heirs & assigns for Ever to the True Intent & meaning that my said Son, ENOCH, aforesaid his heirs and assigns may from time to time & at all times for ever hereafter have hold possess & enjoy the said premises with their appurtenances

without the lett disturbance or molestation of me the said DANIEL BRADFORD my heirs
or assigns or any other person In Witness whereof I the said DANIEL BRADFORD have
hereunto set my hand & seal this 18th day of November 1782
in the presence of us   DANIEL BRADFORD
   At a Court held for Culpeper County the 18th day of November 1782
This Indenture was acknowleged by the within DANIEL BRADFORD & ordered to be
recorded

pp.   (On margin: Yage & Ux. to Smith Dld. 1790)
230-   THIS INDENTURE made the 15th day of September in year of our Lord One thou-
233   sand seven hundred and Eighty two Between SOLOMON YAGER & ELIZABETH his
         Wife of County of Culpeper of one part & MICHAEL SMITH of County aforesaid of
other part Witnesseth that SOLOMON YAGER and ELIZABETH his Wife for and in consideration of the sum of Forty pounds current money of Virginia to them in hand paid
by these presents do bargain & sell unto MICHAEL SMITH one certain Tract of land
lying in said County & containing by estimation One hundred acres and bounded Begining at a Poplar and a red Oak, Corner to ZACHARIAH BLANKENBEKER, Extending
thence South fifty degrees West twenty two poles up a Ridge of a Mountain to a Chesnut
and Spanish Oak, Corner to NICHOLAS WILHOITEs line, thence South thirty one degrees
East two hundred and twenty two poles to three Hickories Corner in another line of the
said WILHOITE, thence South sixty two degrees East forty nine poles to two Dogwoods a
Locust and red Oak saplins near a Branch in the Hallow of a Mountain, thence North
fifteen degrees West Two hundred and twenty six poles to a Hickory and Poplar, Corner
to the said BLANKENBEKER, thence with his line South fifty degrees West eighty four
poles to a Poplar and white Oak another Corner of BLANKENBEKERs thence with another of said BLANKENBEKERs lines North fifty five West to the first mentioned Beginning, Togather with all houses fences priviledges and advantages whatseover
belonging To have & to hold the said tract of land with all & every of its appurtenances
unto MICHAEL SMITH his heirs and assigns and SOLOMON YAGER and ELIZABETH his
Wife do hereby warrent & will forever defend the said tract of land with the appurtenances before mentioned unto MICHAEL SMITH his heirs and assigns free from all
Incumbrances & claims of any persons In Witness whereof the parties to these presents
have hereunto set their hands and seals the day & year above written
in presence of JAMES BARBOUR,   SOLOMON YAGER
         WILLIAM WALKER, SAMUEL MAJOR SENR.,   ELIZABETH YAGER
         FRANCIS MAJOR
   The Commonwealth of Virginia to JAMES BARBOUR & WILLIAM WALKER Gentlemen
Greeting (The Commission for the private Examination of ELIZABETH, the Wife of
SOLOMON YAGER dated at the Courthouse the 30th day of September 1782 and in the
seventh year of the Commonwealth)(Return of examination of ELIZABETH YAGER dated
the fourth day of October 1782 and signed by JAS. BARBOUR and WILLIAM WALKER)
   At a Court held for Culpeper County the 21st day of October 1782
This Indenture was proved by the Oath of WILLIAM WALKER a witness thereto and
ordered to be Certified; And at a Court held for said County the 18th day of November
1782 was fully proved by the Oaths of JAMES BARBOUR & SAMUEL MAJOR SENR. other
witnesses thereto, with the commission thereto annexed & Certificate thereon ordered
to be recorded

pp.   (On margin: Amis to Dolley Amis DD 1790)
233-   TO ALL TO WHOM these presents shall come Greeting. Know ye that I JOSEPH
234   AMIS of County of Culpeper & Parish of Saint Marks for the love and affection

I bear toward my beloved Gran Daughter, DOLLEY AMIS, the Daughter of my Son,
GABRIEL AMISS deced and ELIZABETH his Wife, have given & by these presents do
freely and absolutely give & grant unto DOLLEY AMISS on her arriving to eighteen
years of age, or Lawfull Wedlock, one certain Negro woman named Sarah & her Children named Charles, Fanney and John, togather with all her future Increase, To have
and to hold the said Negro woman & Children and future Increase to the said DOLLEY
AMIS her & her heirs for ever. In Witness whereof I have hereunto set my hand & Seal
this Eighth day of July One thousand seven hundred & Eighty two
in presence of us JAMES JETT,   JOSEPH AMIS
        AUGUSTINE JENNINGS,
        PHILIS DUNCAN JETT
  Memorandum. The within Deed of Gift to be admitted to record on the Proviso of a
certain Instrument of Writing or Note sent Mr. JAS. POLLARD deced upon the marriage
of GABRIEL AMISS Deced & ELIZABETH his Wife
Teste JAMES JETT   July 18th 1782   ELIZABETH FOX
  At a Court held for Culpeper County the 18th day of November 1782
This Deed of Gift was acknowledged by the within mentioned JOSEPH AMIS and ordered
to be recorded

pp.   (On margin: Vicecarver to Vicecarver D D ELIAS WALTER March 1800)
234-   TO ALL TO WHOM these presents shall come Know ye that I TILMON VICECARVER
235   of County of Culpeper for divers good causes me thereunto moving but more
        especially for the natural love & affection which I have and do bear towards my
Son, HERMON VICECARVER of said County and for the consideration of the sum of Five
shillings to me in hand paid have given granted and made over unto my Son, HERMON
VICECARVER & his heirs forever one certain piece or parcel of land lying on each side
of CROOKED RUN in County aforesaid the same being now in the possession or tenure of
my said Son, & bounded by the lines of SAMUEL MORE and WILLIAM FLOURENCE & COLO.
JOHN CARLILE containing Five hundred acres be the same more or less To have and to
hold the said land & premises with all its appurtenances unto my said Son, HERMON
WISECARVER his heirs and assigns In Witness whereof I the said TILMON VICECARVER
hereunto set my hand & Seal this 15th day of November 1782
in presence of us JAMES GAUNT,   TILMON VICECARVER his mark
        JAMES SCOTT, DAVID his mark X ELKIN,
        CORNELIUS his mark X SCOTT
  At a Court held for Culpeper County the 18th day of November 1782
This Indenture was proved by the Oaths of JAMES GAUNT, JAMES SCOTT & CORNELIUS
SCOTT witnesses thereto & ordered to be recorded

pp.   (On margin: Brown & Ux. to Haywood DD 1792)
235-   THIS INDENTURE made this Eighteenth day of November in year of our Lord One
237   thousand seven hundred and Eighty two and the Seventh year of the Common-
        weath Between JOHN BROWN of the County of DUNMORE and State of Virginia &
his Wife of one part and GEORGE HAYWOOD of County of Culpeper and State aforesaid of
other part Witnesseth that JOHN BROWN & his Wife for and in consideration of the sum
of Fifty pounds current money of Virginia to them in hand paid by these presents do
bargain and sell unto GEORGE HAYWOOD his heirs and assigns all that Tract or parcell of
land lying on the East side of MOUNT PONEY in County of Culpeper which the said JOHN
BROWN purchased of NICHOLAS KABLER as by Deed from the said NICHOLAS KABLER &
NANCY his Wife to said JOHN BROWN made bearing date the Sixteenth day of August One
thousand seven hundred & seventy three and duly recorded in the Court of County of

Culpeper will fully appear and containing by Estimation One hundred and sixty two acres be the same more or less and bounded Begining at two white Oaks and Spanish Oak on the side of MOUNT PONEY, Corner to CHRISTOPHER KABLER, thence with his line South sixty eight degrees East two hundred and twenty two poles to a forked white Oak another Corner of said KABLER in MINOR WINNs Line, thence with the said WINNs line North thirty seven degrees East sixty eight poles to a Spanish Oak and white Oak near the said WINNs Plantation, Corner to THOMAS BROWN, thence with said BROWNs line North sixty two degrees West One hundred and ninety six poles to three Scrubby Oaks near an old CART PATH, thence South eighty six degrees West eighty poles to a forked Poplar and Gum at the foot of the said Mountain, thence North five degrees West seventy six poles to a Dead red Oak & a white Oak, thence West forty poles to two Gums and a Chesnutt Oak on the side of the said Mountain, thence North five degrees West twenty four poles North sixty degrees West twenty two poles to a Chesnut Oak, Ash and Poplar on the side of said Mountain, thence leaving the said BROWNs line South twenty five degrees West sixty poles to three marked trees near the Top of the said Mountain, thence South forty one degrees East one hundred and forty nine poles to the Beginning To have and to hold the appurtenances and priviledges thereunto belonging unto GEORGE HAYWOOD his heirs and assigns forever and JOHN BROWN & MARY his Wife will warrent and forever defend by these presents the said land and premises with all that doth thereunto appurtain unto GEORGE HAYWOOD his heirs and assigns free from all Incumbrances and claims whatever In Witness whereof they said JOHN BROWN and MARY his Wife have hereunto set their hands and Seals the day and year aforesaid
in presence of DENNIS McCARTHEY,   JOHN BROWN
        THOMAS LEWIS, HENRY HIDE,   MARY her mark X BROWN
        (a name in German), WM. C. BROWN,
        JOSEPH HEDGEAR
  The Commonwealth of Virginia to JOHN NORTH and JOHN SNAPP Gentlemen Greeting (Commission for the private Examination of MARY, the Wife of JOHN BROWN, dated at the Courthouse the Twenty ninth day of May 1778 and Third year of the Commonwealth) (Return of private Examination of MARY BROWN dated the 29th of May 1778 and signed by JOHN NORTH and JOHN SNAPP)
  At a Court held for Culpeper County the 18th day of November 1782
This Indenture was acknowledged by the within mentioned JOHN BROWN with Commission thereto annexed & Certificate thereon is ordered to be recorded

pp.   (On margin: Cook & Ux. to Cook D D Self 1805)
238-   THIS INDENTURE made this 21st day of October in year of our Lord One thousand
239   seven hundred & Eighty two Between MICHAEL COOK and KATHARINE his Wife
        of County of Culpeper of one part & PETER COOK of said County of other part Witnesseth that MICHAEL COOK and KATHARINE his Wife for and in consideration of the sum of Five pounds current money of Virginia to them in hand paid by these presents do fully clearly and absolutely give bargain sell & confirm unto PETER COOK & his heirs & assigns forever all that tract or parcell of land containing Forty nine more or less acres of land lying in Culpeper County & on the North side of the JARMON RIDGE & on the Waters of ROBINSON RIVER & is bounded Begining at two white Oaks and a Chesnut standing in the old line, thence North forty one degrees West One hundred and forty six pole to a red and black Oak in the Dividing line of the said Tract, thence with that line South twenty four degrees West seventy one pole to a red and black Oak in another line of the Old Tract, thence with that line South forty degrees East One hundred and forty two poles to a Corner of the Old Tract, thence with that line North twenty degrees East to the beginning. And all the houses orchards gardens and meddows pastures and all

other the appurtenances belonging To have and to hold the aforesaid land and premises from all incumbrances As Witness our hands and seals the day and year above
written
in presence of   MICHAEL COK
  At a Court held for Culpeper County the 18th day of November 1782
This Indenturewas acknowledged by the parties and ordered to be recorded

pp.   (On margin: Back &c. Deed to Wayland D D. Mr. P. LIGHTFOOT 1815)
240-   THIS INDENTURE made this Fourteenth day of January in year of our Lord One
243   thousand seven hundred and Eighty three Between JOHN BACK and MARGARET
        his Wife and PETER CLORE and MARY his Wife of the State of Virginia and County
of Culpeper of one part and JOHN WAYLAND JUNR. of the aforesaid County of the other
part Witnesseth that for and in consideration of the sum of Ten pounds current money
of Virginia to them the said JOHN BACK and MARGARET his Wife and PETER CLORE and
MARY his Wife well and truly in hand paid have bargained & sold unto JOHN WAYLAND
JUNR. his heirs and assigns for ever a certain parcel of land lying in the aforesaid
County and lying on both sides of DEEP RUN containing by Estimation Twenty acres
more or less & boundeth beginning at two white Oaks on the West side of DEEP RUN near
the said Run Corner with JOHN BACK, running thence North forty eight degrees East
fifty eight poles to two Pines in TILMAN HUFFMANs line, thence with his line South
forty degrees East twenty eight poles to DEEP to a Maple & parcimon, thence up the said
RUN four poles crossing the RUN to BUMGARDNERs Corner, thence with BUMGARD-
NERs line South fifty East twelve pole to two red Oak saplings and one Pine, thence
South thirty five West forty four pole to a Pine, thence South seventy five West thirty
five pole to a white Oak and Dogwood, thence North thirty eight West twelve pole to
DEEP RUN, thence down the several courses of said RUN to the beginning, Together
with all woods, waters courses, houses & all other appurtenances belonging To have and
to hold all the aforesaid Land and premises with every part thereof from all Incumbrances whatsoever to be the only use of him the said JOHN WAYLAND his heirs and
assigns forever As Witness our hands and Seals the day and year above written
in presence of JOHN HANBACK,   JOHN BACK
         ZACHARIAS SIMS   MARGARET her mark + BACK
                                              PETER CLORE
                                              MARY her mark + CLORE
  Received of JOHN WAYLAND the full sum of Ten pounds current money of Virginia the
consideration of the within Deed. In Witness whereof we have hereunto set our hands
& Seals this Fourteenth of January One thousand seven hundred and Eighty three
in presece of us JOHN HANBACK,   JOHN BACK
         ZACHARIAS SIMS   PETER CLORE
  The Commonwealth of Virginia to ROBT. ALCOCK, HENRY HILL and WILLIAM WALKER
Gent. Greeting (The Commission for the private Examination of MARGARET, the Wife of
JOHN BACK, and MARY, the Wife of PETER CLORE Witness DAVID JAMESON, Deputy Clerk
of our said Court, at the Courthouse the 16th day of Janaury 1783 and the Seventh year
of the Commonwealth) (Return of the private Examinations dated the 26th day of
March 1783 and signed by ROBT. ALCOCK, HENRY HILL)
  At a Court held for Culpeper County the 20th day of January 1783
This Indenture was acknowledged and ordered to be recorded with Commission thereto
annexed & Certificate thereon

pp,   THIS INDENTURE made in the 17th day of February in the year of our Lord Christ
243-   One thousand seven hundred and Eighty three Between BENJAMIN STINNETT of
244   County of Culpeper of one part & AMON BOHANNON RICE and ANNA his Wife of
        said County of other part Witness for and in consideration of a certain tract of
land which the said STINNETT bought of the said AMON BOHANON RICE which he doth
hereby acknowledge by these presents doth bargain and sell unto BENJAMIN STINNETT
his heirs and assigns forever a part of the land the said piece now lives on One hundred
more or less Binding Beginning at three white Oaks at the Corner of ROBERT SLAUGH-
TERs land and running on JOHN BUTLERs line to BEN: PULLIAMs from thence to WIL-
LIAM JONES to the Corner to a Black Haw and Maple on the Bank of BEAVER DAM RUN,
from thence on JONES's line to the top of a Mountain with the new line on the top of the
said Mountain to the said SLAUGHTERs line again, Together with all houses orchards
watercourses profits and appurtenaces to the same belonging To have and to hold the
above mentioned land with the appurtenances unto BENJAMIN STINNETT his heirs and
assigns for ever & AMON BOHANNON RICE & ANNA his Wife their heirs and assigns &
with the mentioned and granted lands and premises with the appurtenances will warrant & forever defend against the lawful claim of every person whatever In Witness
whereof we the said AMON BOHANNON RICE & ANNA his Wife have hereunto set their
hands and Seals the day and year above mentioned
in the presence of   AMON BOHANNON RICE
                                                ANNA RICE
   At a Court held for Culpeper County the 17th day of February 1783
This Indenture was acknowledged by the within AMON BOHANNON RICE & ordered to be
recorded, And at a Court held for the aforesaid County the 21st day of April 1783 the said
ANNA RICE came into Court and acknowledged her right in the said Conveyance, she
being first privily examined as the Law directed

pp,   (On margin: Stinnett to Rice DD PHILIP GAINES 1789)
244-   THIS INDENTURE made the 17th day of February in the year of our Lord Christ
245   One thousand seven hundred and Eighty three Between BENJAMIN STINNETT &
        JARUSAY his Wife of County of Culpeper of one part & AMON BOHANNON RICE of
the County aforesaid of other part Witnesseth that for and in consideration of a Certain
tract of land which the said RICE bought of the said BENJAMIN STINNETT which he doth
hereby acknowledge by these presents doth bargain & sell unto AMON BOHANNON RICE
his heirs & assigns forever all that tract or Dividend of land containing One hundred &
sixty five acres being the same Land that the said STINNETT now lives on lying in County of Culpeper & Parish of Bromfield & premises with the appurtenances the aforesaid
BENJAMIN STINNETT and JARUSAY his Wife their heirs and assigns shall warrant and
forever defend by these presents against all persons whatever and BENJAMIN STINNETT
and JARUSAY his Wife doth covenant with said AMON BOHANNON RICE his heirs and
assigns shall forever hereafter peaceably and quietly have possess and enjoy the
aforesaid land with the appurtenances thereto belonging without the least suit or
hindrances of any person whatsoever and the aforesaid One hundred and sixty five
acres of land shall forever hereafter remain unto the said AMON BOHANNON RICE his
heirs and assigns forever In Witness whereof the parties to these presents hath In-
terchangable hereto set their hands and fixt their seals this day and year first mentioned
in presence of   BENJAMIN STINNETT
                                                JERUSAY her mark ⊥ STINNETT

At a Court held for Culpeper County the 17th day of February 1783
This Indenture was acknowledged by the within mentioned parties and ordered to be
recorded the said JERUSA being first privily examined as the Law directs

pp.   (On margin: Coones Senr. to Coones Junr. D D to Self 1788)
246-   THIS INDENTURE made the seventeenth day of March in year of our Lord One
248   thousand seven hundred and Eighty three Between JOSEPH COONES SENR. and
       ELIZABETH his Wife of County of Culpeper and Commonwealth of Virginia of one
part and JOSEPH COONES JUNR. of the County & State aforesaid of other part Witnesseth
that JOSEPH COONES SENR. and ELIZABETH his Wife for and in consideration of the sum
of Thirty five pounds current money to them in hand paid by these presents do bargain and sell unto JOSEPH COONES JUNR. his heirs and assigns forever a Certain Tract of
land lying in County of Culpeper in the Little Fork of RAPPAHANNOCK RIVER and being
a tract of land granted by the Lord Proprietor of the Northern Neck unto JOSEPH COONES
SENR as by Patent bearing date the Eighth day of December One thousand seven hundred and forty seven Beginning at two old Corner white Oaks, Corner to a tract of land
granted to WILLIAM DETHERAGE run thence South seventy nine degrees East two hundred & eight poles to two old Corner white Oaks, thence North fifty four degrees East
fifty six poles to a white Oak and agreed Corner between the said COONES and JOHN
CRIMM (now GEORGE's) thence along their agreed dividing line North thirty eight degrees West One hundred and four poles to two red Oak saplins, thence along another Dividing line North sixty degrees West ninety poles to one red Oak & one white Oak saplins in an old line of Marked Trees & another agreed Corner, thence with the said line
South forty two degrees West One hundred and fifty eight poles to the Beginning containing One hundred & twenty seven and half acres (be the same more or less, together
with all houses Inclosures water courses profits advantages whatsoever to the said land
belonging and all Right title Interest and demand whatsoever of them the said JOSEPH
COONES SENR. and ELIZABETH his Wife of in and to the said bargained premises To have
and to hold the said One hundred twenty seven and a half acres of land with the appurtenances unto JOSEPH COONES JUNR. his heirs and assigns and will warrant & forever
defend by these presents against any person whatsoever In Witness whereof the parties to these presents have Interchangably set their hands & Seals the day and year
first above written
in presence of   JOSEPH his mark (COONES SENR.
                                      ELIZA. her mark (COONES
   At a Court held for Culpeper County the 17th day of March 1783
This Indenture was acknowledged by the within mentioned JOSEPH COONES SENR. and
ordered to be recorded & at a Court held for said County the 19th day of May 1783,
ELIZABETH COONES, Wife to said JOSEPH, came into Court and acknowledged the same
being first privily examined according to Law

pp.   TO ALL TO WHOM these presents shall come Know ye that I SAMUEL SCOTT of the
248-   County of Culpeper for divers good causes me thereto moving, but more especi-
250   ally for the natural love and affection which I have and do bear towards my Son
       CORNELIUS SCOTT of the said County as for the consideration of the sum of Five
shilings to me in hand paid have given granted & made over to my said Son, CORNELIUS
SCOTT & his heirs forever one certain piece or parcel of land lying in the LITTLE FORK
of RAPPAHANNOCK RIVER & County aforesaid, the same being now in the possession &
tenure of my said Son & being the place my Father, ANTHONY SCOTT, lived on, only the
GRAVE YARD be free for any person to bury their Dead & the said piece or parcel of
land is bounded beginning at a white Oak corner to ROBERT SCOTTs near the head of the

SNAKE BRANCH running thence with said line to a red Oak, corner of said ROBERT SCOTT in the old line of ANTHONY SCOTTs, thence with said old line to the beginning containing One hundred acres be the same or or less To have and to hold the said land and premises with all the improvements & appurtenances unto my said Son, CORNELIUS SCOTT, his heirs and assigns, the said CORNELIUS SCOTT is to pay Two hundred pounds of Tobacco to said SAMUEL SCOTT every as long as SAMUEL SCOTT lives & no longer. In Witness I the said SAMUEL SCOTT have hereunto set my hand and Seal this 17th day of February 1783

in presence of us EDMOND BASYE,   SAMUEL SCOTT
        ELIZEMON BASYE, HARMAN his mark X WISECARVER
        WALTER STALLARD, JAMES GAUNT, JAMES SCOTT
    At a Court held for Culpeper County the 17th day of April 1780
This Indenture was partly proved by the Oaths of two of the Witnesses thereto which is to be Certified, And at a Court held for the aforesaid County the 17th day of March 1783 was fully proved by the Oath of another witness thereto and ordered to be recorded

pp.   (On margin: Scott Deed of Gift to Scott D D THO. SPINDLE 1805)
250-   TO ALL TO WHOM these presents shall come Know ye that I SAMUEL SCOTT of the
251   County of Culpeper for divers good causes me thereto moving but more especi-
       ally for the natural love & affection which I have and do bear towards my Son,
JAMES SCOTT, of said County as for the consideration of Five shillings to me in hand paid have given granted & made over to said Son, JAMES SCOTT, and his heirs forever, one certain piece or parcel of land lying in the Little Fork of RAPPAHANNOCK RIVER & County aforesaid the same being now in the possession & tenure of my said Son & bounded beginning at a red Oak, Corner to JOHN SCOTT in my line, thence running with his line to a Pine, a Corner of said JOHN SCOTTs in my line, thence with my lines to the beginning containing One hundred and forty acres be the same more or less with all reversions rents issues and profits thereof To have and to hold the said land with all its Improvements and appurtenances unto my said Son, JAMES SCOTT, his heirs and assigns excepting the House and Apple Orchard & the Land to my said Son's Spring Branch I am to keep possession as long as I live & at my decease he takes possession of the said House Orchard and land in Witness I the said SAMUEL SCOTT have hereunto set my hand & Seal this 17th day of February 1783

in presence of WALTER STALLARD,   SAML. SCOTT
        JAMES GAUNT, CORNELIUS his mark X SCOTT
    At a Court held for Culpeper County the 17th day of March 1783
This Indenture was proved by the Oaths of WALTER STALLARD and JAMES GAUNT & COR-NELIUS SCOTT, witnesses thereto, & ordered to be recorded

pp.   (On margin: Johnston Deed to Walker D D 1788)
251-   THIS INDENTURE made this Eighth day of February in year of our Lord Christ
253   One thousand seven hundred & Eighty three Between ANDREW JOHNSTON of
       County of Culpeper and Colony of Virginia of one part & MERRY WALKER of said
County & Colony of Virginia of other part Witnesseth that ANDREW JOHNSTON for and in consideration of the sum of One hundred pounds current money of Virginia to him in hand paid by these presents doth bargain and sell unto MERRY WALKER his heirs & assigns forever one certain tract of land and premises situate lying and being in County and Colony aforesaid being part of a Patent granted to MICHAEL WILHOITE bearing date the Twenty eighth day of September 1728 for 289 acres and is bounded beginning at Maples on the West side of MUDDY RUN in ADAM WAYLAND thence with the said line North eighty five degrees East eighty pole to a red Oak white Oak & Spanish Oak

a corner to the said WAYLAND in a line of WILHOITEs Patent, thence with that line
North five degrees West One hundred poles to a red Oak & white Oak saplin in the said
line thence South eighty five West eighty pole to a Pine in a Branch of the said Run,
thence down the several courses thereof to the begining containing Sixty two acres be
the same more or less To have and to hold the aforesaid Tract of land & premises with all
of its appurtenances unto him the said MERRY WALKER his heirs and assigns forever
and ANDREW JOHNSTON doth further agreed to and with MERRY WALKER his heirs and
assigns that I will forever warrant and defend the said land with all its appurtenances
from the claim or demand of every other person and that the same is freely and clearly
discharged of all Incumbrance whatsoever. In Witness whereof the parties to these
presents hath set their hands and Seals the day and date first above written
in presence of us WILLIAM WALKER   AND. JOHNSTON
         WILLIAM WALKER JUNR., JAMES WALKER,
         JOHN WALKER
  At a Court held for Culpeper County the 17th day of March 1783
This Indenture was proved by the Oaths of WILLIAM WALKER, WILLIAM WALKER
JUNR. & JOHN WALKER, witnesses thereto, & ordered to be recorded

pp.   (On margin: Johnston to Walker Power of Atto. D D 1788)
253-   THIS IS TO CERTIFY that I ANDREW JOHNSTON of Culpeper County do Impower
254   MERRY WALKER of said County to collect the Debts due from WILLIAM BOUGHER,
         WILLIAM DICKENSON, JOHN RICE, JOHN GLASSWELL, THOS. WALKER GRAIG,
SAMUEL LEATHERS and also all and every other person due to me and to commence any
sute or sutes in my name for the recovery of the same and to prosecute dismiss discontinue or Compromise in any other manner as to him the said MERRY WALKER shall
seem most advisable for the recovery of the aforesaid Debts, And I do hereby oblige
myself and my heirs to confirm whatever the said Attorney shall due in the premises
aforesaid As Witness hereof I set my hand & Seal this 1st day of January One thousand
seven hundred and Eighty three
in presence of WILLIAM WALKER,   AND. JOHNSTON
         WILLIAM WALKER JUNR.
  At a Court held for Culpeper County the 17th March 1783
This Power of Attorney was proved by the Oaths of WILLIAM WALKER & WILLIAM WAL-
KER JUNR. witnesses thereto & ordered to be recorded

pp.   (On margin: Elkins Deed to Alexr. Accreat 19th July 1784)
254-   THIS INDENTURE made the Eighteenth day of November in year of our Lord One
257   thousand seven hundred & Eighty two Between BENJAMIN ELKINS & PHILLIS his
         Wife of County of Culpeper and State of Virginia of one part and ALEXANDER
ACREAT of County of KING GEORGE and State aforesaid of other part Witnesseth that for
and in consideration of the sum of One hundred and fifty pounds current money of
Virginia to them in hand paid by said ALEXANDER ACREAT by these presents do bargain
& sell unto ALEXANDER ACREAT his heirs & assigns all that Dividend tract or parcel of
land lying in Culpeper County (it being part of a Tract of Four hundred acres granted
by the Proprietor of the Northern Neck to Mr. RICHARD FOOTE and Mrs. MARGARET
GRANT, Executor & Executrix to Capt. JOHN GRANT, by Patent bearing date the Nineteenth day of July One thousand seven hundred and forty eight) and bounded Beginning at three white Oak saplins, Corner to Patent, thence North twenty five degrees East
One hundred and sixty poles to five white Oaks standing on the South side of a small
Branch, thence leaving Patent Line North sixty five degrees West Two hundred poles to
2 Pines & a white Oak saplin in GREEN's line, thence with the same South twenty five

degrees West One hundred and sixty poles to a white Oak in said line & Corner to Patent, thence leaving GREENs line and with Patent South sixty five degrees East Two hundred poles to the beginning containing Two hundred acres Together with all houses gardens orchards meadows pastures and appurtenances whatsoever to the same belonging To have and to hold all the said premises with the appurtenances hereby bargained and sold or meant or intended to be hereby conveyed to said ALEXANDER ACREAT his heirs and assigns forever and BENJAMIN ELKINS and PHILLIS his Wife doth for themselves their heirs warrant and forever defend the said premises with appurtenances against the claim or demand of any other persons and clear of any Incumbrances whatsoever In Witness whereof the said BENJAMIN ELKIN & PHILLIS his Wife have hereunto set their hands & affix'd their Seals the day and year first above written
in presence of us EMMANUEL ELKINS,   BENJAMIN ELKINS
        NATHANIEL ELKINS, SARAH ELKINS
    Received of the within named ALEXANDER ACREAT the full and just sum of One hundred and fifty pounds Virginia currency it being the consideration money within mentioned to be paid by him to us on the perfection of the within Deed. Witness our hands & Seals this 18th day of Novr. 1782
Witness   EMMANUEL ELKINS,   BENJAMIN ELKINS
        NATHANIEL ELKINS
    At a Court held for Culpeper County the 17th March 1783
This Indenture was acknowledged by the within BENJAMIN ELKINS and ordered to be recorded

p.   (On margin: Thomas Deed to Thomas D D W. Thomas 1796)
257   TO ALL PEOPLE to whom these presents shall come I JOHN THOMAS send Greeting.
        Know ye that I the said JOHN THOMAS of the Parish of Bromfield in the County of Culpeper for divers good causes and considerations but more especially for and in consideration of the natural love good will and affection which I have and do bear towards my Grandson, WILLIAM THOMAS, of the County of SULLIVAN in NORTH CAROLINA, have given and by these presents do freely and absolutely give and grant unto the said WILLIAM THOMAS his heirs and assigns one Negro girl named Mima, To have and to hold the said Negro Mima to him the said WILLIAM THOMAS his heirs or assigns from henceforth as his or their own property, absolutely without any manner of condition In Witness whereof I have hereunto set my hand and Seal this Sixteenth day of February One thousand seven hundred & Eighty three
in presence of THOS. WALLACE,   JOHN his mark ✗ THOMAS
        WILLIAM LEWIS
    At a Court held for Culpeper County the 17th March 1783
This Deed of Gift was proved by the Oaths of THOMAS WALLACE & WILLIAM LEWIS, Witnesses thereto, and ordered to be recorded

pp.   (On margin: Minor Deed to Beale D D. ROBT. C. CARTER 1806)
258-   THIS INDENTURE made this Seventeenth day of March in year of our Lord Christ
261   One thousand seven hundred and Eighty three Between ARMISTEAD MINOR of
        the County of Culpeper & Colony of Virginia of one part and REUBEN BEALE of the County and Colony aforesaid of the other part Witnesseth that ARMISTEAD MINOR for and in consideration of the sum of twenty five thousand pounds of Tobacco to him the said ARMISTEAD in hand paid by these presents doth bargain and sell unto REUBEN BEALE his heirs and assigns for ever one certain tract of land lieing in the County and Colony aforesaid in the Fork of the RAPID ANN and ROBINSON RIVERs and is bounded Beginning at two Poplars on a Branch, Corner to JAMES ARCHER, and runneth thence

South Twenty five degrees West Two hundred and eighty poles crossing BEAUTIFUL RUN to a black Oak, Corner to said ARCHER, thence South fifty degrees East One hundred and ninty poles, thence South twenty five degrees East One hundred and sixty poles to a Pine and white Oak, Corner on a Branch, thence crossing the Branch to a white Oak and black, Corner to AMBROSE BOHANNON, thence North thirty degrees West two hundred & fifty five poles to the first mentioned beginning, Together with all the profits commodities and appurtenances to the said land and premises belonging and all Estate, right, title, Interest and demand in and to the same belonging To have and to hold the aforesaid Tract of land and premises with all its appurtenances unto him the said REUBEN BEALE his heirs and assigns forever and the sd ARMISTEAD and MARGARET his Wife for themselves their heirs &c. doth farther covenant and agree to and with said REUBEN his heirs &c. that sd ARMISTEAD and MARGARET will forever warrent and defend the said Land and premises with every of its appurtenances unto said REUBEN his heirs and assigns forever and that by virtue of these presents the sd land and premises with all its appurtenances is become the actual possession of him the said REUBEN his heirs and assigns forever and further the same is clearly and freely discharged of & from every manner of Incumbrance In Witness whereof the parties to these presents have set their hands and Seals the day and the date of the first above written
in presence of us EPHRAIM RUCKER,   ARMISTEAD MINOR
    ELLIOTT RUCKER, JULIUS RUCKER   MARGERET MINOR
  Memorandum that on the day and date within mentioned free and quiet possession & seizen was had and taken of and from the said ARMISTEAD MINOR by the within mentioned REUBEN BEALE according to the true intent purport & meaning of the within written Deed
in presence of us EPHRAIM RUCKER   ARMISTEAD MINOR
    ELLIOT RUCKER, JULIUS RUCKER   MARGRET MINOR
  The Commonwealth of Virginia to (blank) Gent. Greeting: (Commission for the private Examination of MARGARET, Wife of ARMISTEAD MINOR dated at the Courthouse the 17th day of March 1783 and in the seventh year of the Commonwealth) (The return of the private examination of MARGARET MINOR is not shown - space left)
  At a Court held for Culpeper the 17th day of March 1783
This Indenture was acknowledged by the parties & with Commission thereto annexed is ordered to be recorded

pp.   THIS INDENTURE made this Seventeenth day of March in year of our Lord One
261- thousand seven hundred and Eighty three between WILLIAM SIMS and MILLEY
265   his Wife and ZACHARIAS SIMS and ELIZABETH his Wife of the State of Virginia
      and County of Culpeper of one part and SAMUEL DELPH of the aforesd County of the other part Witnesseth that for and in consideration of the sum of One hundred and Twenty pounds current money of Virginia to the said WILLIAM SIMS & MILLY his Wife and ZACHARIAS SIMS & ELIZABETH his Wife in hand paid have bargained and sold unto SAMUEL DELPH his heirs and assigns for ever a certain piece or parcel of land lying in the aforesaid County containing by estimation One hundred and Sixty & a half acres of land more or less and boundeth beginning at a Spanish Oak on the ROBERTSON RIVER Corner to GEORGE RASOR running thence with RASORs line South fifty four degrees West One hundred and twenty pole to two red oaks thence South thirty degrees West eight pole thence with RASORs line South East One hundred and eighteen pole to two Maples & red Oak on LITTLE DARK RUN thence up the RUN north Eighty two degrees West eight pole, thence South fifty eight degrees West twenty six pole to a white and red Oak on the said RUN at the mouth of the Spring Branch, thence up the Spring Branch to three Maples, thence South sevinty degrees West twenty two poles to three red Oaks

thence North fifteen degrees West thirty poles to two white Oaks & one red Oak thence North forty sevin degrees West forty four pole to two red Oaks, thence North five degrees East sixteen pole to two white Oaks on the branch, thence North twenty degrees West thirty two pole, thence North forty degrees West sixty sevin pole, thence North eighty three degrees West twenty six pole the same Course continued ninety four pole further to RUSSELLs line to one white and red Oak in the said RUSSELLs line, thence North thirty degrees East One hundred and thirty eight pole to a red Oak and Dogwood on the RIVER, thence down the several courses of the RIVER to the beginning, Together with all woods ways watercourses houses & all other appurtenances belonging with all rents and reversion of rents & all other the Estate, right & title that may now or ever hereafter appurtain to the same from from all trouble or molestation of any person whatsoever lawfully claiming the same To have and to hold all the aforesaid Land from all Incumbrances to be the only use of him the said SAMUEL DELPH his heirs and assigns forever As Witness our hands and Seals the day and year above written
in presence of   WM. SIMS
                                   ZACHARIAS SIMS
                                   ELIZABETH SIMS

The Commonwealth of Virginia to
(blank) Gent. greeting (The Commission for the private Examination of MILLEY, Wife of WILLIAM SIMS dated at the Courthouse the (blank) day of (blank) 1783 & seventh year of the Commonwealth signed by D. JAMESON JUNR., Deputy Clerk) (The return of the examination is as follows: "Given under our hands and Seals this 14th day of March 1783 signed by WILLIAM McDOWELL and REUBIN HARRISON")
At a Court held for Culpeper County the 17th day of March 1783
This Indenture was acknowledged by the parties and ordered to be recorded with commission thereto annexed and Certificate thereon

pp.   THIS INDENTURE made the 17th day of March in year of our Lord Christ One
265-   thousand seven hundred and Eighty three Between BOWLES ARMISTEAD of the
269   County of Culpeper Gent. and MARY his Wife of one part and BASIL NOE of the
          aforesaid County of other part Witnesseth that the said BOWLES ARMISTEAD and
MARY his Wife for and in consideration of the sum of fifteen thousand pounds current money to them in hand paid by these presents doth bargain and sell unto BASIL NOE his heirs and assigns all that tract of land lying in the County aforesaid being part of a large tract of land whereon the said BOWLES ARMISTEAD now lives, lying at the upper end of the same, which part or parcel hereby bargained and sold contains One thousand One hundred and Eighty three acres and is bounded Beginning on the RAPPADAN RIVER at the Mouth of PATRICKS RUN, thence North twenty four degrees West ninety six pole to a white Oak & Dogwood, thence North forty three degrees East twenty six pole to a Gum & Poplar, thence North thirty degrees East fifty three poles to a red Oak on a Hill, thence North twenty degrees East one hundd. and five poles to two white Oaks by a Run, thence North fifty three poles to a red Oak on the edge of low ground, thence North forty three degrees East fifty three pole to three Hickorys by the Road side, thence up the Road to a black Oak in PATTON's Line by the Road, thence West One hundred and forty six poles to Four Pines in the head of ARMISTEAD RUN, thence North fifty nine degrees West One hundred & twenty pole to two black Oaks in the Old Road, thence South fifty five degrees West three hundred & twenty four pole to a white Oak standing on the RIVER side, thence down the several meanders of the RIVER to the Beginning, Together with all ways woods houses, mines, minerals, profits and appurtenances thereunto belonging with the Reversions rents and profits and all the Estate in fee Simple unto BASIL NOE his heirs and assigns from the said BOWLES ARMISTEAD &

MARY his Wife free and clear of all Incumbrances warranting and forever defending
the said Land and premises from all claims sutes, Mortgages or other things vesting in
BASIL NOE his heirs and assigns in full peaceable and absolute possession to all intents
and purposes In Witness whereof the said BOWLES ARMISTEAD and MARY his Wife for
their and either of their heirs Executors Administrators & assigns have hereunto set
their hands and seals as their act & deed the day & year first above written
in presence of   BOWLES ARMISTEAD
                                                     MARY ANNE ARMISTEAD
    The Commonwealth of Virginia to SAMUEL CLAYTON, JAMES HORD and ROBERT
SLAUGHTER Gent. Greeting (The commission for the private examination of MARY,
Wife of BOWLES ARMISTEAD dated at the Courthouse the 18th day of March 1783) (The
return of the Examination dated the 18th day of March 1783 and signed by SAM. CLAY-
TON and JAMES HORD)
    At a Court held for Culpeper County the 17th day of March 1783
This Indenture was acknowledged by the within mentioned BOWLES ARMISTEAD &
ordered to be recorded with Commission thereto annexed & Certificate thereon

pp.   TO ALL PEOPLE TO WHOM these presents shall come I MICHAEL LAWLER of the
270-   County of Culpeper and State of Virginia sends Greeting. Know ye that for and
272   in consideration of the love good will and affection which I have and do bear
       towards my well beloved Son, JOHN LAWLOR of the County and State aforesaid,
hath given and granted and by these presents do fully freely and absolutely give grant
and confirm unto my said Son, JOHN LAWLOR, his heirs and assigns forever all that
tract of land lying in the County aforesaid and on which I now live containing by estimation Two hundred and two acres be the same more or less and bounded Beginning at
JAMES CANNONs Corner (now JAMES DUNCAN) a white Oak and two pines on a hill,
thence North seventy eight degrees West One hundred and twenty four poles to three
Pines on a Hill near the River, thence down the River the several Courses until it in-
tersects a line that bears South fifty two degrees West to the Beginning Together with
the following Slaves (Vizt) Sam, Jinny, Hannah, Beck, Sam, Bob, George and one not yet
named, Will, Lill, Will, Clary, Doll, Benson, Celia & Phebe and one other not yet named
and all the future increase as also all my stock of horses, cattle, hogs, sheep and all
working tools and household furniture and furniture of any kind whatsoever and
every other article whatsoever of my property either Real Estate or Personal and all
houses buildings gardens orchards meadows and appurtenances whatsoever to the same
belonging To have and to hold all the lands and premises together with the slaves and
all other articles above mentioned with their and every of their appurtenances unto
my said Son, JOHN LAWLOR, his heirs and assigns forever and I the said MICHAEL
LAWLOR do hereby the land and premises together with the slaves and all other the
article above mentioned with the appurtenances unto my said Son, JOHN LAWLOR, his
heirs and assigns against me or any persons whatsoever warrents and forever defends
by these presents to the true intent and meaning that my said Son, JOHN LAWLOR, his
heirs and assigns shall and may after the sealing and delivery of these presents be
possessed of a good sure perfect and Indefeasable right in fee simple of all the land and
premises together with the slaves and other the articles above mentioned In Witness
whereof I have hereunto set my hand and seal this 14th day of December in year of our
Lord One thousand seven hundred and Eighty two
in presence of JOHN BRADFORD   Provided Always and it is my intent that my said
         JOHN STROTHER JUNR.   Son, JOHN, shall not bar or hinder my or my Wife
         WILLIAM DUNCAN JUNR.   using for my ease or sustenance any of the land or
         JAMES DUNCAN   premises abovementioned during my or her

CHARLES BROWNING   natural life any thing above to the contrary not-
                                      withstanding   MICHAEL his mark ꓷ LAWLOR
   At a Court held for Culpeper County the 17th day of March 1783
This Indenture was proved by the Oaths of JOHN BRADFORD, WM. DUNCAN JUNR. &
CHARLES BROWNING, Witnesses thereto, & ordered to be recorded

pp.   (On margin: Lawler Deed to Butler DD SPENCER BUTLER Mar. 1796)
272-   THIS INDENTURE made this Twenty fifth day of Decr. in year of our Lord One
275   thousand seven hundred and Eighty two Between JOHN LAWLOR and SUSANNAH
       his Wife of the County of Culpeper and State of Virginia of one part and WIL-
LIAM BUTLER of County & State aforesaid of other part Witnesseth that JOHN LAWLOR
and SUSANNAH his Wife for and in consideration of the sum of Twenty pounds current
money of Virginia to them in hand paid by these presents do bargain and sell unto
WILLIAM BUTLER his heirs and assigns one certain piece or parcel of land containing
One hundred and fifty acres (be the same more or less) & bounded Beginning at a white
Oak standing on the Bank of BATTLE RUN on the So. side thereof & runs down the
several courses thereof South forty seven degrees East sixty eight pole South sixty six
degrees Twenty eight pole, South thirty six degrees East thirty pole to a Locust & an Ash
standing on the bank of said RUN, thence leaving the RUN South thirty nine degrees
West Two hundred pole to a line made for WILLIAM ROBERTS, thence with the same
North thirty degrees West One hundred and thirty nine pole to three red Oaks on a Spur
of AARON MOUNTAIN on the East side thereof, thence North East One hundred and Sixty
poles to the Beginning, it being a tract of land sold to JOHN LAWLOR by JAMES WALL &
recorded in the records of Culpeper County, the Deeds bearing date the 26th day of
March 1773, Together with all houses gardens Orchards & Emoluments to the same belonging To have and to hold the said tract of land with the appurtenances to the said
WILLIAM BUTLER his heirs and assigns forever and JOHN LAWLOR & SUSANNAH his
Wife & their heirs the said tract of land and premises to the sd WILLIAM BUTLER his
heirs and assigns will warrent & forever defend by these presents against every person whatsoever freed and discharged of and from all Incumbrances of any kind whatsoever In Witness whereof the parties to these presents have hereunto set their hands
& Seals the day and year first above written
in the presence of us   JOHN LAWLOR
   At a Court held for Culpeper County the 17th day of March 1783
This Indenture was acknowledged by the within mentioned JOHN LAWLOR and ordered
to be recorded

pp.   THIS INDENTURE made the Seventeenth day of February One thousand seven
275-   hundred and Eighty three Between ALEXANDER WAUGH JUNIOR of Culpeper
277   County of one part and THOMAS PORTER JUNIOR of the same County of other part
       Witnesseth that Whereas ALEXANDER WAUGH JUNIOR for and in consideration of
the sum of One hundred and thirteen pounds to him in hand paid by these presents do
bargain and sell unto THOMAS PORTER JUNR. his heirs and assigns one tract of land
lying in the County of Culpeper containing One hundred and thirteen acres and
bounded Beginning at a Pine, Corner to ALEXANDER WAUGH against WILLIAM CLARKE's
on FRY's ROAD, from thence down the meanders of said Road to the Ford across GREAT
RUN, thence down the meanders of the said RUN to the Mouth of HAWK BRANCH in POR-
TER's MILL POND, thence North ten degrees West twenty six poles to a white Oak, Corner
to WAUGH on HAWK BRANCH, thence North sixty four degrees West One hundred and
sixty poles to the Beginning, Together with all houses orchards & improvements of the
land belonging and also all the Estate, right, title and Interest of him the said ALEXAN-

DER WAUGH JUNR. of the land hereby conveyed with the appurtenances To have and to
hold the above mentioned land with the appurtenances unto THOMAS PORTER JUNR. his
heirs and assigns and ALEXANDER WAUGH JUNR. for himself his heirs and against the
claim of all other persons whatever shall warrent and defend by these presents In
Witness whereof the said ALEXANDER WAUGH JUNR. hath hereunto set his hand and
affixed his Seal the day and year first above written
in presence of   ALEXR. WAUGH
   At a Court held for Culpeper County the 17th day of March 1783
This Indenture was ackowledged by the within ALEXANDER WAUGH and ordered to be
recorded

pp.   (On margin: Slaughter & Ux. to Latham D D to Thos. Latham)
277-   THIS INDENTURE made the 20th day of Septr. in year of our Lord One thousand
280   seven hundred and eighty two Between ROBERT SLAUGHTER the Younger and
       LUCY his Wife of the Parish of Bromfield & County of Culpeper of one part and
THOS. LATHAM of the Parish of St. Mark and County aforesaid of the other part Witness-
seth that ROBERT SLAUGHTER the Younger & LUCY his Wife for and in consideration of
the sum of Four thousand seven hundred pounds to them in hand paid by these presents do bargain and sell unto THOS. LATAM his heirs & assigns forever two tracts of
land lying in County aforesaid and on HUNGARY RUN all which lands (Except seventeen
acres) was given by Will to THOMAS MORRISS by his Father, WILLIAM MORRISS deceased, & the whole by the said THOMAS MORRIS conveyed to JOHN POINDEXTER & by him
conveyed to the said ROBERT SLAUGHTER Younger, And is bounded Beginning at the
Mouth of QUARRY BRANCH on HUNGARY RUN, thence up FLOYDS OLD PATH to the back
line, thence South thirty five degrees Thirty west to two Pines, thence North fifty three
degrees West Twenty pole to three Pines, thence South Eighty degrees East two hundred poles to two red & one white Oak in SPOTWOODs Line, th. North sixty six degrees East
to HUNGARY RUN, thence up the said RUN to the Beginning, the Seventeen acres of
land is bounded Beginning at a white Oak in SPOTWOODs line, North Twenty West seven
poles to a large Pine in HENNINGs Line, thence with his line South Twenty five degrees
West One hundred and Eighteen poles to some marked Dead and Down Pines in SPOTS-
WOODs Line, th. with his line to the Beginning containing in the whole Two hundred
acres be the same more or less Together with all houses Orchards watercourses Profits
and Commodities whatsoever to the same belonging To have and to hold the said two
tracts of land and premises with the appurtenances unto THOMAS LATHAM his heirs
and assigns forever and the said ROBERT SLAUGHTER the Younger and LUCY his Wife
for themselves their heirs the said lands and appurtenances to the said THOS. LATHAM
his heirs and assigns against them the said ROBT. SLAUGHTER the Younger and LUCY
his Wife & their heirs and against the claim of any other person whatsoever will warrant and forever defend by these presents unto THOS. LATHAM his heirs and assigns
forever In Witness whereof the said ROBERT SLAUGHTER the Younger & LUCY his Wife
have hereunto set their hands and Seals this day and year within written
in presence of JOHN SLAUGHTER,   ROBERT SLAUGHTER
       HENRY HILL, BENJAMIN LILLARD   LUCY SLAUGHTER
   Then received of THOMAS LATHAM the full and just Sum of Four thousand Seven
hundred pounds this 20th day of Sept. 1782.
       JOHN SLAUGHTER,   Recd p   ROBERT SLAUGHTER
       HENRY HILL, BENJAMIN LILLARD
   The Commonwealth of Virginia to JOHN SLAUGHTER, HENRY FIELD & HENRY HILL
Gentlemen Greeting (The Commission for the private Examination of LUCY, the Wife of
ROBERT SLAUGHTER dated at the Courthouse of the said County the 20th day of Sept. 1782

in the Seventh year of the Commonwealth) (Return of the Private Examination of
LUCY SLAUGHTER dated the 20th day of Sept. 1782 and signed by JOHN SLAUGHTER and
HENRY HILL)
At a Court held for Culpeper County the 18th day of November 1782
This Indenture was proved by the Oaths of JOHN SLAUGHTER & HENRY HILL, witnesses
thereto, which is to be Certified, And at a Court held for Culpeper County the 17th day of
March 1783, was fully proved by the Oath of BENJAMIN LILLARD, another Witness
thereto, and ordered to be recorded with the Commission thereto annexed & Certificate
thereon

pp.   THIS INDENTURE made the Seventeenth March in year of our Lord One thousand
281-   seven hundred and Eighty three Between WILLIAM GRANT and SARAH his Wife
283   of County of PRINCE WILLIAM of the one part and CATLETT TIFFEE of the County
       of Culpeper of other part Witnesseth that WILLIAM GRANT and SARAH his Wife
for and in consideration of the sum of Sixteen pounds current money of Virginia to
them in hand paid by these presents do bargain and sell unto CATLETT TIFFEE my right
of a Tract or parcel of land lying in County of Culpeper containing Ninety acres and is
bounded beginning at two Hickorys and a black Gum, Corner to FREDERICK ZIMMER-
MAN, running thence South Ten and a half degrees East One hundred and twenty seven
poles to the line of JOHN ASHER, thence North seventy degrees East One hundred and
fifty two poles to the line of SAMUEL WRIGHT, thence North Eleven degrees East thirty
six poles to a white Oak on the side of a Stony Hill, thence North fifty three degrees West
along the line of RICHARD WRIGHT forty six poles to four white Oaks, corner to said
ZIMMERMON, thence along his line to the Beginning, And all houses Orchards profits
commodities and appurtenances whatsoever and also all Estate, right, Interest and
demand whatsoever of the said WILLIAM GRANT of in & to the premises and all Deeds,
Evidences & Writings touching or in any ways concerning the same To have and to
hold my right of the said tract or parcel of land and all premises hereby granted &
released and every of the appurtenances unto CATLETT TIFFEE his heirs and assigns and
WILLIAM GRANT and SARAH his Wife their heirs and all and every person claiming
under them will warrent and forever defend by these presents In Witness whereof the
said WILLIAM GRANT and SARAH his Wife hath hereunto set their hands & Seals the day
and year first above written
in the presence of WILLIAM ALLEN,   WILLIAM GRANT
      JOHN BROWN, WILLIAM KABLER   SARAH GRANT
At a Court held for Culpeper County the 17th day of March 1783
This Indenture was acknowledged by the parties and ordered to be recorded, previous to
which the said SARAH was first privately examined as the Law directs

pp.   (On margin: Kirtley Deed of Gift to Barnes D D Self 1808)
283-   TO ALL CHRISTIAN PEOPLE to whom these presents shall come I JAMES KIRTLY
284   of County of Culpeper for and in consideration of the love and good will and
       affection which I bear towards my Son in Law, CHARLES BARNS and my Daugh-
ter, MARY BARNS, and to the Survivour of them during their natural lives, have given
and by these presents do freely clearly and absolutely give and grant unto CHARLES
BARNES and to the Survivour of them and to their heirs lawfully begotten between
their bodies, the use of one Negro girl called Sheby and her Issue which said Negro girl
and her Issue aforesaid after the decease of my Son in Law, CHARLES BARNS, and my
Daughter, MARY BARNS, I give to be equally divided amongst the Children of the said
CHARLES BARNS that he shall have by my said Daughter, To have and to hold the said
Negro girl and her issue unto said CHARLES BARNS and MARY BARNS and their heirs as

aforesaid from henceforth as their right In Testimony whereof I have set my hand and
Seal this 19th day of April in the Eighth year of the American Independence and in the
year of our Lord Seventeen hundred & Eighty three
in the presence of us JOHN BARNS,   JAMES KIRTLY
     JOS. SANFORD, JOHN STONE
  At a Court held for Culpeper County the 21st day of April 1783
This Deed of Gift from JAMES KIRTLEY to CHARLES BARNS &c. was proved by the Oaths of
JOHN BARNES & JOSEPH SANFORD two of the Witnesses thereto and ordered to be
recorded

pp.   (On margin: Leatherer Deed of Gift to Leatherer D. D. to Self 1783)
284-   TO ALL PEOPLE to whom these presents shall come I PAUL LEATHERER do send
286   Greeting. Know ye that I PAUL LEATHERER of the Parish of Bromfield in County
       of Culpeper for divers good causes and considerations but more especially for
and in consideration of love good will and natural affection which I have and do bear
towards my Loving Son, JOSHUA LEATHERER, of the foresaid Parish and County do give
grant and make over unto him, the said JOSHUA LEATHERER, the tract of land and Plantation whereon I now live also two other tracts one bought of JOHN & MICHAEL CLORE of
100 acres, the other bought of ADAM CLORE of 13 acres, Together with one Negro boy
named Ben, One half of my stock of Horses, cattle, hogs and of all other of my Stock of
all kinds, Also one bed and furniture which said Bed is now called his now, the above
mentioned land and Plantation together with the articles above mentioned I do hereby
freely give grant make over and confirm unto said JOSHUA LEATHERER his heirs and
assigns forever to be possessed by him his heirs &c. after my decease and my Wife,
MARGARETs decease (and not before) in consideration of which the said JOSHUA
LEATHERER doth hereby oblige himself to find me and my Wife, MARGARET LEATHER, a
proper and sufficient support of all kinds during our natural lives and after our
decease to be by him possessed all the above articles I do hereby Warrent and forever
defend to him the said JOSHUA LEATHERER his heirs and assigns forever In Witness
whereof I do set my hand & Seal this Fourth day of November One thousand seven hundred & Eighty
in presence of. JNO. HUME,   PAUL LEATHERER
     JAMES his mark C CRAIN,
     JOHN his mark X YOWELL
  At a Court held for Culpeper County the 18th day of December 1780
This Indenture was partly proved by the Oath of JAMES CRAIN, a witness thereto, &
ordered to be certified.
  At a Court held for the aforesaid County the 16th day of April 1781 was further proved
by the Oath of JOHN HUME, another witness thereto, which is to be certified
  And at a Court held for the said County the 21st day of April 1783 was fully proved by
the Oath of JOHN YOWELL and ordered to be recorded

pp.   (On margin: Starr & Ux. Deed to Mauk D D 1792)
286-   THIS INDENTURE made this 21st day of April in year of our Lord One thousand
288   seven hundred & Eighty three Between JASPER STARR and KATHARINE his Wife
       of County of Culpeper of one part and DANIEL MAUK of County of SHENANDOAH
Witnesseth that for and in consideration of the sum of Fifty pounds current money of
Virginia to him the said JASPER STARR and KATHARINE his Wife well and truly in hand
paid have bargained and sold unto DANIEL MAUK his heirs and assigns forever a certain parcel of land lying in County of Culpeper containing by estimation Two hundred
acres be the same more or less lying on the South side of the ROBINSON RIVER and

bounded Beginning at two white Oaks and a Poplar, thence South fifty degrees West One hundred and eighty eight poles to a Spanish and red Oak, thence North seventy two degrees West eighty two poles to two red Oaks, thence North thirty degrees East fifty two poles to a white Oak on a branch, thence North One hundred & ninety six poles to the mouth of QUAKER RUN, thence down the said RUN and River to the Beginning Together with all woods ways houses orchards and all other appurtenances belonging and all other the Estate, Right and Title that may now or ever hereafter appertain to the same from the trouble hindrance or molestation of any person whatsoever lawfully claiming the same To have and to hold all the aforesaid land and premises from all Incumbrances of Mortgages Dower Reversions by or from us or from any other person whatsoever and to be the only use of him the said DANIEL MAUK his heirs and assigns forever As Witness my hand and Seal the day and year above written

in presence of   JASPER his mark⊙𝄁⌡ STARR
                                                   KATHARINE her mark ⌡ STARR

At a Court held for Culpeper County the 21st of April 1783
This Indenture was acknowledged by the within parties and ordered to be recorded, previous to which the said KATHARINE was first privily examined as the Law directs

pp.   (On margin: Sims to Bobo D the ord. of the heirs of NANCY POWELL May 1821)
288-   THIS INDENTURE made this fifth day of April One thousand seven hundred and
289   Eighty three Between THOMAS SIMS of County of Culpeper of one part and AMY
       BOBO (Daughter of the said THOMAS SIMS) of the County aforesaid of other part
Witnesseth that THOMAS SIMS for and in consideration of love and affection which he has for his said Daughter and also for and in consideration of Five shillings current money to him in hand paid by said AMY BOBO the Receipt whereof he doth hereby acknowledge hath lent to said AMY BOBO during her natural life Five slaves now in the possession of her Husband, ABSALOM BOBO, to wit, One Negro woman named Cate, two Negro boys, Sons of the said Cate, named Henry and Oliver, Two Negro girls, Daughters of the said Cate, named Jenny and Hannah, the said THOMAS SIMS doth lend unto ABSALOM BOBO two of the said slaves during his natural life and after the death of ABSALOM BOBO and AMY his Wife, then the said slaves above mentioned to return to my Grann Daughter, NANCY POWELL, and her lawfull heirs forever, and the said THOMAS SIMS doth hereby oblige himself & his heirs to warrent and defend the right and title of the said slaves and their future Increase to said NANCY POWELL her heirs and assigns forever against the claim of him the said THOMAS SIMS & her heirs and against the claims of any person claiming under him in Witness whereof the said THOMAS SIMS hath hereunto set his hand and affixed his Seal the day and year above written

in presence of us LEWIS GRAVES,   THOMAS SIMS
       GEORGE SIMS, WILLIAM POWELL
At a Court held for Culpeper County the 21st day of April 1783
This Indenture was proved by the Oaths of LEWIS GRAVES, GEORGE SIMS & WILLIAM POWELL, witnesses thereto, and ordered to be recorded

pp.   (On margin: Thomas Deed of Gift to Piper D D to Self 1787)
289-   KNOW ALL MEN by these presents that I RICHARD THOMAS do give grant and by
290   these presents have given granted & confirmed to my beloved Son in Law, JOHN
       PIPER, as well for the natural love and affection which I have & do bear him the
said JOHN PIPER as for the sum of Five shillings to me in hand paid, the receipt whereof I do hereby acknowledge, do give the following Negro slaves (to witt) Reuben & Sambo together with one equal half of the rest of my Stock, Household furniture & working utensils to him the said JOHN PIPER his heirs & assigns To have and to hold forever

Sealed with my Seal & dated this sevinth day of October One thousand seven hundred and eighty two
in presence of JAMES THOMAS,   RICHARD THOMAS
      JOSHUA BROWNING, GEORGE THOMAS
   At a Court held for Culpeper County the 21st day of April 11783
This Deed of Gift was proved by the Oaths of JAMES THOMAS & GEORGE THOMAS, witnesses thereto, & ordered to be recorded

pp.   (On margin: Bradford Deed to Bradford D D your Son WM. BRADFORD 1804)
290-   THIS INDENTURE made this 17th day of May in year of our Lord One thousand
292   seven hundred and Eighty two Between JOHN BRADFORD of County of Culpeper &
        State of Virginia of one part and DANIEL BRADFORD of County of FAUQUIER &
State aforesaid of other part Witnesseth that for and in consideration of the sum of Five pounds current money of Virginia to him in hand paid by DANIEL BRADFORD by these presents do bargain and sell unto DANIEL BRADFORD his heirs and assigns for ever all that tract or parcel of land lying in County of Culpeper bounded Beginning at a Sycamore tree standing on BATTLE RUN & Corner to said DANIEL BRADFORD and ENOCH BRADFORD, thence with the line of the former North forty five East ninety poles passing said DANIEL's Corner to a Pine and red Oak, thence North sixty seven West twenty eight poles to a white Oak & Ash standing on the Bank of BATTLE RUN, thence down the same the several Courses thereof to the Beginning Containing 20 acres more or less, Together with all houses buildings gardens Orchards Meadows water courses mines minerals Quarries profits and appurtenances whatsoever to the same belonging To have and to hold all the said premises with the appurtenances unto DANIEL BRADFORD his heirs and assigns forever and the said JOHN BRADFORD doth for himself his heirs and assigns all and singular the premises above mentioned unto the said DANIEL BRADFORD his heirs & assigns Warrant and for ever defend by these presents against every persons In Witness whereof the said JOHN BRADFORD hath hereunto set his hand & affixed his Seal the day and year first above written
in the presence of us   JOHN BRADFORD
   Received of the within named DANIEL BRADFORD the sum of Five pounds Virginia Currency it being the consideration money mentioned to be paid by him to me on perfection of the within Deed. Witness my hand & Seal this 17th day of May 1783
                                                    JOHN BRADFORD
   At a Court held for Culpeper County the 19th day of May 1783
This Indenture was acknowledged by the within mentioned JOHN BRADFORD & ordered to be recorded

pp.   (On margin: Redding Deed to Hand D D to Self 1786)
293-   THIS INDENTURE made the 19th day of May in year of our Lord One thousand
295   seven hundred and Eighty three Between WM. REDDING & CLARY his Wife of the
        County of Culpeper of the one part & THOMAS HAND of County of SHENANDOA of
other part Witnesseth that WILLIAM REDDING & CLARY his Wife for and in consideration of the sum of Six pounds current money of Virginia to them in hand paid by these presents do bargain and sell unto THOMAS HAND his heirs &c. one certain tract of land lying in County of Culpeper and bounded Beginning at two Poplars two white Oaks & a Gum on the South side of the main HEDGMAN RIVER corner to WILLIAM WITHERS, thence up the RIVER North five degrees East fourteen poles, thence North seventy degrees West seven poles, thence South eighty degrees West six poles, thence North fifty three degrees West eleven poles, thence North sixty five degrees West Twelve poles to a Poplar standing by the MAIN ROAD, thence South five degrees West thirty six poles to a

red Oak, thence South twenty eight degrees West ten poles to three Sassafras Bushes in or near WILLIAM WEATHERS's line, thence with the said Line to the beginning, Containing six acres be the same more or less Together with all ways profits commodities & appurtenances whatsoever to the same belonging and also all the Estate, Right, Title Interest and demand whatsover of them the said WILLIAM REDDING & CLARY his Wife their heirs or assigns To have and to hold the said tract or parcel of land with the appurtenances unto THOMAS HAND his heirs & assigns and WILLIAM REDDING & CLARY his Wife their heirs and assigns the above mentioned granted land and premises with the appurtenances unto THOMAS HAND & his heirs shall warrant and forever defend against the claim of every person whatsoever In Witness whereof the said WILLIAM REDDING and CLARY his Wife have hereunto set their hands and Seals the day and year first above written

in presence of

WILLIAM his mark X REDDING
CLARY her mark X REDDING

Received of the within named THOMAS HAND the full sum of Six pounds the consideration mentioned in the within deed

WILLIAM his mark X REDDING

At a Court held for Culpeper County the 19th day of May 1783
This Indenture was acknowledged by the parties and ordered to be recorded, the said CLARY being first privily examined as the Law directs

p. (On margin: Thomas Deed of Gift to Geo. Thomas D D to Self 1787)
295 KNOW ALL MEN by these presents that I RICHARD THOMAS do give grant and by these presents hath given granted & confirmed to my Beloved Son, GEORGE THOMAS as well for the natural love and affection which I have and do bear to him the said GEORGE THOMAS as the sum of Five shillings to me in hand paid the receipt whereof I do hereby acknowledge do give the following slaves, to wit, Jerry, Doll and Sall, together with my two Horses & one equal half of the rest of my Stock, household furniture and working Utensils to him the said GEORGE THOMAS his heirs & assigns to have and to hold forever. Sealed with my Seal and dated this sevinth day of October One thousand sevin hundred & eighty two

In the presence of JAMES THOMAS   RICHARD THOMAS
JOSHUA BROWNING, JOHN PIPER
At a Court held for Culpeper County the 19th day of May 1783
This Deed of Gift was proved by the Oaths of JAMES THOMAS & JOHN PIPER, Witnesses thereto, & ordered to be recorded

pp. (On margin: Rogers Deed & Com. to Taliaferro D D. to Jno. Taliaferro 1786)
296- THIS INDENTURE made this seventh day of September and in the year of our Lord
300 One thousand seven hundred and Eighty two Between WILLIAM ROGERS & ANNEY his wife of Culpeper County of one part and JOHN TALIAFERRO of ALBEMARLE COUNTY of other part Witnesseth that WM. ROGERS & ANNEY his Wife for and in consideration of the Sum of Four hundred and thirty five pounds current money of Virginia to him in hand paid by JOHN TALIAFERRO and for divers good causes and valuable consideration him thereunto moving by these presents doth bargain and sell unto JOHN TALIAFERRO his heirs & assigns one Tract or parcel of land containing by Estimation Four hundred and thirty five acres be the same more or less, lying and being on the Branches of the RAPPADAN RIVER and the County of Culpeper and is bounded Beginning at four Sarsaphrass in the Old Field on the ROLING PATH, thence North nineteen degrees East Three hundred and eighty six poles to three pines, Corner to JOSEPH ROGERS & JOHN BEAL on a Ridge, thence South eighty eight degrees West One hundred

and sixty four poles to two Pines & a Hickory, thence South eighteen poles to three
pines in JOHN LEWIS's line, thence North Eighty degrees West One hundred & eighty
poles to a Beach & Pine on the East side of SMITHS RUN, thence North two degrees West
thirty poles, thence South eighty nine degrees East nineteen poles, thence South thirty
four degrees East twenty four poles, thence South ten degrees East seventy eight poles,
thence South fifty poles mouth of WHITE OAK RUN, thence seventy two degrees West to
BLUNTs line twelve poles, thence with said BLUNTs line South fifteen degrees East ten
poles to three Pines in said BLUNTs line, thence with said BLUNTs line South thirty
three degrees East hundred & twenty six poles to three red Oaks & one white Oak, Corner
to FRANCIS BLUNT, JAMES QUIN & BENEJAH RICE, from thence to the beginning, To
have and to hold the said granted lands & premises with the appurtenances unto said
JOHN TALIAFERRO his heirs and assigns forever and WILLIAM ROGERS & ANNEY his
Wife their heirs & assigns to the said granted premises with the appurtenances unto
JOHN TALIAFERRO his heirs and assigns and shall warrent and forever defend against
all persons whatsoever claiming any Right or Title to the same In Witness whereof the
said WILLIAM ROGERS & his Wife, ANNEY, hath hereunto Interchangably set their
hands & affix'd their Seals the day & year first above written
in presence of us BENJAMIN JOHNSTONE,   WILLIAM ROGERS
        JOHN STOCKDELL, JOHN STOCKDELL JUNR.,   ANNEY ROGERS
        JAS. BARBOUR, WILLIAM WALKER,
        ELIJAH KIRTLEY, MERRY WALKER
    Memorandum That Quiet & Peaceable possession & Seizen of the within mentioned
lands & premises was had & taken by the within named JOHN TALIAFERRO of & from the
within named WILLIAM ROGERS and ANNEY his Wife according to form & effect of the
within written Deed on the day and year within mentioned
to the presence of JAS. BARBOUR,   WILLIAM ROGERS
        WILLIAM WALKER, ELIJAH KIRTLEY,
        MERRY WALKER
    The Commonwealth of Virginia to JAMES BARBOUR, WM. WALKER & ELIJAH KIRTLEY
Gent. Greeting. (The Commission for the private Examination of ANNEY, the Wife of
WILLIAM ROGERS dated at the Courthouse the 20th day of September 1782 and in the
Sevinth year of the Commonwealth) (The return of the private Examination of ANNEY
ROGERS dated the 16th day of May 1783 and signed by JAMES BARBOUR, WILLIAM WAL-
KER and ELIJAH KIRTLEY)
    At a Court held for Culpeper County the 19th day of May 1783
This Indenture was acknowledged by the parties and ordered to be recorded with Com-
mission thereto annexed & a Certificate thereon

pp.   (On margin: Johnston & Ux. Deed to Taliaferro D D to Self)
300-   THIS INDENTURE made the 20th day of May in year of our Lord One thousand
305   seven hundred & Eighty three Between JOHN JOHNSTON and MARY his Wife of
        County of Culpeper of one part & HARRY TALIAFERRO of the aforesaid County of
the other part Witnesseth that for and in consideration of the sum of Fifteen pounds &
Fifteen thousand pounds of Tobacco by the said HARRY TALIAFERRO to said JOHN JOHN-
STON well and truly in hand paid by these presents the said JOHN JOHNSTON and MARY
his Wife doth bargain and sell unto HARRY TALIAFERRO his heirs and assigns a certain
tract or parcel of land lying in County of Culpeper containing by estimation Two hun-
dred acres more or less and bounded Beg.g at two Chesnut Oaks and Pine, Corner to Colo.
CHARLES CARTER, thence running down the several Courses of the OLD ROAD to a white
Oak Corner, thence South twenty degrees West thirty nine pole to a Hickory, thence
South sixty four degrees East sixty two poles to three Box Oaks, thence North twenty two

and a half degrees East six poles to a Box Oak, Corner to HENRY FIELD's, thence North
Eight degrees East One hundred & sixty two poles to a red and white Oak, Corner to
LAWRENCE SLAUGHTER, thence North thirty eight degrees West One hundred and two
poles to JOHN CARDERs Corner, thence along the said CARDERs line North fifty four degrees West One hundred and forty four poles to a red Oak, Corner to ABIL STOUT & HANES
in CARTERs line thence along the said CARTERs line to the beginning, Together with
all woods watercourses & appurtenances whatsoever to the said parcel of land in any
wise appurtaining And all Estate, Right, Title and demand of said JOHN JOHNSTON &
MARY his Wife of or to the same belonging To have and to hold the said piece or parcel
of land and premises hereby bargained and sold unto HARRY TALIAFERRO his heirs and
assigns and JOHN JOHNSTON & MARY his Wife shall warrant & forever defend by these
presents In Witness whereof we have hereunto set our hands and Seals the day and
year first above written
in presence of JNO. WILLIAM JUNR.   JOHN JOHNSTON
        SAM. CLAYTON, RICHARD GAINES   MARY her mark JOHNSTON
   The Commonwealth of Virginia to WM. McCLANAHAN, JAMES BROWNING & JOHN WIG-
GINTON Gent. Greeting. (Commission for the private Examination of MARY, Wife of
JOHN JOHNSTON, dated at the Courthouse the 16th day of June 1783 & in Seventh year of
the Commonwealth.)(The return of the private Examination of MARY JOHNSTON dated
the 26th day of July 1783 and signed by WM. McCLANAHAN and JAS. BROWNING)
   At a Court held for Culpeper County the 19th day of May 1783
This Indenture was acknowledged by the within JOHN JOHNSTON and ordered to be recorded and on the motion of the said JOHNSTON a commission is ordered to issue to take
the private examination of MARY, his Wife, which when returned with Certificate
thereon is also ordered to be recorded

pp.   THIS INDENTURE made the third day of May in year of our Lord One thousand
305-   seven hundred & Eighty three Between the Honble. ALEXANDER SPOTSWOOD of
307   County of SPOTSYLVANIA and ELIZABETH his Wife of one part and CHARLES
        BRUCE of County of ORANGE of other part Witnesseth the said Honble. ALEXAN-
DER SPOTSWOOD and ELIZABETH his Wife for and in consideration of the sum of 16
pounds Currency of Virginia in hand paid by these presents doth bargain & sell to the
said CHARLES BRUCE his heirs & assigns all that tract of land lying in Parish of (blank)
in Culpeper County containing six acres bounded Beginning at a small heap of Stone at
the Upper End of the ISLAND, thence down the several Courses of the South Prong of
the River to the Lower end of do. to a small Burch, thence up the several courses of the
North Prong of said River to the Beginning, Together with all dwelling as well as out
houses, fences woods feedings and all other appurtenances benefits and advantages
whatsoever belonging to said Land and the said Honble ALEXANDER SPOTSWOOD and
ELIZABETH his Wife for themselves & their heirs do covenant and agree unto said
CHARLES BRUCE that they shall forever defend the said land & premises hereby granted
unto said CHARLES BRUCE his heirs and assigns against the claims of all persons whatsoever In Witness whereof the said Honble. ALEXANDER SPOTSWOOD & ELIZABETH his
Wife have hereunto set their hands and Seals this day & year above written and before
the following witnesses   ALEXANDER SPOTSWOOD
        FRANCIS HUGHS, ADAM GOODLET,
        RICHARD LONG, WILLIAM his mark X CHISM,
        ARTEMINUS ROBINSON
   Received of CHARLES BRUCE the within mentioned sum of Six pounds in full of all demands for the within mentioned ISLAND
Teste ADAM GOODLET   ALEXANDER SPOTSWOOD

At a Court held for Culpeper County the 19th day of May 1783
This Indenture was proved by the Oaths of FRANCIS HUGHS, ADAM GOODLET &
ATEMINUS ROBINSON three of the witnesses thereto and ordered to be recorded

pp.
308-
309

THIS INDENTURE made the 19th day of May in year of our Lord One thousand
seven hundred & Eighty two by & Between JACOB CRIM of County of Culpeper &
Parish of Bromfield of one part and GEORGE THEAD of same County & Parish of
other Witnesseth that JACOB CRIM for and in consideration of the sum of Twenty
pounds current money of Virginia to him in hand paid by the aforesaid GEORGE THEAD
hath bargained & sold unto said GEO. THEAD a Certain piece or parcel of land which said
land is lying in the aforesaid County and Parish of Bromfield and is bounded Beginning
at two white Oaks in the line of a Patent formerly JOHN KILBY's at the head of a Branch,
thence down the sd Branch South sixty six and half degrees East fifty five poles to 2
white Oaks, thence South fifty three degrees East One hundred poles to two red Oaks and
a Pine another line of the said KILBYs & thence with KILBYs line the several courses to
the beginning South fifteen degrees West fifty poles to two red Oaks, thence North fifty
six degrees West One hundred and seventy three poles to a Stake, formerly a Corner of
the said KILBYs, from thence to the Beginning containing by estimation Forty eight
acres of land, Together with all houses timber Orchards priviledges profits and advantages to the same belonging To have and to hold the aforesaid land & premises freed
from all Incumbrances Dowers, Mortgages or molestation of any kind or sort whatsoever and hereafter held by him the said GEO. THEAD his heirs and assigns In Witness
whereof I have hereunto set my hand & Seal the day month and year above written
in presence of   JACOB CRIM
At a Court held for Culpeper County the 19th day of May 1783
This Indenture was acknowledged by the within mentioned JACOB CRIM and ordered to
be recorded

pp.
310-
312

(On margin: Miller & Ux. Deed to Noe. D. D. to BENJA. McKENSEY 18th May 84)
THIS INDENTURE made this 25th day of April in year of our Lord Christ One thousand seven hundred and Eighty three Between FRANCIS MILLER and ELIZABETH
his Wife of County of Culpeper in Colony of Virginia of one part and GEORGE NOE
of STATE of MARYLAND of other part Witnesseth that FRANCIS MILLER and ELIZABETH
his Wife for & in consideration of the sum of Three hundred and ninety seven pounds
Current money of Virginia by these presents doth bargain and sell unto GEORGE NOE his
heirs and assigns for ever one certain tract of land lying in County and Colony aforesaid & bounded Beginning at 2 white Oaks and a Pine in GEO. THEADs line on FOLING RUN
thence up the said RUN to JAMES FRY line, thence South sixty three degrees East to a
Chesnut tree, thence North eight degrees East to two red Oaks, thence to the beginning,
containing Eighty eight acres more or lesss Together with all houses Inclosures water
courses profits and Emoluments whatsoever to the same belonging also the Estate, Right
title & Interest of me the said FRANCIS MILLER of in and to the said Eighty eight acres
of land and premises To have and to hold the said tract of land with the appurtenances
thereunto belonging to the said GEORGE NOE his heirs and assigns and I the said FRAN-
CIS MILLER my heirs and assigns the said Tract of land to the said GEORGE NOE his heirs
& assigns shall and will warrant and forever defend by these presents against all persons whatsoever and the said eighty eight acres shall forever hereafter remain unto
GEORGE NOE his heirs and assigns freed and discharged of and from all former rights,
titles Debts or sales whatsoever In Witness whereof we the said FRANCIS MILLER and
ELIZABETH his Wife hath hereunto set our hands and fixed our seals the day and year

above written

                                              FRANCIS MILLER
                                              ELIZABETH MILLER
  Received this 25th day of April Seventeen hundred and Eighty three of Mr. GEORGE
NOE the just sum of three hundred and ninety seven pounds current money of Virginia
it being the consideration money of the within Deed by me FRANCIS MILLER
  At a Court held for Culpeper County the 19th day of May 1783
This Indenture was acknowledged by the parties and ordered to be recorded, previous to
which the said ELIZABETH was examined as the Law directs

pp.   THIS INDENTURE made the Twenty Third day of August in year of our Lord One
312-   thousand seven hundred and Eighty One Between ROBERT TERILL & JUDAH his
315   Wife of the County of Culpeper of one part & JOHN TERRILL of the County of the
        other part Witnesseth that they the said ROBERT TERRILL & JUDY his Wife for
and in consideration of the sum of Four thousand pounds current money of Virginia by
these presents do bargain and sell unto JOHN TERRILL his heirs and assigns forever a
certain tract or parcel of land situate lying and being in the County aforesaid and on
the North side of the ROBINSON RIVER containing Two hundred and sixty acres more or
less Beginning at Locust in LEWIS CONNERs line, running thence with said line South
Fifty degrees East sixty five poles to the ROBINSON RIVER, thence up the several Courses
of the sd RIVER three hundred & ninety pole to a Maple, Corner to ADAM UTZ, running
thence UTZ line North sixty degrees East two hundred and fifty two Pole to a red Oak and
Hickory Corner to JOHN PINCE and LEWIS CONNER, thence with CONNERs line One hundred and sevinty Pole to the beginning and all houses orchards profits & appurtenances whatsoever to the said premises hereby granted To have and to hold the said
Two hundred & sixty and a half acres of land be the same more or less and all the other
the premises hereby granted with the appurtenances unto JOHN TERRILL his heirs and
assigns forever and ROBERT TERRILL will forever warrent and defend by these
presents In Witness whereof the said ROBERT TERRILL and JUDAH his Wife hath
hereunto set their hands and Seals the day and year first above written
in presence of HUMPHREY SPARKS,   ROBERT TERRILL
        LEWIS CONNER, JOHN PHILLIPS   JUDY + TERRILL
  At a Court held for Culpeper County the 19th day of May 1783
This Indenture was proved by the Oaths of HUMPHREY SPARKS, LEWIS CONNER & JOHN
PHILLIPS witnesses thereto and ordered to be recorded

pp.   THIS INDENTURE Witnesseth that THOMAS TRIPLET of Culpeper County doth put
315-   himself an Apprentice to BAYLOR BANKS, Carpenter & Joiner, of said County to
316   learn his art or mystery, and with him after the manner of an Apprentice to
        serve till he is twenty one years old during all which time the said Apprentice
his said Master faithfully shall serve, his secrets keep & all his lawfull commands every
where gladly obey, he shall do no damage to his said Master nor see it done by others
without letting or giving notice thereof to his said Master, he shall not waste his Masters goods nor lend them unlawfully to any; he shall not contract Matrimony during
the said Term, he shall not play at Cards or Dice or any other unlawfull game whereby
his Master may be damag'd with his own goods nor with the goods of others, he shall
not absent himself day or night from his Masters service unlawfully but in all things
behave himself as a faithfull Apprentice in the trade or mystery he now followeth and
the said Master shall do his true Endeavour to teach or cause to be taught unto the said
Apprentice the art of Carpentry & Joinery & shall procure & provide for him sufficient
meat drink lodging & washing during the said Term, And for the true performance of

all and every the said Covenants and agreements either of the said Parties bindeth himself unto the other firmly by these presents. In Witness whereof they have hereunto
set their hands and Seals this (blank)

                              THOMAS TRIPLETT
                              BAYLOR BANKS
    At a Court held for Culpeper County the 19th day of May 1783
This Indenture was ackowledged by the parties and ordered to be recorded

pp.   (On margin: Fry Deed to Noe D D to BENJA. McKENSEY 18th May 1784)
316-   THIS INDENTURE made this twenty fourth day of April in year of our Lord One
318   thousand seven hundred and Eighty three Between JAMES FRY of County of
        SAINT MARYS in the State of MARYLAND of one part and GEORGE NOE of County
and State aforesaid of other part Witnesseth that JAMES FRY for & in consideration of
the just sum of Twenty eight thousand pounds of Tobo. by these presents doth bargain
and sell unto GEORGE NOE his heirs and assigns forever one certain tract or parcell of
land situated lying and being in County of Culpeper and Colony of Virginia & bounded
Adjoining THOS. SPARKS, BENJAMIN HAWKINS, JACOB MANSPOIL, JOHN BROILES containing One hundred & Ninety two acres more or less Together with all Houses Inclosures profits and Emoluments whatsoever to the same belonging and all the Estate,
Right title and Interest of JAMES FRY of in and to the said One hundred and ninety two
acres of land and premises To have and to hold the said Tract of land with the appurtenances thereunto belonging to GEORGE NOE his heirs and assigns and I JAMES FRY my
heirs and assigns the said Tract of land to the said GEORGE NOE his heirs and assigns
shall warrant and forever defend by these presents against any person whatsoever and
the said Tract of One hundred and ninety two acres of land shall forever hereafter remain unto the said GEORGE NOE his heirs and assigns freed and discharged of and from
all former rights titles debts bargains or sales whatsoever In Witness whereof I the said
JAMES FRY hath hereunto set my hand and affixed my Seal the day and year above
written in presence of H. HILL,   JAMES FRY
        ZACHARIAH WALL, GEORGE PASSONS
    Received the 24th day of April One thousand seven hundred and Eighty three of Mr.
GEORGE NOE the sum of Twenty eight thousand pounds of Tobo. it being the consideration sum of the within Deed by me   JAMES FRY
        H. HILL
        ZACHARIAH WALL, GEORGE PASSONS
    At a Court held for Culpeper County the 19th day of May 1783
This Indenture was proved by the Oaths of the Witnesses thereto & ordered to be
recorded

pp.   (On margin: Kilby Deed to Noe D D to BENJA. McKENSEY 17th May 1784)
318-   THIS INDENTURE made the 19th day of April in the year of our Lord One thou-
319   sand seven hundred and Eighty three made & entered into Between JAMES KILBY
        of the County of Culpeper of one part and GEORGE NOE of MARYLAND of other
part Witnesseth that JAMES KILBY for and in consideration of the sum of One hundred
pounds current money of Virginia to him in hand paid by these presents bargain and
sell unto GEORGE NOE his heirs & assigns a certain tract or parcel of land laying being
in the County of Culpeper & bounded Beginning at a Chesnut Oak & one red Oak Saplin, a
Corner of ZACHARY WALL & running thence North seventeen degrees West One hundred & thirty three poles to a red Oak and Pine, WILLIAM THOMPSONs & JOHN REYNOLDS
Corner, and Corner to the sd KILBYs old line and thence with said line South sevin degrees West to the Dividing Line between MICHAEL KILBY and ADAM KILBY thence with

said line to the beginning containing Twenty One acres of land, Together with all houses Orchards watercourses & appurtenances to the same belonging or in any wise appurtaining with all the Right, Title Interest & demand of him the said JAMES KILBY in and to the same To have and to hold the said Tract of land & premises with the appurtenances hereby granted unto GEORGE NOE his heirs & assigns forever freed & cleared from all Incumbrances whatsoever and JAMES KILBY for himself his Executors & Administrators the aforesaid tract of land with the appurtenances unto the sd GEORGE NOE his heirs &c. against the claim of every person whatsoever the same will forever warrant & defend by these presents In Witness whereof the said JAMES KILBY have hereunto set their hands & Seals the day & year first above written
in the presence of H. HILL,   JAMES his mark ┼ KILBY
        ZACHARIAH WALL, GEORGE PASSONS
    Received of GEORGE NOE One hundred pounds current money in full for the above consideration money
Teste   H. HILL,   JAMES his mark ┼ KILBY
        ZACHARIAH WALL, GEORGE PASSONS
    At a Court held for Culpeper County the 19th of May 1783
This Indenture was proved by the Oaths of the witnesses thereto & ordered to be recorded

pp.   (On margin: Colvin Deed to Miller D D 1787)
320-   THIS INDENTURE made this 19th day of May in the year of our Lord One thousand
321   seven hundred and Eighty three Between MASON COLVIN of Culpeper of one part
        and FRANCIS MILLER of other part of County of Culpeper Witnesseth that MASON
COLVIN for and in consideration of the sum of fifty pounds current money of Virginia to him in hand paid by these presents doth bargain and sell unto FRANCIS MILLER his heirs and assigns a Tract or parcel of land containing One hundred & forty sevin & a half acres lying in County of Culpeper bounded Beginning at a Pine & small Chesnut on the South side of THORNTONS ROAD & Corner to SMITH thence South (blank) pole to two Pines in a bottom thence South (blank) poles to two Pines on South side of a branch thence (this entry was not completed - space left) Together with all woods trees profits commodities and appurtenances whatsoever to the same belonging and also all the Estate, Right, Title, Interest & demand whatsoever of them the said MASON COLVIN to the same To have and to hold the said One hundred & forty seven and a half acres of land with the appurtenances unto FRANCIS MILLER his heirs and assigns and MASON COLVIN doth hereby covenant and agree to and with FRANCIS MILLER his heirs and assigns the said Tract of land and premises with appurtenances unto the said FRANCIS MILLER will warrant & forever defend by these presents In Witness whereof the said MASON COLVIN hath hereunto set his hand and Seal the day and year above written
in presence of   MASON COLVIN
    At a Court held for Culpeper County the 19th day of May 1783
This Indenture was acknowledged by the within mentioned MASON COLVIN & ordered to be recorded

pp.   (On margin: Green to Corbin D D yr. Son JERIAH CORBIN 1818)
321-   THIS INDENTURE made this 6th day of August in year of our Lord Christ One
324   thousand seven hundred & Eighty two Between JOHN GREEN, Son and Heir at Law
        of DUFF GREEN deceased, of County of FAUQUIER of one part & WILLIAM CORBIN
of County of Culpeper of other part. Whereas the said DUFF GREEN in his life time bargained and sold to the said WILLIAM CORBIN the Fee Simple Estate of Four hundred acres of land lying in County of Culpeper in the Little Fork of RAPPAHANNOCK RIVER which

said Four hundred acres of land was never conveyed by the said DUFF GREEN in his life
time to said WILLIAM CORBIN, And Whereas the said WILLIAM CORBIN did after the decease of the said DUFF GREEN Exhibit his Bill in Chancery in Culpeper County Court
against WILLIAM GREEN and JOHN GREEN Administrators of DUFF GREEN deceased and
JOHN GREEN, Son and Heir of said deceased & party hereto, praying they might be com-
pelled to convey the said Land and appurtenances to him in Fee Simple, Whereupon it
was ordered & Decreed by the said Court that the Complainant should be Quieted in his
Seisen and possession of the said land & premises and that JOHN GREEN, Heir of the said
Deceased, should on his arriving to the age of Twenty one convey the said land and premises to the said WILLIAM CORBIN his heirs or assigns in fee simple with a warranty,
NOW THIS INDENTURE WITNESSETH that JOHN GREEN, Son and Heir at Law of the said Deceased for and in consideration of the said Decree doth convey and confirm unto WIL-
LIAM CORBIN all that said Tract of land now in the possession of the said CORBIN con-
taining by Patent Four hundred acres and is bounded Begining at three white Oaks on a
branch of CROOKED RUN and corner to ANTHONY SCOTT, thence down the several
courses of the said Branch to four white Oaks by the mouth of a small branch, thence
South twenty degrees West One hundred and twenty poles to two white Oaks, thence
South seven degrees East sixty six poles to two red Oaks & two white Oaks, thence South
East eighty two poles to two red and one white Oaks, thence North Sixty five degrees East
sixty poles to two white Oaks and a Hickory, thence North ten degrees East sixty poles to
white Oaks and a Hickory, thence North East twenty six poles to two Hickorys & two
white Oaks, thence South fifteen degrees East two hundred poles, thence South Eighty
five degrees East Two hundred and twelve poles, thence North Elevin degrees West four
hundred poles to two white Oaks & a red Oak, thence North fifteen degrees West One
hundred and sixty poles to two Hickories and a red Oak, thence North fifteen East One
hundred & twenty poles to a Poplar & two White Oaks on a Branch, thence down the
several course of the same to two white Oaks and a Hickory, Corner to ANTHONY SCOTT,
thence with the said SCOTT's line South fifteen degrees East two hundred poles South
three hundred and ten poles, West ninety poles and North fifteen degrees West Three
hundred & sixty two poles to the beginning, Together with all houses Improvements
and appurtenances whatsoever to the same belonging To have and to hold the said tract
of Land and all the premises with the appurtenances unto WILLIAM CORBIN his heirs
and assigns forever and JOHN GREEN doth hereby warrant and forever defend the said
land & premises unto WILLIAM CORBIN his heirs or assigns against the claim of any
person whatsoever In Witness whereof the said JOHN GREEN hath hereunto set his hand
and seal the day and year first above written
 6th August 1782 I hereby acknowledge all Right & Title that I may have to the above
Recited tract of land as Heir at Law to DUFF GREEN deceased as witness my hand and seal
Test   ROBERT LATHAM,   JOHN GREEN JUNR.
        JOHN WILLIAMS, ROBT. GREEN
 At a Court held for Culpeper County the 21st day of April 1783
This Indenture was partly proved by the Oaths of ROBERT LATHAM and JOHN WILLIAMS,
witnesses thereto, which is to be certified; And at a Court held for the aforesaid County
the 19th day of May 1783 was full proved by the Oath of ROBERT GREEN, another witness
thereto, & ordered to be recorded

pp.   (On margin: Weaver Deed to Hardin D D to Geo. Hardin 1788)
324-   THIS INDENTURE made the 27th day of September in year of our Lord One thou-
327   sand seven hundred and Eighty Two Between PHILLIP WEAVER and ANNA his
       Wife of Culpeper County in the Colony of Virginia of one part and GEORGE HAR-
DIN of the same County & Colony of other part Witnesseth that PHILLIP WEAVER and

ANNA his wife for and in consideration of the full and just sum of Twenty pounds current money of Virginia to them in hand paid by the said GEORGE HARDIN by these presents doth bargain & sell unto GEORGE HARDIN his heirs and assigns one certain piece or parcel of land containing Two hundred and forty acres situate lying and being in Bromfield Parish & Culpeper County in the Great Fork of RAPPAHANNOCK RIVER the same being Two hundred and Forty acres of land granted to WILLIAM DUNCAN the Younger & JOHN DAVIS by the right Honourable THOMAS LORD FAIRFAX, Proprietor of the Northern Neck of Virginia, by Deed from the Proprietors Office bearing date the Seventh day of December One thousand seven hundred & seventy eight And the said Two hundred and forty eight acres of land is bounded Begining at three Pine, corner to WILLIAM COON, thence with his line North fifty nine West One hundred and Ten pole to three red Oak saplins by a Branch in the WIDOW GREEN's line, thence with her lines South twenty five degrees West three hundred and seventy two poles to a white Oak by a branch, thence North sixty five West ninety six poles to a forked white Oak by the said Branch marked W G thence South thirty West two hundred poles to two blazed red Oak saplings, thence North eighty five East One hundred and two poles to two Pines, Corner to GEORGE WILLIAM FAIRFAX Esqr., and to the said GREEN and COON, thence with said COON's line North forty East two hundred and ninety eight poles to an Imaginary Corner, thence North twenty West forty poles to a Pine & thence North forty seven East two hundred & twenty two poles to the Beginning Place with all houses buildings and water courses profits & Emoluments whatsoever to the same belonging and all the Estate, Right, Title & Interest whatsoever of them the said PHILLIP WEAVER and ANNA his Wife of in and to the said Bargained premises To have and to hold the said tract of Two hundred & forty acres of land with the appurtenances unto the said GEORGE HARDEN his heirs & assigns forever and PHILLIP WEAVER & ANNA his Wife and theirs the said tract of land with the appurtenances unto the said GEORGE HARDIN his heirs and assigns shall and will warrent and forever defend by these presents against any person whatsoever In Witness whereof the parties to these presents have set their hands & fixt their Seals the day and year first above written
in the presence of us JOHN GOLDEN, PHILLIP his mark + WEAVER
GEORGE CARDER, JOHN SHINGLETON ANN her mark X WEAVER
Memorandum That on the 27th day of September One thousand seven hundred & eighty two Peaceable and Quiet possession and Seizen of the land & premises within mentioned was held & taken by the within named PHILLIP WEAVER and by him was delivered unto the within named GEORGE HARDIN to be held by him his heirs and assigns forever according to the true intent & meaning of the within Deed Witness my hand & seal the day and year first above written
PHILLIP his mark + WEAVER
At a Court held for Culpeper County the 21st day of October 1782
This Indenture was aproved by the Oaths of JOHN GOLDEN & JOHN SHINGLETON Witnesses thereto & ordered to be Certified; And at a Court held for the aforesaid County the 19th day of May 1783, This Indenture was acknowledged by the parties & ordered to be recorded

p.   TO ALL TO WHOM these presents shall come Know ye that I JAMES ABBITT of the
328   County of Culpeper and State of Virginia being about to remove from the said
        County and it being altogether inconvenient for me to attend to the settlement
of my Business in the said County, Therefore I do by these presents Constitute and appoint my Friend, WILLIAM BRADLEY, of said County my sole and Lawfull Attorney to act and do for me in all things as to him shall seem convenient and necessary for the settleling and adjusting my affairs, And more especially do impower my said Attorney to

sell & convey any or all of my land or lands in said County and to convey the same in
my name to any person to which he may think fit, and also to bring commence prosecute or defend any Suit or Suits in Law for the recovery of any just Debts or preventing
fraud or Injustice to my Estate, And Lastly do by these bind myself and my heirs to Rati-
fy & confirm all his proceedings in my behalf done or executed. In Witness whereof I
have hereunto set my hand & Seal this 27th day of March 1783
in presence of FRANCIS HUME,   JAMES ABBITT
            JOSEPH ROSSON
   At a Court held for Culpeper County the 16th day of June 1783
This Power of Attorney was proved by the oath of FRANCIS HUME and JOSEPH ROSSON
witnesses thereto & ordered to be recorded

pp.   (On margin: Lawson & Ux. Deed to Freeman D D 1791)
328-   THIS INDENTURE made the twenty seventh day of December in year of our Lord
331   One thousand seven hundred and Eighty two Between GAVIN LAWSON and SU-
       SANNA his Wife of County of Culpeper of one part and ROBERT FREEMAN JUNIOR
of the same County of other part Witnesseth that the said GAVIN & SUSANNA for and in
consideration of the sum of Six hundred pounds Specie by these presents do bargain &
sell unto ROBERT FREEMAN JUNIOR one certain tract or parcell of land in said County of
Culpeper at present in the possession of the said GAVIN LAWSON and containing by Estimation Five hundred acres be the same more or less and is part of a larger tract of land
which belonged to ROBERT FREEMAN SENIOR and parcelled out amongst his Sons, HUGH
FREEMAN and others,& sold and conveyed by the said HUGH to the said GAVIN LAWSON
and is bounded agreeable to the lines in the Deed of Conveyance from the said ROBERT
FREEMAN, the Father, to the said HUGH, as by the same and the Deed made by the said
HUGH to the said GAVIN will more fully appear Together with all the Right Title Interest
Claim or property of the said GAVIN LAWSON & SUSANNA his Wife of in and to the same
with the appurtenances to the said ROBERT FREEMAN JUNIOR and his heirs forever free
from the claim of said GAVIN LAWSON and his heirs and GAVIN LAWSON and his heirs
the aforesaid Tract of land with the appurtenances shall and will warrant & forever
defend from the claim of him the said GAVIN LAWSON and his heirs In Witness whereof
the said GAVIN LAWSON and SUSANNA LAWSON have hereunto set their hands & Seals
the day & year first above written
in presence of JOHN WIGGINTON,   GAVIN LAWSON
          WM. McCLANAHAN, JOHN DILLARD,   SUSANNA LAWSON
          GEORGE GRASTY
   December 27th 1782 Then received the sum of Six hundred pounds being the consideration within mentioned
          (same witnesses)   GAVIN LAWSON
   The Commonwealth of Virginia to WM. McCLANAHAN, JOHN WIGGINTON & JAMES
PENDLETON Gent. Greeting. (The Commission for the private Examination of SUSANNA,
the Wife of GAVIN LAWSON, dated at the Courthouse the 28th day of December 1782) (The
return of the private Examination of SUSANNA LAWSON dated the 3 day of January 1782
and signed by WM. McCLANAHAN and JOHN WIGGINTON)
   At a Court held for Culpeper County the 16th day of June 1783
This Indenture was proved by the Oaths of JOHN WIGGINTON, JOHN DILLARD & GEORGE
GRASTY Witnesses thereto and ordered to be recorded with Commission thereto annexed
& Certificate thereon is also ordered to be recorded

pp.   (On margin: Parker & Ux. Deed to Lewis D D 1787)
331-   THIS INDENTURE made this Nineteenth day of July in year of our Lord One thou-
333   sand seven hundred and eighty three Between RICHARD PARKER & GRISSELL
        his Wife of County of Culpeper of one part and WILLIAM LEWIS of the aforesaid
County of other part Witnesseth that for and in consideration of the sum of One hun-
dred & seventy pounds current money of Virginia to them the said RICHD. PARKER and
GRISSELL his Wife well and truly in hand paid have bargained and sold unto WILLM.
LEWIS his heirs and assigns forever a Certain tract of land containing by Estimation
Two hundd. & fifty acres more or less lying in the foresaid County and on the Waters of
MOUNTAIN RUN and bounded Begining at a Pine, Corner to JOHN SMITH deced, thence
with his line South sixty degrees East 88 poles, Corner to a red Oak & Pine by JAMES
YOWILLs Fence, thence with his line North twenty five degrees East One hundred and
Eighteen poles, Corner to said YOWILL a Pine by a Bridge on the upper side of a Run,
thence with the said YOWILLs line North five degrees West thirty four poles to three
Pines on a point, Corner to said YOWELL, thence North sevinty degrees East forty four
poles to a Stump in the said YOWILLs Plantation, thence North eight degrees West two
hundred poles to a Pine, Corner to JAMES GARNET, thence North eighty degrees West
One hundred and thirty eight poles to three Pines, Corner to ELIJAH SIMS, thence with
his line South two hundred and sixty poles to a white red & Spanish Oaks Corner to the
said SIMS, thence West forty poles to three Hickorys Corner to the said SIMS, thence
South fifteen degrees West ninety two poles to a Hickory and red Oak, Corner to the said
JOHN SMITH deced line, thence with his line to the beginning, Together with all woods,
ways, houses, Orchards and other appurtenances belonging & all other the Estate, Right
and title that may now or ever hereafter appertains to the same free from the Trouble
Hindrance or Molestation of any person whatsoever To have and to hold the aforesaid
Land & premises from all Incumbrances or from any person whatsoever As Witness our
hands & Seals the day and year above written
in presence of JOHN HUME,   RICHARD PARKER
     JAS. YOWELL, HENRY LEWIS 33   GRISSELL her mark ─┼─PARKER
  Received full satisfaction for this Within Written Indenture. Witness my hand this
Nineteenth day of July 1783   RICHARD PARKER
                                              GRISSELL her mark ─┼─ PARKER
  Memorandum that on the same day of the date of the within written Indenture Quiet
and peaceable possession of the said Land and premises within mentioned was made and
given by the said RICHARD PARKER & GRISSELL his Wife to him the said WILLIAM
LEWIS in presence of us whose names are under written
                                   JOHN HUME
                                   JAS. YOWELL
                                   HENRY LEWIS
  At a Court held for Culpeper County the 21st day of July 1783
This Indenture was acknowledged by the parties & ordered to be recorded, previous to
which the said GRISSELL was first privately examined as the Law directs

p.   TO ALL PEOPLE to whom these presents shall come Greeting. Know ye that I
334   GEORGE DILLARD of the County of Culpeper for the love I bear towards my Son,
        MAJOR DILLARD of the County aforesaid have given and granted & by these pre-
sents do fully freely clearly and absolutely give and grant the said MAJOR DILLARD one
Negro named Charles to have and to hold the said Negro boy unto said MAJOR DILLARD
his heirs &c. from henceforth to his own proper use without any manner of Condition.
In Witness whereof I the said GEORGE DILLARD have hereunto set my hand and Seal this
(blank) day of (blank) One thousand seven hundred & Eighty three

in presence of W. ROBERTSON,   GEORGE DILLARD
         WILLIAM CHOWNING, CHAS. DUNCAN
    At a Court held for Culpeper County the 21st day of July 1783
This Deed of Gift was proved by the Oath of WILLIAM CHOWNING & CHAS. DUNCAN, witnesses thereto, and ordered to be recorded

pp.   (On margin: Vawter Deed to Broiles D D. Z. WALL 1787)
334-   THIS INDENTURE made this Fourteenth day of Decr. in year of our Lord One thou-
 336   sand seven hundred and Eighty two Between JOHN VAWTER of the State of NORTH
         CAROLINA and County of SURRY of one part and JOHN BROILES of the State of
Virginia and County of Culpeper and Parish of Bromfield of other part Witnesseth that
the said JOHN VAWTOR for and in consideration of the sum of Sevinty five pounds current money of Virginia and for other good causes & considerations him thereunto
moving, by these presents do bargain & sell unto JOHN BROILES his heirs & assigns one
tract of land lying and being in the said County of Culpeper and Parish of Bromfield
bounded Begining at three red Oaks Corner to ZACHARIAS WALL in the old line, thence
with the said Line South thirty nine degrees West One hundred & sixty four pole to
three Pines, Corner to said BROILES, thence North Sevinty nine degres West thirty eight
pole to a Blaz'd Pine and red Oak, thence North twenty nine degrees East One hundred &
sixty pole to two red Oaks, thence South sixty sevin degrees East, sevinty one pole to the
Begining, With all profits and benefits with all waters & watercourses, woods and
underwoods, fences, gardens, Orchards, houses with all buildings and Improvements
being on the said Tract of land belonging And the said JOHN VAWTOR for himself his
heirs & assigns do by this Deed Warrant the said Tract of land to the said JOHN BROILES
his heirs & assigns forever from claim or claimes of any other persons whatsoever In
Witness whereof have hereunto set my hand & Seal this day and year above written
in presence of JOHN WAYLAND JUNR.,   JOHN VAWTER
         SAMUEL DELPH, JOHN SWINDLE
    Received of JOHN BROILES the full sum of Sevinty five pounds current money of Vir-
ginia the consideration of the within Deed In Witness thereof I have hereunto set my
hand & Seal this 14th day of December One thousand sevin hundred and Eighty two
in presence of JOHN WAYLAND JUNR.,   JOHN VAWTER
         SAMUEL DELPH, JOHN SWINDLE
    At a Court held for Culpeper County the 21st day of July 1783
This Indenture was proved by the Oaths of the witnesses thereto & ordered to be
recorded

pp.   (On margin: Vawtor Deed to Wall D D to Self)
336-   THIS INDENTURE made the Elevinth day of December in year of our Lord One
338   thousand seven hundred and Eighty two Between JOHN VAWTER of County of
         SURRY and STATE of NORTH CAROLINA of one part and ZACHARIAS WALL of the
Colony of Virginia of other part Witnesseth that JOHN VAWTER for and in consideration
of the full & just sum of Six thousand pounds current money of Virginia to them in
hand paid by said ZACHARIAS WALL by these presents doth bargain and sell unto the
said ZACHARIAS WALL his heirs or assigns one certain Tract of land containing Fifty
acres lying in Culpeper County & Brumfield Parish in the Great Fork of RAPPAHAN-
NOCK RIVER and bounded Begining at a Hickory standing in JOEL WILHOITEs Plantation
thence with the Old Line South thirty nine degrees West One hundred & two pole to
three red Oaks, thence North sixty sevin degrees West sevinty one pole to two red Oaks
in the Old Line, thence with said line North twenty nine degrees East sixty poles to two
pines and a Hickory, thence North fourteen degrees West forty pole to a red Oak and

Hickory, thence South sevinty two East to the Begining place, with all houses orchards fences profits and Emoluments to the same belonging and all the Estate, Right, Title & Interest whatsoever of the said JOHN VAWTER of in and to the bargained lands with the appurtenances thereto belonging unto the said ZACHARIAS WALL his heirs and assigns and JOHN VAWTER and his heirs the aforesaid tract of land unto the said ZACHARIAS WALL his heirs and assigns shall warrant & forever defend by these presents against any person whatsoever and the said tract of Fifty acres of land with the appurtenances thereto belonging shall forever hereafter fully and clearly unto ZACHARIAS WALL his heirs and assigns freed and discharged of an from all Incumbrances claims or demand of any person whatsoever In Witness whereof I have set my hand & Seal the day and year first above written

> JOHN WAYLAND JUNR.,   JOHN VAWTER
> SAMUEL DELPH, JOHN SWINDLE

  Received of ZACHARIAS WALL the just & full sum of Six hundred pounds current money of Virginia the consideration of the within Deed, In Witness whereof we have hereunto set my hand & seal this Fourteenth day of December One thousand sevin hundred and eighty two

in presence of us JOHN WAYLAND JUNR.,   JOHN VAWTER
> SAMUEL DELPH, JOHN SWINDLE

  At a Court held for Culpeper County the 21st day of July 1783
This Indenture was proved by the Oaths of the Witnesses thereto & ordered to be recorded

pp.   (On margin: Wiscarver & Ux. Deed to Basye D D HARMAN VISCARVER 1789)
338-   THIS INDENTURE made this fifth day of August in year of our Lord One thousand
341   sevin hundred & Eighty Between HARMAN VISCARVER & BRIDGET his Wife of
        Culpeper County of one part and ELIZAMON BASIE of said County of other part
Witnesseth that HARMON VISCARVER for and in consideration of the sum of Eight hundred pounds in hand paid by these presents do bargain & sell unto the said ELIZAMON BASIE his heirs and assigns one piece or parcel of land on CROOKED RUN in said County containing Fifteen acres more or less and bounded Begining at white Oak and two Spanish Oaks in a line of JNO. COONES's on the West side of BROAD BRANCH, thence with the said COONES's line down said RUN till it comes to two Pines and one white Oak Corner to said COONES & MOORE on the East side of said RUN, thence with said MOORE's line down said RUN to one forked white Oak on West side of said RUN, Corner to said MOORE & SIGNEs, thence with said SIGNEs line up CROOKED RUN to two white Oaks in said line on the South side of a small Branch of CROOKED RUN & on the West side of CROOKED RUN, thence with a Blaized line to the begining containing Fifteen acres more or less with all houses Orchards meadows profits Emoluments to the same belonging To have and to hold the said land and premises with the appurtenances unto the said ELIZAMON BASIE his heirs or assigns forever against the claims of us our heirs or any person whatsoever and we do warrant and defend the said BASYE in the Peaceable possession of the same In Witness whereof we have hereunto set our hands and Seals the day and year above written

in presence of us JAMES PENDLETON,   HERMON his mark X VISCARVER
> WM. McCLANAHAN, JOHN BOWLINE,   BRIDGET her mark X VISCARVER
> JOHN PULLER

  The Commonwealth of Virginia to JAMES PENDLETON, WM. McCLANAHAN & JONO. WIGGINTON Gentlemen Greeting (The Commission for the private Examination of BRIDGET, Wife of HERMON VISCARVER, dated at the Courthouse this fifth day of August 1780) (Return of the private Examination of BRIDGET VISCARVER dated the 5th day of

August 1780 and signed by JAMES PENDLETON and WM. McCLANAHAN
   At a Court held for Culpeper County the 21st day of August 1780
This Indenture was partly proved by the Oaths of WM. McCLANAHAN & JOHN PULLER,
witnesses thereto, and ordered to be Certified, And at a Court held for the aforesaid
County the 21st day of July 1783, This Indenture was fully proved by the Oath of JAMES
PENDLETON, another witness thereto, & ordered to be recorded with Commission thereto
annexed & certificate thereon

pp.   (On margin: Monroe Deed to Samuel D D REUBEN SAMUEL 1805)
341-   THIS INDENTURE made this fourteenth day of June in year of our Lord One thou-
343   sand seven hundred and Eighty three Between ALEXANDER MONROE & MARGA-
         RET his Wife of County of FAUQUIER of one part and JAMES SAMUEL of County of
Culpeper of other part Witnesseth that for and in consideration of the sum of One hundred & ten pounds current money of Virginia to the said ALEXANDER MONROE in hand
paid by these presents do bargain and sell unto JAMES SAMUEL his heirs and assigns
forever all that tract or parcel of land lying in Parish of St. Marks & in the County of
Culpeper and bounded Begining at a Pine in the Old Line on a Hill joining the land of
ABSALOM ADAMS, thence Runing South fifty two degrees East sevinty two poles to a
large Pine in JOHN PICKETs Line, thence with said PICKETTs line South forty one degrees West Twinty poles South fifty two degrees East One hundred & fifty Pole to REY-
NOLDs Line, thence with the said Line South forty degrees West Two hundred and thirty
pole to two white Oaks joining WM. WHITESIDES, thence West twinty pole to a Dead Pine
near the said WHITESIDES's House, thence with the Old line to the Begining containing
by Estimation Two hundred and five acres which Tract of Land the said ALEXANDER
MONROE & MARGARET his Wife do grant bargain and sell to said JAMES SAMUEL with all
houses buildings, yards gardens orchards profits commodities & appurtenances whatsoever to the same belonging and all the Estate, right Title and demand whatsoever of
them the said ALEXANDER MONROE and MARGARET his Wife of in and to the same To
have and to hold all the premises with appurtenances hereby bargained and sold to the
said JAMES SAMUEL his heirs and assigns and ALEXANDER MONROE and MARGARET his
Wife shall warrant and forever defend against all persons whatsoever In Witness
whereof the said ALEXANDER MONROE and MARGARET his Wife have hereunto set their
hands and Seals the day and year first above written
in presence of JOHN WHITESIDES   ALEXANDER his mark + MONROE
               JOHN COONES,   MARGARET her mark + MONROE
               JACOB his mark + HANDBACK
   Received the Fourteenth day of June 1783 of the within named JAMES SAMUEL the sum
of One hundred and Ten pounds Currt. money it being the consideration within mentioned to be paid to me
Witness JOHN COONES,   ALEXANDER his mark + MONROE
         JOHN WHITESIDES
   At a Court held for Culpeper County the 21st day of July 1783
This Indenture was proved by the Oaths of the Witnesses thereto & ordered to be
recorded

pp.   (On margin: Hume Deed to Yowell D D JOEL YOWELL Feby 1796)
344-   THIS INDENTURE made this fifteenth day of February in year of our Lord One
345   thousand seven hundred and Eighty three Between GEORGE HUME of County of
         Culpeper of one part and JOHN YOWELL of the aforesaid County of other part,
Witnesseth that for and in consideration of the sum of Fifty pounds current money of
Virginia to him the said GEORGE HUME well & truly in hand paid have bargained and

sold unto JOHN YOWELL his heirs and assigns forever a certain piece or parcell of land lying in County of Culpeper containing by estimation Three hundred twenty two acres be the same more or less lying on the FORK MOUNTAIN on the Waters of the ROBINSON RIVER and bounded Begining at two white Oaks & Chesnut on the East side of the Fork in the foresaid County and runing thence North sixty six degrees West two hundred and twenty poles to two Chesnuts & Spanish Oak thence South twenty four degrees West One hundred and Twelve poles to a Chesnut Oak and two Chesnuts and Mahogany, thence South Twenty two Degrees East Two hundred & twenty eight poles to two Chesnuts, thence South Sixty six degrees East Eighty poles to four white Oaks on the South side of the FORK MOUNTAIN, thence North nineteen degrees East two hundred & sivinty four poles to the Begining, Together with all woods and underwoods, houses orchards and all other appurtenances belonging and all other the Estate right and title that may now or ever hereafter appertain to the same free from the trouble hindrance or molestation of any persons whatsoever To have and to hold the aforesaid Land & premises from all Incumbrances of Mortgages Dowers and Reversions by or from us whatsoever As Witness my hand and Seal the day and year above written

in presence of JOHN CAMPBELL,   GEORGE HUME
           AMBROSE GARRIOTT

At a Court held for Culpeper County the 27th day of July 1783
This Indenture was acknowledged by the within mentioend GEORGE HUME & ordered to be recorded

pp.   (On margin: Green & Ux. to Green D.D. to Wm. Green Exr. of H. Green 1786)
345-   THIS INDENTURE made the twelfth day of August 1783 Between WILLIAM GREEN
347   and BETSY his Wife of Culpeper County of one part and HENRY GREEN of the
           County of FAUQUIER of the other part Witnesseth that WILLIAM GREEN and
BETSY his Wife for & in consideration of the sum of One hundred & twenty pounds to them in hand paid by the said HENRY GREEN hath bargained and sold by these presents a certain tract or parcel of land containing by Estimation Five hundred acres more or less joining WOODs Tract of land & bounded Begining at two red Oaks and a Pine marked R. G. on a Ridge on the East side of the WHITE OAK RUN & extending South Twenty five degrees West two hundred & sixty two poles three white Oaks near the Main Branch of the WHITE OAK RUN in the Patent Line, thence with the dividing line North sixty five degrees West three hundred & six poles to a Pine red Oak & Chesnut on MERINGO MOUNTAIN to Patent Line, thence with the same North twenty five degrees East two hundred & sixty two poles to a Pine near the foot of JOBBERS MOUNTAIN, thence South sixty five degrees East three hundred and six poles to the beginning and all houses water courses profits and Emoluments whatsoever to the same belonging To have and to hold the said tract of land with the appurtenances to the said HENRY GREEN his heirs or assigns forever and WILLIAM GREEN & BETSY his Wife doth bind themselves their heirs firmly by these presents to support the above title in Witness we have hereunto set our hands & Seals   WILLM. GREEN
                                                                          BETSEY GREEN

Memom. that on the day and year within mentioned peaceable & Quiet possession and seizen of the within land was hand & taken by the within WILLIAM GREEN by him was delivered to the within named HENRY GREEN to be held by him his heirs & assigns for ever according to the intent and meaning of the within Deed Witness my hand and Seal the Date within written   WILLM. GREEN
                                                                          BETSY GREEN

Recd the within sum in full it being One hundred & Twenty pound Currencey, the consideration of the in Deed   W. GREEN

At a Court held for Culpeper County the 18th day of August 1783
This Indenture was acknoweldged by the parties & ordered to be recorded, previous to
which the said BETSY GREEN was first examined as the Law directs

pp.   (On margin: Head & Ux. Deed to Canaday D D RD. TUTT 1797)
347-   THIS INDENTURE made the fifteenth day of August in year of our Lord One thou-
349   sand seven hundred and Eighty three Between HADLEY HEAD of Culpeper Coun-
         ty and MILDRED his Wife of one part and WHORTON CANADY of the said County of
the other part Witnesseth that HADLEY HEAD and MILDRED his Wife for and in consideration of the sum of Seventeen pound Ten shillings current money of Virginia to
him the said HADLY HEAD in hand paid by these presents doth bargain and sell unto
WHORTEN CANEDY his heirs and assigns forever one certain tract of land lying and
being in Parish of Bromfield and in the County of Culpeper & containing by Estimation
eighty eight acres be the same more or less and bounded Begining at three black Oaks a
Hickory and two Pines, Corner to JOHN BEAL, thence with his line South seventy five
degrees East eighty pole to three small red Oaks & Pine, another Corner to said BEAL,
thence with his line to a white Oak red Oak and Pine, a Corner claimed by the said BOBO
thence South sevinty four degrees East forty poles, thence South sixty one degrees East
forty one poles to two Pines and white Oak Corner to AMBROSE BARNETT, thence North
seven degrees West thirty two poles to three Pines on the North side of the head of a
Branch, one of which is marked F F formerly a Corner to GIBBINs now LYNEs thence
North five Degrees West One hundred and forty six pole to three Pines on the North side
of MEDLEYS ROAD, Corner in a line belonging to JOHN MEDLEY's Orphans, thence South
fifty four degrees West One hundred and Eighty poles to the Beginning with all the appurtenances thereunto belonging and all right Title Interest and demand whatsoever
of them the said HADLEY HEAD, MILDRED his Wife of in and to the premises To have and
to hold the premises aforesaid with the appurtenances to WHORTON CANDADEY his heirs
and assigns forever and HADLEY HEAD and MILDRED his Wife their heirs doth covenant
and agree with said WHORTON CANADAY his heirs and assigns that at all times hereafter
to peaceably and Quietly have hold possess and enjoy the said premises with appurtenances without the lawfull Lett Suit Hindrance disturbance of said HADLEY HEAD &
MILDRED his Wife their heirs or assigns free and clearly discharged of all Incumbrances whatsoever In Witness whereof the parties to these presents have Interchangably set their hands and Seals the day & year first above written
in presence of us THOMAS CANADAY,   HADLEY HEAD
        WILLIAM CARTER, EDMUND ARCHER   MILDRED HEAD
   At a Court held for Culpeper County the 18th day of August 1783
This Indenture was acknowledged by the parties and ordered to be recorded, previous to
which the said MILDRED was first privately examined as the Law directs

pp.   (On margin: Wallace Deed to Wallace D.D. to Self 21 April 1787)
349-   THIS INDENTURE made this Eighteenth day of August in year of our Lord One
351   thousand seven hundred and Eighty three Between WILLIAM BROWN WALLACE
         of County of STAFFORD of one part and JOHN WALLACE of County aforesaid of
other part Witnesseth that said WILLIAM BROWN WALLACE for and in consideration of
the sum of Two hundred and fifty pounds current money of Virginia to him in hand
paid by JOHN WALLACE by these presents do bargain and sell unto JOHN WALLACE a
certain tract or parcel of land lying in County of Culpeper in the Great Fork of RAPPA-
HANNOCK RIVER bounded as by Survey thereof made by Mr. GEORGE HUME Begining at
three white Oaks corner to CHARLES CAVENAUGH in JOHN YANCEYs line, thence with
the said YANCEYs line South ten degrees West sixty four poles to a Pine and two white

Oak saplings standing on the North side of the MOUNTAIN ROAD below STONE HOUSE
MOUNTAIN, thence South fifty degrees West One hundred and Eighty four poles to two
Pines, thence North Forty degrees WEst two hundred and thirty poles to two red Oak
saplins, thence North fifty degrees East two hundred & thirty two poles to three Pines
in CHARLES CAVENAUGHs Line, thence with his line South forty degrees East One hundred and ninety six poles to the begining containing Three hundred acres be the same
more or less which said Tract was granted by the Right Honble. THOMAS LORD FAIRFAX
&c. &c. unto CAPT. JOHN FROG & DOCTOR MICHL. WALLACE by a Pattent bearing date the
Ninth day of Decr. One thousand sevin hundred & forty nine Registered in the Proprietors Office in Book G, Folio 315, and by the Last Will and Testament of said MICHAEL
WALLACE the same descended to his Son, WILLIAM B. WALLACE, party to these presents,
as will more fully appear referance being had to the Records of KING GEORGE COUNTY
Together with all houses gardens priviledges profits whatsoever to the said Tract of
land appertaining To have and to hold the said Tract or parcel of land above mentioned
and hereby intended to be granted bargained & sold unto said JOHN WALLACE his heirs
&c. forever In Witness whereof I have hereunto set my hand & Seal this day and year
first above mentioned or written
in presence of us   WM. B. WALLACE
   Received of the within named JOHN WALLACE the within mentioned sum of Two hundred and fifty pounds current money being the consideration in the within Deed to be
paid by him to me on the perfection thereof. Witness my hand this 18th day of August
1783
                                 WM. B. WALLACE
   At a Court held for Culpeper County the 18th day of August 1783
This Indenture was acknowledged by the within mentioned WM. B. WALLACE & ordered
to be recorded

pp.   (On margin: Banks Deed to Earley Dd. Joel Early)
351-   THIS INDENTURE made the 18th day of August in year of our Lord One thousand
353   seven hundred and Eighty three Between ADAM BANKS & GRACY his Wife of
       County of Culpeper of the one part and JOEL EARLEY of the aforesd County of
other part Witnesseth that for and in consideration of the Quantity of Ten thousand
pounds of Nett Crop Tobacco to him the said ADAM BANKS well & truly in hand paid
have bargained & sold in fee unto JOEL EARLY his heirs and assigns forever a certain
piece or parcel of land containing Two hundred and Twenty four acres be the same
more or less lying in the aforesaid County at the head of WILSONS RIVER a branch of
STANTON RIVER bounded Beg: at a Wild Cherry tree and three Chesnut trees on the side
of a Mountain nigh the head of the said WILSONS RIVER and running North thirty five
degrees West One hundred and twenty poles to two white Oaks and one Chesnut tree on
the side of a Mountain, th: South fifty five degrees West Two hundred and forty poles to
three Spanish Oaks, th: South thirty five degrees East One hundred and sixty two poles to
three Chesnut trees in ISAAC SMITHs old line, th: North sixty degrees East One hundred
and Ten poles to a Wild Cherry tree Maple and white Oak on the said WILSONS RIVER, th:
up the several courses of the same to the Beg: Together with all houses, fences,
orchards and all appurtenances belonging To have and to hold the aforesaid premises
with every part and parcel from all incumbrance of Mortgage, Dowers & reversions &
to be only to the use of him the said JOEL EARLY his heirs and assigns As Witness our
hands and Seals the day and date above written
in presence of   ADAM BANKS
   Received full satisfaction for the within written Indenture as Witness my hand this
18th day of August 1783   ADAM BANKS

At a Court held for Culpeper County the 18th day of August 1783
This Indenture was acknowledged by the within mentioned ADAM BANKS and ordered
to be recorded

pp.   THIS INDENTURE made this Eighteenth day of August in year of our Lord One
353-   thousand seven hundred and Eighty three Between MICHAEL ZIMMERMON &
355   SARAH his Wife of the County of Culpeper of one part & CHRISTOPHER ZIMMER-
       MON of the said County of other part Witensseth that MICHAEL ZIMMERMON and
SARAH his Wife for and in consideration of the sum of seventy pounds to them in hand
paid by these presents doth bargain and sell unto CHRISTOPHER ZIMMERMON all the
premises of a certain tract or parcel of land containing Seventy acres be the same more
or less lying and being in Culpeper County & Parish of Bromfield in the Great Fork of
RAPPAHANOCK RIVER and the same is bounded Begining at two white Oaks and one red
Oak in AMBROSE HUFFMANs line and runs thence with his line North five degrees East
One hundred & Eighteen pole to one white Oak & two red Oaks on a Ridge in the said line,
thence North eighty five degrees West ninety five Pole to a red Oak and a Pine in said
CHRISTOPHER ZIMMERMON's Line, thence with his line South five degrees West One
hundred and Eighteen pole to one red Oak & two white Oaks in HUFFMANs Line, thence
with his line South eighty five degrees East Ninety five pole to the Begining place; with
all houses orchards Improvements fences meadows profits & Emoluments to the same
belonging and all the Estate, Right, Title & Interest whatsoever of us the said MICHAEL
ZIMMERMON & SARAH his Wife of in and to the said land & premises To have and to hold
the aforesaid Tract of Seventy acres of land and all the premises with the appurtenances thereunto belonging unto CHRISTOPHER ZIMMERMON his heirs and assigns and
MICHAEL ZIMMERMON & SARAH his Wife will warrant and forever defend by these presents from and against all persons whatsoever In Witness whereof the said MICHAEL
ZIMMERMON and SARAH his Wife hath hereunto set their hands and Seals this Eighteenth day of August 1783
in presence of us WM. HERNDON   MICHAEL ZIMMERMON
                                  SARAH her mark + ZIMMERMON
  1783 August 18th. Received the within contents in full
                                  MICHAEL ZIMMERMON
At a Court held for Culpeper County the 18th day of Augst. 1783
This Indenture was acknowledged by the parties & ordered to be recorded, to which the
said SARAH was first privily examined as the Law directs

pp.   (On margin: Hackley &c. Deed to Pendleton D.D. to P. Pendleton 14th June 1784)
355-   THIS INDENTURE made the 21st day of July in year of our Lord One thousand
358   seven hundred and Eighty three Between JAMES HACKLEY and ELIZABETH his
       Wife and SUSANNA DANIEL of the County of Culpeper of one part and PHILLIP
PENDLETON of said County of the other part Witnesseth that said JAMES HACKLEY and
ELIZABETH his Wife and SUSANNA DANIEL for and in consideration of the sum of Three
hundred pounds current money of Virginia to them in hand paid by these presents do
bargain and sell unto PHILLIP PENDLETON his heirs and assigns one certain tract or
parcel of land lying and being in County aforesaid in the GOURDVINE FORK of RAPPA-
HANNOCK RIVER and bounded Begining at sevin marked Pines on the North side of the
SOUTH RIVER of GOURDVINE, Corner to BENJAMIN FARGUSON, thence with his line
North twenty four degrees West three hundred and twenty poles to a white Oak sup-
posed to be Corner to the said FARGUSON, thence South fifty five degrees West three
hundred and twenty poles to a red Oak and one Hickory Saplins Corner to JAS. THOMAS
thence with the said THOMAS's line South twenty degrees East Two hundred and ninety

poles to one white and one red Oak on the river, another corner to JAMES THOMAS, thence down the several courses of the said River to the Begining containing Five hundred and ninety acres be the same more or less and all ways profits commodites and appurtenances whatsoever to the same belonging and also all the Estate right Interest and demand whatsoever of them the said JAMES HACKLEY and ELIZABETH his Wife & SUSANNA DANIEL their heirs and assigns of in or to the aforesaid granted land To have and to hold the said Tract or parcel of land with the appurtenances unto PHILIP PENDELTON his heirs and assigns and JAMES HACKLEY and ELIZABETH his Wife and SUSANNA DANIEL shall warrant and forever defend against the claim of any person whatsover In Witness whereof the said JAMES HACKLEY and ELIZABETH his Wife and SUSANNA DANIEL have hereunto set their hands & Seals the day and year first above written

in presence of JAMES SLAUGHTER,   JAMES HACKLEY
        JOHN WILLIAMS, H. PENDLETON,   ELIZABETH HACKLEY
        JOHN PIPER for S. DANIEL. ackd.,   SUSANNA DANIEL
        N. PENDLETON, JAMES PENDLETON,
        JAMES PENDLETON JUNR.

    Received of PHILLIP PENDLETON the sum of Three hundred pounds current money of Virginia, the consideration of the within deed mentioned

                                                            JAMES HACKLEY

    The Commonwealth of Virginia to NATHANIEL PENDLETON, JAMES PENDLETON & JOHN WIGGINTON Gent. Greeting: (The private Examination of ELIZABETH, the Wife of JAMES HACKLEY, witness DAVID JAMESON Deputy Clerk of our said Court at the Courthouse the 23d day of July 1783 and 8th year of the Commonwealth) (Return of the private Examination of ELIZABETH HACKLEY dated the 23d day of July 1783 and signed by N. PENDLETON and JAMES PENDLETON)

    At a Court held for Culpeper County the 18th day of Augst. 1783
This Indenture was acknowledged by the within mentioned JAMES HACKLEY and proved by the Oaths of NATHL. PENDLETON, JAMES PENDLETON & JAMES PENDLETON JUNR. as to SUSANNA DANIEL & ordered to be recorded with Commission thereto and Certificate thereon

pp.   KNOW ALL MEN by these presents that I MARY HEAD of the County of Culpeper
358-   for divers good causes and considerations but more Especially for the love and
359   affection which I bear unto my Son, JOHN ALFRED HEAD, of said County have
        given and granted and by these presents do give and grant unto said JOHN AL-
FRED HEAD One Bay Mare named Phillis, with all her increase also all and whole of the articles of household and kitchen furniture left with the above Mare in the possession of the said JOHN ALFRED at the death of his Father, ALFRED HEAD, together with all the Crops and benefits arising from the Services of a negro wench named Judah from and after the death of the said ALFRED, To have and to hold the same to him his heirs or assigns forever to his and their proper use and against the claims or demands of any person whatsoever shall warrant & forever defend by these presents in Witness whereof I have hereunto set my hand and Seal this Seventeenth day of May One thousand seven hundred and Eighty three

in presence of WILLIAM ROBIRTSON,   MARY her mark ⦿ HEAD
        JOHN ROBERTSON, ALEXR. DAWNEY

    At a Court held for Culpeper County the 18th day of August 1783
This Indenture was proved by the oaths of the witnesses thereto & ordered to be recorded

pp.   THIS INDENTURE made this Twentieth day of October in the year of our Lord One
359-   thousand seven hundred and Seventy Seven Between CHARLES PAYTON and
362   LETTICE his Wife of County of FREDERICK & Colony of Virginia of one part and
        CHARLES MAUZINGO of County of Culpeper & Colony aforesaid of other part
Witnesseth that CHARLES PAYTON & LETTICE his Wife for and in consideration of the
sum of sixty pounds Current money of Virginia to them in hand paid by the said
CHARLES MAUZINGO by these presents do fully freely & absolutely grant bargain & sell
unto said CHARLES MAUZINGO his heirs & assigns forever a certain piece or parcell of
land lying and being in the aforesaid County of Culpeper containing 391 acres &
bounded Begining at three Pines and a Chesnut on South side of CANNONS RIVER Corner
to WM. DUNCAN & MICHL. LAWLOR & runs up the River North eighty five degrees West
twenty two pole South sixty one West thirty poles, North nineteen degrees West twenty
pole, North thirty six West forty six pole, South sevinty nine Degrees West sevinty six
pole, North forty six degrees West twelve pole, South fifty six West twenty four pole to a
white Oak on the River side then leaving the River South thirty five degrees West
Three hundred Eighty five pole to a Chesnut & Spanish Oak on DUNCANS MILL RUN &
Corner to WM. DUNCAN, thence down the said RUN North sevinty one degrees East One
hundred and twenty pole South sixty two degrees East sevinty sevin pole North forty
five degrees East eighty six poles North Sevinty three degrees East Sevinty pole, North
forty eight degrees East forty eight pole to three white Oaks & a Double Pine on the said
Run in DUNCAN's line, thence with his line North ten degrees West One hundred and
four pole to two pines and a red Oak, Corner to DUNCAN, thence with his line to the
begining Together with all houses gardens orchards meadows mines minerals quarries
and appurtenances whatsoever to the same belonging and also all Estate right title and
demand of him the said CHARLES PAYTON & LETTICE his Wife or either of them
of in or to the said premises with the appurtenances To have and to hold the said lands
with their appurtenances unto CHARLES MAUZINGO his heirs & assigns forever and
CHARLES PAYTON & LETTICE his Wife shall warrant and forever defend by these
presents that CHARLES MAUZINGO his heirs and assigns shall at all times forever
hereafter have hold occupy and enjoy the said premises with the appurtenances
without the lett hindrance or molestation of him the said CHARLES PAYTON & LETTICE
his Wife In Witness whereof the said CHAS. PAYTON & LETTICE his Wife have hereunto
set their hands & seals the day & year first above written

in the presence of us JAMES DUNCAN,   CHAS. PAYTON
     JOHN LAWLOR, SHADRACH BARNES,   LETTICE her mark ⌐PAYTON
     SHADRACH BARNES, CHARLES MUZINGO

    Received of the within named CHARLES MAUZINGO the sum of Sixty pounds Current
money of Virginia being the consideration money within mentioned to be paid by him
to us on the perfection of the within Deed. Witness our hands & Seals this (blank) One
thousand seven hundred & Seventy Seven 1777.

                             CHAS. PAYTON

    At a Court held for Culpeper County the 18th day of August 1783
This Indenture was proved by the oaths of JAMES DUNCAN, JOHN LAWLOR & SHADRACH
BARNES witnesses thereto & ordered to be recorded

pp.   (On margin: Norman Deed to Norman D. D. JOHN MINOR 1797)
362-   THIS INDENTURE made this Eighteenth day of July One thousand seven hundred
364   and Eighty three Between COURTNEY NORMAN of the Parish of Bromfield and
        County of Culpeper of one part and JOHN NORMAN of the Parish & County afore-
said of other part Witnesseth that COURTNEY NORMAN for and in consideration of the
sum of Twenty pounds Virginia money to him in hand paid by JOHN NORMAN by these

presents doth bargain and sell unto JOHN NORMAN and his heirs forever one tract or parcel of land lying in the Parish & County abovementioned containing Twenty acres & is bounded Beginning at a Gum and Spanish Oak standing near a large Rock & Corner to REUBEN NORMAN, thence South forty six degrees West fifty six poles to the Road that leads to CHESTERS GAP, thence down the same the several courses thereof to the said JOHN NORMANs line, thence leaving the Road North twenty five degrees East thirty six poles to two small Chesnut trees in REUBEN NORMANs line and with the same North Twenty five degrees West seventy eight poles to the Begining containing twenty acres be the same more or less together with all woods profits commodities & appurtenances whatsoever to the same belonging and also all the Estate right title and demand of them the said COURTNEY NORMAN of in and to the said premises To have and to hold the said tract or parcel of land herein before mentioned to be hereby sold & conveyed with every of their appurtenances unto JOHN NORMAN & his heirs forever and COURTNEY NORMAN & their heirs shall forever warrant and defend by these presents In Witness whereof the said COURTNEY NORMAN hereunto interchangably set their hands and affixed their Seals the day & year first above written
in the presence of   COURTNEY NORMAN
   At a Court held for Culpeper County the 18th day of August 1783
This Indenture was acknowledged by the party & ordered to be recorded

pp.   THIS INDENTURE made this Sixteenth day of August One thousand seven hundred
364-   & Eighty three Between JOHN NORMAN and ANN his Wife of the Parish of Brom-
365   field & County of Culpeper of one part & JAMES BROWNING of the Parish &
         County aforesaid of other part Witnesseth that JOHN NORMAN and ANN his Wife
for and in consideration of the sum of Fifteen pounds Virginia money to him in hand paid by JAMES BROWNING by these presents doth bargain and sell unto JAMES BROW- NING and his heirs forever one tract or parcel of land lying in the Parish and County above mentioned containing Ten acres & is bounded begining at a white Oak on the No. side of a branch in BROWNINGs Field, thence North four degrees West sevinty poles to a Chesnut & white Oak, thence South forty sevin degrees East sevinty to a Hickory white & Spanish Oak, thence South sixty six degrees West fifty poles to the Begining together with all woods profits commodities and appurtenances whatsoever to the same belonging & also all the Estate, right, Title and demand of them the said JOHN NORMAN & ANN his Wife of in and to the said premises, To have and to hold the said tract or parcel of land herein before mentioned or intended to be hereby sold and conveyed with their appurtenances to JAMES BROWNING and his heirs forever and JOHN NORMAN & ANN his Wife shall forever warrant and defend by these presents In Witness whereof the said JOHN NORMAN and ANN his Wife hereunto interchangeably set their hands and affixed their Seals the day & first above written
in presence of   JOHN NORMAN
   At a Court held for Culpeper County the 18th day of August 1783
This Indenture was acknowledged by the party & ordered to be recorded

pp.   (On margin: Fishback & Ux. Deed to Atwood D. D. Tho. Atwood 1818)
366-   THIS INDENTURE made this Eighteenth day of August One thousand seven hun-
368   dred & Eighty three Between JACOB FISHBACK & PHEBE his Wife of County of Cul-
         peper of one part and JAS. ATWOOD of the same County of other part Witnesseth
that said JACOB FISHBACK & PHEBE his Wife for and in consideration of the sum of Two hundred and fifty pounds current money to them in hand paid or secured to be paid by the said JAMES ATWOOD by these presents do give bargain and sell unto JAMES ATWOOD his heirs & assigns a certain tract or parcel of land lying in the Little Fork of RAPPA-

HANNOCK RIVER & County aforesaid & bounded Beginning at a red Oak white Oak and
Pine near a Path running thence North fifty three & three quarters degrees East Two
hundred & two poles to a white Oak saplin & two red Oaks & Corner to JOHN KAMPER,
thence with his line North fifty seven degrees West One hundred and sixty four poles to
two red Oaks & a Hickory Corner to KAMPER, thence South forty three degrees West One
hundred and seventeen poles, thence South thirteen degrees East One hundred and
nine poles to a large white Oak & Hickory saplin in a Bottom, thence South fifty five and
a half degrees East thirty three poles to the begining containing One hundred & fifty
acres be the same more or less, the said JACOB FISHBACK holds by virtue of a Deed of Gift
from FREDERICK FISHBACK Deced & is a part of a greater tract whereon the said
FREDERICK FISHBACK lately lived, To have and to hold the said land & premises with the
appurtenances unto JAMES ATWOOD his heirs & assigns forever discharged from all
former Incumbrances or conveyance whatsoever In Witness whereof the said JACOB
FISHBACK & PHEBE his Wife have hereunto set their hands & seals the day and year first
above written
in presence of THOS. SPILMAN,   JACOB FISHBACK
        OLIVER CLARK, LEWIS CORBIN
  The Commonwealth of Virginia to (blank) Gent. Greeting: (The private examination of
PHEBE, the Wife of JACOB FISHBACK, Witness DAVID JAMESON Deputy Clerk of our said
Court at the Courthouse the 18th day of August 1783 and 8th year of the Commonwealth)
(No return of the private examination is recorded)
  At a Court held for Culpeper County the 18th day of August 1783
This Indenture was acknowledged by the within mentioned JACOB FISHBACK & ordered
to be recorded with Commission thereto annext & (blank) thereon

                                        Test JOHN JAMESON Cl Cur

Heritage Books by Ruth and Sam Sparacio:

Abstracts of Account Books of Edward Dixon, Merchant of
Port Royal, Virginia, Volume I: 1743–1747

Abstracts of Account Books of Edward Dixon, Merchant of
Port Royal, Virginia, Volume II

Albemarle County, Virginia Deed and Will Book Abstracts, 1748–1752

Albemarle County, Virginia Deed Book Abstracts, 1758–1761

Albemarle County, Virginia Deed Book Abstracts, 1761–1764

Albemarle County, Virginia Deed Book Abstracts, 1764–1768

Albemarle County, Virginia Deed Book Abstracts, 1768–1770

Albemarle County, Virginia Deed Book Abstracts, 1776–1778

Albemarle County, Virginia Deed Book Abstracts, 1778–1780

Albemarle County, Virginia Deed Book Abstracts, 1780–1783

Albemarle County, Virginia Deed Book Abstracts, 1787–1790

Albemarle County, Virginia Deed Book Abstracts, 1790–1791

Albemarle County, Virginia Deed Book Abstracts, 1791–1793

Augusta County, Virginia Land Tax Books, 1782–1788

Augusta County, Virginia Land Tax Books, 1788–1790

Amherst County, Virginia Land Tax Books, 1789–1791

Caroline County, Virginia Appeals and Land Causes, 1787–1794

Caroline County, Virginia Committee of Safety and
Early Surveys, 1729–1762 and 1774–1775

Caroline County, Virginia Land Tax Book Alterations, 1782–1789

Caroline County, Virginia Land Tax Book Alterations, 1792–1795

Caroline County, Virginia Land Tax Book Alterations, 1795–1798

Caroline County, Virginia Order Book Abstracts, 1765

Caroline County, Virginia Order Book Abstracts, 1767–1768

Caroline County, Virginia Order Book Abstracts, 1768–1770

Caroline County, Virginia Order Book Abstracts, 1770–1771

Caroline County, Virginia Order Book, 1764

Caroline County, Virginia Order Book, 1765–1767

Caroline County, Virginia Order Book, 1771–1772

Caroline County, Virginia Order Book, 1772–1773

Caroline County, Virginia Order Book, 1773

Caroline County, Virginia Order Book, 1773–1774

Caroline County, Virginia Order Book, 1774–1778

Caroline County, Virginia Order Book, 1778–1781

Caroline County, Virginia Order Book, 1781–1783

Caroline County, Virginia Order Book, 1783–1784

Caroline County, Virginia Order Book, 1784–1785

Caroline County, Virginia Order Book, 1785–1786

Caroline County, Virginia Order Book, 1786–1787

Caroline County, Virginia Order Book, 1787, Part 1

Caroline County, Virginia Order Book, 1787, Part 2

Caroline County, Virginia Order Book, 1787–1788

Caroline County, Virginia Order Book, 1788

Culpeper County, Virginia Deed Book Abstracts, 1769–1773

Culpeper County, Virginia Deed Book Abstracts, 1778–1779

Culpeper County, Virginia Deed Book Abstracts, 1781–1783

Culpeper County, Virginia Deed Book Abstracts, 1785–1786

Culpeper County, Virginia Deed Book Abstracts, 1788–1789

Culpeper County, Virginia Deed Book Abstracts, 1791–1792

Culpeper County, Virginia Deed Book Abstracts, 1795–1796

Culpeper County, Virginia Land Tax Book, 1782–1786

Culpeper County, Virginia Land Tax Book, 1787–1789

Culpeper County, Virginia Minute Book, 1763–1764

Digest of Family Relationships, 1650–1692, from
Virginia County Court Records

Digest of Family Relationships, 1720–1750, from
Virginia County Court Records

Digest of Family Relationships, 1750–1763,
from Virginia County Court Records

Digest of Family Relationships, 1764–1775, from
Virginia County Court Records

Essex County, Virginia Deed and Will Abstracts, 1695–1697

Essex County, Virginia Deed and Will Abstracts, 1697–1699

Essex County, Virginia Deed and Will Abstracts, 1699–1701

Essex County, Virginia Deed and Will Abstracts, 1701–1703

Essex County, Virginia Deed and Will Abstracts, 1745–1749

Essex County, Virginia Deed and Will Book, 1692–1693

Essex County, Virginia Deed and Will Book, 1693–1694

Essex County, Virginia Deed and Will Book, 1694–1695

Essex County, Virginia Deed and Will Book, 1701–1704

Essex County, Virginia Deed, 1753–1754
and Will Book 1750

Essex County, Virginia Deed Abstracts, 1721–1724

Essex County, Virginia Deed Book, 1724–1728

Essex County, Virginia Deed Book, 1728–1733

Essex County, Virginia Deed Book, 1733–1738

Essex County, Virginia Deed Book, 1738–1742

Essex County, Virginia Deed Book, 1742–1745

Essex County, Virginia Deed Book, 1749–1751

Essex County, Virginia Deed Book, 1751–1753

Essex County, Virginia Land Trials Abstracts,
1711–1716 and 1715–1741

Essex County, Virginia Order Book Abstracts, 1695–1699

Essex County, Virginia Order Book Abstracts, 1699–1702

Essex County, Virginia Order Book Abstracts, 1716–1723, Part 1

Essex County, Virginia Order Book Abstracts, 1716–1723, Part 2

Essex County, Virginia Order Book Abstracts, 1716–1723, Part 3

Essex County, Virginia Order Book Abstracts, 1716–1723, Part 4

Essex County, Virginia Order Book Abstracts, 1723–1725, Part 1

Essex County, Virginia Order Book Abstracts, 1723–1725, Part 2

Essex County, Virginia Order Book Abstracts, 1725–1729, Part 1

Essex County, Virginia Order Book Abstracts, 1727–1729

Essex County, Virginia Order Book, 1695–1699

Essex County, Virginia Will Abstracts, 1730–1735

Essex County, Virginia Will Abstracts, 1735–1743

Essex County, Virginia Will Abstracts, 1745–1748

Fairfax County, Virginia Deed Abstracts, 1799–1800 and 1803–1804

Fairfax County, Virginia Deed Abstracts, 1804–1805

Fairfax County, Virginia Deed Book Abstracts, 1799

Fairfax County, Virginia Deed Book, 1798–1799

Fairfax County, Virginia Land Causes, 1788–1824

Fauquier County, Virginia Minute Book Abstracts, 1759–1761

Fauquier County, Virginia Minute Book Abstracts, 1761–1762

Fauquier County, Virginia Minute Book Abstracts, 1762–1763

Fauquier County, Virginia Minute Book Abstracts, 1763–1764

Fauquier County, Virginia Minute Book Abstracts, 1764–1766

Fauquier County, Virginia Minute Book Abstracts, 1766–1767

Fauquier County, Virginia Minute Book Abstracts, 1767–1769

Fauquier County, Virginia Minute Book Abstracts, 1769–1771

Fredericksburg City, Virginia Deed Book, 1782–1787

Fredericksburg City, Virginia Deed Book, 1787–1794

Fredericksburg City, Virginia Deed Book, 1794–1804

Hanover County, Virginia Land Tax Book, 1782–1788

Hanover County, Virginia Land Tax Book, 1789–1793

Hanover County, Virginia Land Tax Book, 1793–1796

King George County, Virginia Order Book Abstracts, 1721–1723

King George County, Virginia Deed Book Abstracts, 1721–1735

King George County, Virginia Deed Book Abstracts, 1735–1752

King George County, Virginia Deed Book Abstracts, 1753–1773

King George County, Virginia Deed Book Abstracts, 1773–1783

King George County, Virginia Will Book Abstracts, 1752–1780

King William County, Virginia Record Book, 1702–1705

King William County, Virginia Record Book, 1705–1721

King William County, Virginia Record Book, 1722 and 1785–1786

Lancaster County, Virginia Deed and Will Book, 1652–1657

Lancaster County, Virginia Deed and Will Book, 1654–1661

Lancaster County, Virginia Deed and Will Book, 1661–1702 (1661–1666 and 1699–1702)

Lancaster County, Virginia Deed Book Abstracts, 1701–1706

Lancaster County, Virginia Deed Book, 1710–1714

Lancaster County, Virginia Order Book Abstracts, 1656–1661

Lancaster County, Virginia Order Book Abstracts, 1662–1666

Lancaster County, Virginia Order Book Abstracts, 1666–1669

Lancaster County, Virginia Order Book Abstracts, 1670–1674

Lancaster County, Virginia Order Book Abstracts, 1674–1678

Lancaster County, Virginia Order Book Abstracts, 1678–1681

Lancaster County, Virginia Order Book Abstracts, 1682–1687

Lancaster County, Virginia Order Book Abstracts, 1729–1732

Lancaster County, Virginia Order Book Abstracts, 1736–1739

Lancaster County, Virginia Order Book Abstracts, 1739–1742

Lancaster County, Virginia Order Book, 1687–1691

Lancaster County, Virginia Order Book, 1691–1695

Lancaster County, Virginia Order Book, 1695–1699

Lancaster County, Virginia Order Book, 1699–1701

Lancaster County, Virginia Order Book, 1701–1703

Lancaster County, Virginia Order Book, 1703–1706

Lancaster County, Virginia Order Book, 1732–1736

Lancaster County, Virginia Will Book, 1675–1689

Loudoun County, Virginia Order Book, 1763–1764

Loudoun County, Virginia Order Book, 1764

Louisa County, Virginia Deed Book, 1744–1746

Louisa County, Virginia Order Book, 1742–1744

Madison County, Virginia Deed Book Abstracts, 1793–1804

Madison County, Virginia Deed Book, 1793–1813, and Marriage Bonds, 1793–1800

Middlesex County, Virginia Deed Book, 1679–1688

Middlesex County, Virginia Deed Book, 1688–1694

Middlesex County, Virginia Deed Book, 1694–1703

Middlesex County, Virginia Deed Book, 1703–1709

Middlesex County, Virginia Deed Book, 1709–1720

Middlesex County, Virginia Order Book Abstracts, 1686–1690

Middlesex County, Virginia Order Book Abstracts, 1697–1700

Middlesex County, Virginia Record Book, 1721–1813

Northumberland County, Virginia Deed and Will Book, 1650–1655

Northumberland County, Virginia Deed and Will Book, 1655–1658

Northumberland County, Virginia Deed and Will Book, 1658–1662

Northumberland County, Virginia Deed and Will Book, 1662–1666

Northumberland County, Virginia Deed and Will Book, 1666–1670

Northumberland County, Virginia Deed and Will Book, 1670–1672 and 1706–1711

Northumberland County, Virginia Deed and Will Book, 1711–1712

Northumberland County, Virginia Order Book, 1652–1657

Northumberland County, Virginia Order Book, 1657–1661

Northumberland County, Virginia Order Book, 1665–1669

Northumberland County, Virginia Order Book, 1669–1673

Northumberland County, Virginia Order Book, 1680–1683

Northumberland County, Virginia Order Book, 1683–1686

Northumberland County, Virginia Order Book, 1699–1700

Northumberland County, Virginia Order Book, 1700–1702

Northumberland County, Virginia Order Book, 1702–1704

Orange County, Virginia, Chancery Suits, 1831–1845

Orange County, Virginia Deeds, 1743–1759

Orange County, Virginia Deed Book Abstracts, 1759–1778

Orange County, Virginia Deed Book Abstracts, 1778–1786

Orange County, Virginia Deed Book Abstracts, 1795–1797

Orange County, Virginia Deed Book Abstracts, 1797–1799

Orange County, Virginia Deed Book Abstracts, 1799–1800

Orange County, Virginia Deed Book Abstracts, 1800–1802

Orange County, Virginia Deed Book Abstracts, 1786–1791, Deed Book 19

Orange County, Virginia Deed Book Abstracts, 1791–1795, Deed Book 20

Orange County, Virginia Land Tax Book, 1782–1790

Orange County, Virginia Land Tax Book, 1791–1795

Orange County, Virginia Order Book Abstracts, 1747–1748

Orange County, Virginia Order Book Abstracts, 1748–1749

Orange County, Virginia Order Book Abstracts, 1749–1752

Orange County, Virginia Order Book Abstracts, 1752–1753

Orange County, Virginia Order Book Abstracts, 1753–1754

Orange County, Virginia Order Book Abstracts, 1755–1756

Orange County, Virginia Order Book Abstracts, 1756–1757

Orange County, Virginia Order Book Abstracts, 1757–1759

Orange County, Virginia Order Book Abstracts, 1759–1762

Orange County, Virginia Order Book Abstracts, 1762–1763

Orange County, Virginia Will Abstracts, 1778–1821

Orange County, Virginia Will Abstracts, 1821–1838

Orange County, Virginia, Will Digest, 1734–1838